'This is a terrific book. Veronica Bidwell's long exper expertise is readily evident. She is able to link th date knowledge of the science of neurodevelopmen the extent to which various difficulties often exist . complemented by her vivid case studies. There is much for parents in here, with practical advice which has been tested in the field. Yet this is more than a book just for parents. Those who teach children with specific learning difficulties will find this an illuminating read and I recommend it to them too.'

— *Professor Peter Hill MA MB BChir FRCP FRCPCH FRCPsych,*
Consultant Child and Adolescent Psychiatrist

'A treasure trove of useful information and practical advice for the parents of children with specific learning difficulties and anyone who teaches them. Difficult concepts are explained in ways that are easy to understand and chapters conclude with helpful key points. Filled to the brim with inspiring and interesting case studies that make it a fascinating read. It really is a must-have.'

— *Claudine Goldingham BA LLB (Dist.), a dyslexic and*
mother of two dyslexic and dyspraxic girls

'Veronica Bidwell's inspirational *The Parents' Guide to Specific Learning Difficulties: Information, Advice and Practical Tips*, which will doubtless become the bible for all, touches on a discipline which can, at times, seem over-complex and impenetrable – especially to troubled parents and teachers. Veronica brings her wit, charm and insight to her wealth of experience as an educational psychologist, working in mainstream and specialist schools. She has written what is essentially a textbook that is, not only accessible to all, but also a rollicking good read. I would chain this book to every parent's wrist.'

— *Jo Petty, Director, Dyslexia Teaching Centre, Kensington, UK*

'This is the go-to book for parents with children who have specific learning difficulties. The book explains the varying specific learning difficulties and tells parents how to help. It is informative, practical and accessible without being patronising. It works either as a cover to cover read or as a book to dip into. If parents could spend a week with an educational psychologist asking every question they could think of, the result might be this book!'

— *Jackie Murray, Principal Educational Psychologist, Fairley House School, UK of related interest*

Specific Learning Difficulties – What Teachers Need to Know
Diana Hudson
ISBN 978 1 84905 590 1
eISBN 978 1 78450 046 7

Literacy for Visual Learners
Teaching Children with Learning Difficulties to
Read, Write, Communicate and Create
Adele Devine
Illustrated by Quentin Devine
ISBN 978 1 84905 598 7
eISBN 978 1 78450 054 2

Creative, Successful, Dyslexic
23 High Achievers Share Their Stories
Margaret Rooke
Foreword by Mollie King
ISBN 978 1 84905 653 3
eISBN 978 1 78450 163 1

The Essential Manual for Asperger Syndrome (ASD) in the Classroom
What Every Teacher Needs to Know
Kathy Hoopmann
Illustrated by Rebecca Houkamau
ISBN 978 1 84905 553 6
eISBN 978 0 85700 984 5

Dyslexia and Mental Health
Helping People Identify Destructive Behaviours and Find Positive Ways to Cope
Neil Alexander-Passe
ISBN 978 1 84905 582 6
eISBN 978 1 78450 068 9

Understanding Dyscalculia and Numeracy Difficulties
A Guide for Parents, Teachers and Other Professionals
Patricia Babtie and Jane Emerson
ISBN 978 1 84905 390 7
eISBN 978 0 85700 754 4

Beating Dyspraxia with a Hop, Skip and a Jump
A Simple Exercise Program to Improve Motor Skills at Home and School
Geoff Platt
ISBN 978 1 84905 171 2
eISBN 978 0 85700 416 1

THE PARENTS' GUIDE TO SPECIFIC LEARNING DIFFICULTIES

INFORMATION, ADVICE AND PRACTICAL TIPS

VERONICA BIDWELL

Jessica Kingsley *Publishers*
London and Philadelphia

First published in 2016
by Jessica Kingsley Publishers
73 Collier Street
London N1 9BE, UK
and
400 Market Street, Suite 400
Philadelphia, PA 19106, USA

www.jkp.com

Copyright © Veronica Bidwell 2016

Front cover image source: Shutterstock®.

Library of Congress Cataloging in Publication Data
A CIP catalog record for this book is available from the Library of Congress

British Library Cataloguing in Publication Data
A CIP catalogue record for this book is available from the British Library

ISBN 978 1 78592 040 0
eISBN 978 1 78450 308 6

Printed and bound in the United States

CONTENTS

PART 2 THE PARENT TOOLKIT – TIPS FOR TEACHING

ACKNOWLEDGEMENTS

My first thanks must go to the many hundreds of children and parents whom I have seen and worked with over the years and who have taught me so much. I have loved my work as an educational psychologist (EP) and particularly the challenge of trying to get an accurate fix on just what might be the underlying causes of parental concerns and pupil difficulties. I have been aware that every individual young person who has come through my door is someone's precious child, and the fact that parents have got as far as requesting an educational psychologist's assessment is an indication of the extent of their worries and their need for understanding, support and advice.

This has often felt a great responsibility. In my early days as an independent EP the advice, insights and coaching which I had from educational psychologist Peter Gilchrist were invaluable, and for that I thank him.

My very particular thanks go to the parents, pupils, students and young adults to whom I have talked as I have been writing and who have allowed me to use their stories for the case studies included at the end of many chapters. They bring the chapters alive, and also provide clear illustrations of how success can be achieved over time, particularly when all are working together.

I would also like to give very specific thanks to the following people who, in their professional capacities, have read and provided astute comments and valuable feedback: consultant child psychiatrist Professor Peter Hill; educational psychologists Lisa Hawking and Jackie Murray (previously head of Fairley House School); Jo Petty, Director of the Dyslexia Teaching Centre, Kensington; school proprietor and dyslexia specialist Josie Cameron; and parents Claudine Goldingham and Juliet Cole. I have also had valuable help from dyslexia specialist Cat Heale; maths specialist Paula Bishop; behavioural optometrist Clare Holland; consultant audiologist Tony Sirimanna; and speech and language therapist Karen Rivlin.

My thanks are also due to educationalist Penelope Penney, literary editor Eleanor Margolies and to my daughter Imogen Palmer. Their encouragement and editorial advice in the early days was essential. Eleanor's gentle feedback and advice were beyond helpful. Imogen did what few other people could have done; she took a pen to my very first draft and was brave enough to send me, kicking and complaining, back to the drawing board.

The combined comments, corrections and suggestions of all those mentioned above as the book has gone from first draft to final copy have been outstanding. I have been kept going by their belief that it was a book worth writing, and the book is undoubtedly all the better for their input. I am only sorry that I have not been able to include all their additional suggestions. Any inaccuracies are entirely my own.

I am thankful also for much practical help. Carol Rosser, who has run my office for many years, has frequently come to the rescue and has been a constant source of support and expertise. Thanks also to Mikey Nicholls, dyslexic printer, neighbour and friend, for printing off draft copies of the book at various stages and at record speed at Leopard Press. It has helped.

Thanks, too, to my agent Jane Graham Maw for all her help and for her belief that it was a book worth publishing. Thanks also to editors Bethany Gower and Kerrie Morton at JKP, who have been hugely helpful and great hand holders.

And, of course, the book would never have made it this far without the encouragement and patience of my incredible husband Robin. I have asked for his views on every chapter, often several times. His, at times painfully, honest feedback has always been of huge value. I do thank him for putting up with me so robustly and for always believing in me.

INTRODUCTION

Dyslexia, dyspraxia, attention deficit disorder, autism spectrum disorder, dyscalculia, auditory processing disorder... This dizzying list of learning difficulties and conditions seems to have emerged over the past few decades. But what do they really mean? Who are the children who experience such difficulties? How can they be helped and, above all, what can parents do?

This book is about the difficulties that many children encounter once they start formal schooling. It is the book that I wanted when I ran an educational psychology practice so that I could hand it to parents as they left my office.

I have worked for many years as an educational psychologist and during this time assessed literally hundreds of children and spent time with one or both of their parents. Although the parent interview time was spent in discussion and was followed up with a comprehensive report, I knew that once they had returned home and digested the results of the educational assessment they would have further concerns and queries.

What I wanted was a book that they and other parents might dip into for guidance and explanations. I wanted a book that would answer some of their questions and help them understand how they could best support their child.

I wanted a book that would explain the nature of their child's difficulties in greater depth. I wanted a book that didn't just describe the problems but would help parents make a plan of action and ensure that appropriate teaching was put in place.

I wanted a book that would enable them to plan ahead; many parents are anxious to know what to expect not just next year but right through the years of education. I wanted a book that could explain that, with the right help and effort, the problems facing their child could be overcome.

And this is that book.

It is a book that I hope will be of help to parents anywhere in the world who have concerns about their child's educational progress. Although I have been London based, my clients have come from far and wide and the learning difficulties described and discussed in this book are not restricted to the UK. The categories and criteria for the identification of difficulties are broadly similar across continents.

Education systems may vary and the terms used to describe specialists like myself may also vary but we share the passion and skills needed to support parents, teachers and, of course, those children who experience learning issues. In the UK we are called educational psychologists; in the USA our equivalents are also known as school psychologists. What we have in common is extensive academic (doctoral or master's degree level) and practical training in psychology and education. We are familiar with social, emotional, educational and behavioural issues. We are familiar with classrooms and the challenges facing teaching staff as well as pupils.

All children learn differently

Children do not all learn in exactly the same way. Some children's minds, brains and ways of learning just don't seem to fit easily into our school systems. We all know bright children with talent in some areas but surprising difficulty in others. One child may, for example, be a whizz at maths but still find it a struggle to read; another may have built a go-cart out of bits and pieces in his father's workshop but be unable to sit still in school; then there is the child who is writing a ten-chapter book at home full of wonderful language, ideas and descriptions but who only ever hands in a bland ten-line story in school. And, of course, there is the child who can talk with authority, who often impresses his teachers with his extensive knowledge and interest in many topics but who hands in messy work which is almost illegible and is limited in structure and quantity.

These are the children who are a puzzle and a worry to both parent and teacher. It is not always easy to work out what is going on and it is likely that parents may start to wonder if their child might have a specific learning difficulty.

Some readers may already know that their child experiences an area of specific difficulty but others of you may just be starting to wonder and perhaps to worry about your child's progress. So before we move on to the specific chapters, it is important to look at the broader context.

In order to learn successfully many things must be in place. These are things which I am sure that you are well aware of, but I think it is worthwhile going over them because it's all too easy to overlook the obvious, particularly when life is busy.

Sight

It is vital that children can see well. For the long- or short-sighted child, information on the board may appear blurred and so too will the useful information which is often displayed on the walls. The child with poor vision will miss out on much essential information.

Even if there are no problems relating to long or short sight, there can be other issues such as poor tracking (that refers to how easily and smoothly the eyes move along a line of print), difficulty with focus, or indeed letters may appear fuzzy or as though they are moving around.

It is helpful for children to have their eyes tested by an orthoptist who can give a full range of tests to check all aspects of vision. The orthoptist can also suggest a programme to improve things such as tracking. This is covered in greater detail in Chapter 10, Visual Processing Difficulty.

Hearing

This too is important to check out. Even if a child has been tested and is hearing well at the time of the test it is important to be aware that there are children who experience an 'intermittent' hearing loss. These are the children who, during early childhood, tend to have numerous colds and catarrh and, as a consequence, often have blocked ears and nose. During the time that they are 'blocked' hearing will be impaired. This intermittent loss is often referred to as glue ear and it can have a very detrimental impact on learning to read. Some children may have good hearing acuity but more subtle difficulties in the interpretation of the incoming sounds. This is considered in Chapter 8, Auditory Processing Disorder.

Physical attributes

Many activities in school involve gross and fine motor skills. Small children need core strength (the core refers to the abdomen, lower back and stomach) and muscle tone to sit at a desk while listening or colouring or writing. They need good fine motor skills to hold and manipulate a pencil (fine motor skills refer to manual dexterity and agility). They need to be aware of their bodies in space if they are to manage to sit still and not to fidget. Any areas of weakness could be causing some difficulty. If you think you need more information, a specialist occupational therapist or physiotherapist could give advice on this. Chapter 4, Dyspraxia, covers many of these issues.

Language

Next on the checklist is 'language'. There are several aspects to language development that may impact on learning. Language involves four distinct elements: the ability to understand the spoken word, the ability to speak in a grammatically correct manner, an understanding of the conventions of interacting and the ability to pronounce speech sounds. This is covered in more detail in Chapter 9, Specific Language Impairment.

Difficulties with any aspect of language can make for difficulty in the classroom and with learning. If parents have any concerns about language development it is important to seek an assessment from a speech and language therapist who can help to work out where difficulties are occurring. Difficulty with some aspects of language is an intrinsic part of many areas of specific learning difficulty. Chapter 9 covers this.

Emotional factors

These can be very real and can get in the way of learning. Anxiety can have a major impact on children's mental availability to take in new information, to concentrate and to learn. It can also impact on confidence. So, if a child is unhappy because of something such as the death of a pet or an ill grandparent or is anxious because the family is going through changes such as moving house, then there is a very real chance that his or her learning will be affected. It is easy for parents to overlook emotional issues, particularly if they are going through a very busy period or experiencing problems of their own. It is always important to let school know of any issues or problems at home that might be worrying a child.

A gap in teaching

A final very obvious, but easy to overlook, cause of difficulty might be lack of appropriate teaching. Children who miss a period of school when any important steps are being taught can fall behind. This can apply to early reading and later on to other subjects such as maths and science. Such children will need someone to help them to go back to the start or wherever they missed out and to fill the gaps. Maybe a child had to move school during some vital period of teaching or perhaps the formal teaching he has received has not been quite so 'joined up' as everyone had imagined.

If there is no obvious cause to a child's difficulty the next level to consider is whether it might be a specific learning difficulty.

What is a specific learning difficulty?

The term specific learning difficulty is an overarching term and has come over the past 20 years or so to encompass an increasing number of specified difficulties. It includes any type of difficulty that affects one or more aspects of learning rather than being a more general learning difficulty. Dyslexia, dyspraxia and dyscalculia all come under this heading. Attention deficit disorder, autism spectrum disorder, auditory processing disorder and specific language impairment are not technically regarded as specific learning difficulties but they do, of course, have a major impact on how easily a child copes with life in the classroom. They are all included in this book and for simplicity I am including them under the umbrella term specific learning difficulties.

Common characteristics

While all these difficulties have different and distinctive characteristics there are some factors which are common to them all:

- *There is evidence that there is a genetic basis to these difficulties.* Frequently one or more members of the family will also experience an area of specific difficulty. Over the years that I have been talking with parents about their child's strengths and difficulties it has been interesting to see just how often one parent will say 'but that's just like me' or 'that is exactly how I was when I was at school'. It is often the case that more than one child in the family has an area of difficulty but they are not necessarily the same.

- *These difficulties are neurologically based differences.* Neuroscientists are beginning to be able to demonstrate through brain scans that the behaviours that have been classified by practitioners as being typically dyslexic or dyspraxic or dyscalculic do indeed reflect different brain activity and patterns and that it is valid to name these different clusters of difficulty.

- *Specific difficulties do not fully disappear.* Although children (and adults) learn to compensate and to find strategies to cope with their areas of weakness, the underlying difficulties do not disappear. A dyslexic will learn to read, but may always be slow and find it tiring. A dyspraxic may rely on checklists forever in order to arrive at the right place with the right equipment.

- *Specific learning difficulties can affect children of all abilities.* Children of all abilities (from gifted through to below average) can experience a specific learning difficulty. They will almost inevitably have difficulty in dealing with some aspect or other of life in the classroom that is independent of their level of intellectual ability.

Specific learning difficulty labels are descriptive rather than diagnostic

Specific learning difficulties can be hard to get to grips with because, unlike mumps or measles, they are not clearly definable diseases with a precise set of symptoms and an underlying medical explanation.

The various terms (dyslexia, dyspraxia, dyscalculia and so forth) with which we have become familiar during the past few years are used to denote particular clusters of difficulty. For example:

- Dyslexia – problems with reading and spelling.

- Dyspraxia – difficulties with physical coordination as well as mental planning and organising.

- Dyscalculia – difficulty with maths.

These terms are more descriptive than precisely diagnostic. In other words, they are the words we use to denote a cluster of difficulties. If we are told that Arabella has mumps we know what to expect. The course of her illness would be the same for her as for others who contract mumps. If we are told that Ben is dyslexic we would have a broad idea that he had some difficulty in acquiring literacy skills but we would not know how serious this was – we wouldn't know the exact nature and extent of the problem. It would require an assessment of his cognitive processes to get a profile of his strengths and weaknesses and he would need good teaching to see how he responded and the extent of his difficulty.

Specific learning difficulties are not mutually exclusive

I have been asked why I have chosen to write a book covering so many areas of difficulty. Surely, anyone who thinks that their child is dyslexic or dyspraxic or has ADHD will want a book devoted entirely to the topic and not one that covers so much.

The answer is simple. The learning difficulties that I have so carefully divided into separate chapters are actually not always well behaved and ready to stay in their own boxes. These specific difficulties are often not mutually exclusive.

In the years that I have been assessing children it has often been the case that the child who is having literacy difficulty and is showing all the signs of dyslexia may also experience difficulties which are associated with ADHD or dyspraxia. Alternatively, a child might be showing a full house of difficulties associated with dyspraxia but his difficulty with social skills may tick the box for mild autism spectrum disorder (ASD). A nice clear identification of, say, dyslexia or dyspraxia can make things feel easier to understand and easier to manage, but in reality many children show a mix of difficulties.

The terms which are generally used to describe this overlap of specific difficulties are co-occurrence or co-morbidity. It is not just practitioners like myself who have noted this overlap; there is extensive research that shows the extent of the phenomena and how common it is. In fact, co-occurring difficulties may often seem to be the rule rather than the exception.

In my experience there is generally a primary or lead problem but with additional difficulties in the frame. Consequently, I have frequently found myself explaining to parents that while I think that their child is experiencing dyslexia or dyspraxia (or whatever), he does, in addition, appear to be showing traits associated with an additional area of difficulty.

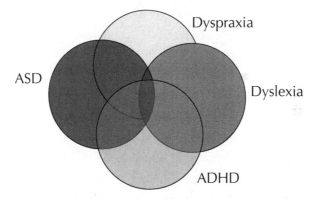

Figure I.1 The overlap of behaviours associated with dyslexia, dyspraxia, ADHD and ASD

From time to time I have seen children who are confusing everyone because they have a bit of this and a bit of that and no clear label seems to really fit. This can be difficult for parents. It is so much easier to be able to explain to the rest of the world that a child is dyslexic or dyspraxic than to have to describe their differences. I remember talking to the parents of such a child and saying that, frustratingly, there really was no good 'label' or shorthand for their child's difficulties when his mother laughed and said that they had been discussing this with their GP who had suggested that 'spaghetti soup' would be the best description. What was actually much more important than the label was being clear as to how this child's various difficulties could be addressed.

Another mother whose son's difficulties did not fit neatly into one category or another gave some interesting insights. First she stressed the damage that can be done to the child–parent relationship if the parents continue to seek a 'diagnosis' and to tout the child from professional to professional in the search for one. However, she then said that without a clear label it is difficult to communicate the child's needs to school.

Why naming these areas of specific learning difficulty is generally helpful

The learning difficulty labels do help in that they provide socially and academically acceptable shorthand as to what the child's key difficulties are. If a teacher is told that a pupil in her class is dyspraxic or dyslexic then she can make the necessary arrangements to support that child. She can make sure that she does not ask the dyslexic child to read aloud in class. She can encourage rather than chastise the dyspraxic child when he is last to get his clothes on after PE. At the very least the teacher knows that she may have to modify her teaching and give well-targeted support.

A named difficulty can also be of value to individual children. Many children with a particular learning difficulty have started to feel in some way inadequate or lacking in ability. For these children it can be a huge relief to know that they are bright and capable but that they have a recognised area of specific difficulty which is not their fault and which they can be helped to manage. It can also be a relief to know that their teachers can be helped to understand them better.

Despite this it can still feel miserably frustrating to need this special treatment.

It is important that children do not start to feel that they are defined by their learning difficulty label and that this is who and what they are. They need plenty of opportunities to shine in other areas, and we need to remember that while a particular child may experience a specific learning difficulty which is extreme and which may make learning a real struggle, this child's disability is only a handicap within certain situations (mainly school) and during certain activities. I cannot sing in tune, but as it is not a required daily activity no one has so far suggested that I have a developmental singing disorder and neither have I been identified with dyscantatia.

It is also important that adults who live and work with children with an area of learning difficulty are thoughtful about the language used to describe the issues. It is, for example, preferable to talk about the identification of a difficulty rather than diagnosis.

The word diagnosis has medical connotations and it is not necessary to regard the specific learning difficulties discussed in the following chapters as illnesses or disorders. They are information processing and behavioural differences, which can impact to a greater or lesser degree on educational progress and social interactions. It is unfortunate, too, that several of these areas of difficulty have been appended with the word disorder.

The identification of a difficulty is so much more positive than the diagnosis of a disorder. Difficulties can be overcome.

Case studies

The 30 or so case studies and the examples that pop up within various chapters are based on real-life children and parents. In order to ensure that they cannot be identified, names and personal details have been changed and details blended. Some of these case studies are composites (but remain true to real-life experiences). Others are more personal, and where the case story has been specific to a particular child and family I have obtained permission from all involved.

I am immensely grateful to the parents and pupils who have given me permission to use their stories which bring these areas of difficulty alive. Their willingness to talk with me, in some cases many years after the initial assessment, and to share their experiences, illustrates the profound impact that a learning difficulty can have on child and parents alike. It has also been very evident that parental involvement and support are absolutely central to children's progress and success.

Writing style and gender issues

I have endeavoured to keep jargon down to a minimum but this is not always easy or indeed possible. I have used words and terms such as 'multisensory', 'cognitive processing', 'information processing', 'working memory', 'phonological awareness' and so forth where it has seemed necessary and to add to precision. I have tried to ensure that there is a clear explanation of what these terms mean both within the text and in the glossary.

Many authors now write in the plural using they and them rather than him or her. I have found this too clumsy. In some chapters I use the pronoun he and in others she. These are interchangeable and I am not suggesting that the content of the chapter refers only to boys or only to girls, except where stated.

How to read this book

This book is not intended to be read from cover to cover. The individual chapters do stand alone but can usefully be cross referenced. For example, the reader of the chapter on dyslexia may also find it helpful to look at the chapters on reading and ideas for teaching literacy skills.

Terminology for stages and ages

Within the book I make reference to the main phases of education – primary (infants and juniors) and secondary – as classified in the UK. Appendix 1 shows how these groupings relate to our key stages and year groups. It also shows how these match up with grade levels in the USA.

Part 1

UNDERSTANDING SPECIFIC LEARNING DIFFICULTIES

Chapter 1

INFORMATION PROCESSING

My son's teacher said she thinks he is a 'slow processor'. Lucy's mother thinks that Lucy is a non-verbal learner and she asked what kind of learner Peter is. The psychologist who I chatted to at a party last week said that many children who are dyslexic have areas of information processing weakness. What are they all talking about?

Sarah Jane never seems to listen or to remember what she has been told, while her sister Florence has full recall of everything which has been said in her presence, even if it's nothing to do with her. William can never find things, even when they are right in front of his nose, while his sibling, James, can reproduce the details of a building passed once on the bus. Phillip, who is a bright boy, is surprisingly slow to complete mental tasks, whether it is assimilating information or copying from the board. Jasmine is always trying things out and has to pull it to pieces or turn it upside down before she is satisfied, while her sister likes to think things through before acting. Parents are generally very much aware of how their individual children take in and absorb information.

Children will take these information processing preferences, strengths or weaknesses into the classroom with them. The good listener will be way ahead. Much of what goes on in class requires children to listen either to the teacher or to media or discussion. If the teacher makes good use of wall displays, if she accompanies her teaching with visual aids (pictures, diagrams, a visual timetable and so forth), then the poor listener who has good visual skills will be well supported. If she plans for and builds in plenty of practical experience and the chance to move around the classroom she will aid the learning of the child who likes to learn through doing.

One mother explained to me that only one out of her four children was what she termed a 'normal' learner. What she meant was that only one of them seemed to find the classroom an easy place in which to learn. The others all needed some back up from home. Two had mild difficulty with attention and concentration, which meant that they were often to be found daydreaming. Their difficulties were not, however, sufficiently marked to be labelled as a specific learning difficulty. The third child had difficulty with a number of physical activities; for him practical activities such as science experiments, painting, writing, sports and gym were all a challenge. He needed much encouragement and support if he was to manage to produce extensive written work. However, his difficulties were not sufficiently marked to warrant a learning difficulty label, even though they shared characteristics with dyspraxia.

There are three key areas of information processing which are in constant use in the classroom: auditory processing, visual processing and kinaesthetic awareness. We will look at them in more detail.

Information processing

Auditory processing

This refers to the speed and accuracy of listening and understanding what has been heard. Difficulty with auditory processing results in poor perception of both speech and non-speech sounds. This has nothing to do with auditory acuity (how good hearing is) but relates to how easily the brain can make distinctions, discriminate and 'understand' sounds.

Several years ago I attended a talk about learning difficulties. The speaker gave the audience a hearing test. First he delivered a series of bleeps, which he varied in pitch and volume. Those of us who had heard all these sounds were 'passed' as having good auditory acuity. No one in the audience appeared to have any hearing difficulty. He then played back some rather muffled speech sounds. Some of the audience had no difficulty in repeating back what they had heard but others found it almost impossible to make head or tail of it. This test had sampled our ability to discriminate speech sounds and make sense of them.

Auditory processing is complex. Between the time that the sound wave hits the ear drum and the moment when it eventually becomes a signal which the brain can interpret in a meaningful way there are a good number of procedures which could be faulty. The full job of processing and making sense of what we have heard also needs the listener to use their working memory and to pay attention.

The chapters on working memory, auditory processing disorder, specific language difficulty and ADHD describe the ways in which children experiencing these areas of difficulty can find it hard to listen effectively. They are often the children who lose track of what teachers are saying and end up gazing out of the window. In contrast, the good auditory processors are likely to find that they can learn through listening (tapes, discussion and lectures). They are at an advantage in the classroom where much of the day requires them to listen to their teacher.

Visual processing

This does not refer to visual acuity, meaning whether a child may be long or short sighted. It refers to the efficiency of the brain component of the visual system when it comes to the speed of discrimination and sequencing of visual information and also to short-term visual memory. A child with poor visual processing might mix up letters, skip words, find it hard to scan and pick up details, or find it difficult to copy from the board. The slow visual/spatial processor will be slow to complete copying tasks and to make visual discriminations. Any weaknesses here are likely to make it hard for the child to learn to read. Children with poor short-term visual memory often do not do well in maths.

The child with good visual processing may like to use visual aids such as mindmaps, diagrams and handouts to help their learning. They may make good use of information displayed on the classroom wall.

Kinaesthetic awareness

Finally, let's look at the impact of poor kinaesthetic awareness. Kinaesthetic awareness refers to the sensations by which bodily positions, weight, muscle tension and movement are perceived. The child with difficulty in any of these areas may be fidgety due to the need for constant feedback from the feel of the objects around him. He may find it hard to maintain a stable body position due to poor muscle tension or strength. This may impact his writing and his concentration.

The child with good kinaesthetic awareness may find that he likes to learn through experience, moving, touching and doing (actively exploring their work, doing science experiments, painting, etc.).

So we see that variation in the efficiency in information processing in these three areas will have a dramatic impact on a child's experience of the classroom and on their progress. Weak auditory, visual and kinaesthetic processing are each associated with areas of specific learning difficulty. For these children it is crucial that their class teacher is adept at presenting information in varied and interesting ways and can adapt her teaching style to meet their strengths and difficulties.

Even the intellectually brightest of children can be slow to process certain types of information whether it is auditory, visual or kinaesthetic. While this does not constitute a formal learning difficulty it is nevertheless frustrating for them, particularly when they are misunderstood or not appropriately supported.

Learning styles

The concept of learning styles is one that has definitely caught the imagination of both parents and teachers in recent years but is controversial. It describes the flip side to information processing deficits in that it focuses on information processing strengths.

One of the most popular theories of 'learning style' suggests that there are three types of learner: the visual learner, the auditory learner and the kinaesthetic or tactile learner.

Proponents of this theory claim that visual learners have a preference for seeing (think in pictures, benefit from visual aids such as mindmaps, diagrams and handouts, etc.). Auditory learners learn best through listening (lectures, discussions, tapes, etc.). Tactile learners prefer to learn via experience, moving, touching and doing (actively exploring their work, doing science experiments, painting, etc.). The idea is that teachers can prepare their lessons in such a way that children with different styles of learning can access new information in their preferred mode. Students can work out their preferred learning style through a range of questionnaires that have been designed for the purpose.

The idea that each of us may have a preferred learning or operating style is very comfortable and feels intuitively to make sense but has not been upheld by research.

Many ideas have been generated about how to enable children to learn using different styles; for example, instead of being taught by the conventional method of listening to a teacher, children might be allowed to wander around, listen to music and even play with balls in the classroom.

It would seem to make good sense for teachers (and parents) to pay attention to how they present information (so that they ensure that it is accessible for children with different strengths in relation to how they process information) and it would seem also to be valuable for pupils to reflect on and to understand how they take in information.

However, critics of the learning styles model say that there is no evidence that identifying a student's learning style and matching the teaching to that style actually produces better outcomes. Neuroscientists remind us that we all use all our senses to learn and that it is unhelpful to categorise children as particular types of learners. Professor Susan Greenfield says that the method of classifying pupils on the basis of 'learning styles' is a waste of valuable time and resources. 'Humans,' she says, 'have evolved to build a picture of the world through our senses working in unison, exploiting the immense interconnectivity that exists in the brain. It is when the senses are activated together that brain cells fire more strongly than when stimuli are received apart.' This is something to keep in mind when supporting children who have areas of weakness.

The learning styles debate has been useful in that it has directed attention to the way in which children process incoming information and what constitutes the most effective learning environment.

The link between learning and information processing

As you will see in the following chapters, poor information processing in one area or another is either causal or goes hand in hand with one or more area of specific learning difficulty; it is for this reason that a general chapter on information processing seemed valuable at the beginning of this section.

If your child experiences any area of information processing weakness, even if it is insufficiently marked to warrant a learning difficulty label, you should find that the suggestions that appear in the specific learning difficulties chapters are relevant and helpful.

Meanwhile here are key ideas for help:

- Multisensory teaching – to support your child with an area of weakness try and engage more than one sense while he is learning. Let him see it, hear it and do it. Do not just teach to the strength. (See Chapter 3, Dyslexia, for more on multisensory learning.)

- For the poor listener – present verbal information in small chunks and allow time for him to digest it before continuing. (See Chapter 2, Working Memory, and Chapter 3, Dyslexia.)

- For the poor visual processor – accompany interpretation of visual data with speech; teach him to talk it through. Give time for copying tasks. (See Chapter 4, Dyspraxia, Chapter 5, Dyscalculia and Other Maths Problems, and Chapter 10, Visual Processing Difficulty.)

- For the poor kinaesthetic learner – allow him to move around while he thinks and works; for example, can he work standing up? (See Chapter 4, Dyspraxia.)

You will know where your child's strengths and weaknesses lie. The important thing is to use the strengths, strengthen the weaker areas and help children to use all sensory input.

KEY POINTS

⇨ Within the classroom children learn through hearing (auditory processing), seeing (visual processing) and doing (kinaesthetic awareness).

⇨ There is variation between children in the speed and efficiency with which their brain interprets in-coming information in each of these domains.

⇨ This variation impacts on how easily they take things in and learn.

⇨ Although strengths and difficulties are important to learning, our senses work best in unison.

⇨ Any areas of weakness can be supported by good multisensory teaching.

Chapter 2

WORKING MEMORY

The working memory capacity of individual pupils has been found to make a remarkable impact on their educational progress. Those children who have a good working memory generally thrive as readers and mathematicians. Conversely, children as young as four or five years old who are identified as having a poor working memory (for their age) are very much at risk of having difficulty in mastering literacy and maths skills.

Working memory is the all-important tool that enables us to keep on track and on task as we go about our daily business. It is the memory system that children need and rely on in the classroom. Working memory capacity has a major influence on how easily and successfully a child learns but it is not related to a child's level of intellectual ability.

Our knowledge about the important role played by working memory in a child's learning has really only come to light in the past decade or two. As you read through this book you will find that working memory is frequently mentioned and that poor working memory is almost invariably associated with poor reading, difficulty with maths, issues related to concentration and many other classroom difficulties. It therefore seemed important to put an explanatory chapter towards the front of the book.

Although working memory capacity is of huge importance in relation to learning, it is not related to a child's level of intellectual ability. It can be confusing for parents when they find that their apparently bright, alert and clever child runs into difficulty in school. School performance may simply not seem to reflect the child's level of intellectual ability, and poor working memory is often the reason for this.

This chapter will cover what we mean by working memory, the implications of poor working memory and the ways in which children with below average working memory can be helped and supported.

What is working memory?

Working memory is an extension of short-term memory, so we need to start by looking at this. Short-term memory is the capacity for holding a small amount of information in mind in an active, readily available state for a short period of time.

It can be helpful to think of short-term memory as a mental whiteboard on which we can keep a temporary store of information which we can use in the here and now.

There are two important features about this mental whiteboard. The board has a limited capacity, and if we are asked to put too much information on the board then everything is wiped clean. The second feature is that if we are interrupted while we are using the information on the board we will also find that it has disappeared when we return to the task in hand.

To illustrate the limited capacity imagine that you stop on a car journey to ask the way. A kind stranger gives directions. By the time he is telling you to go right or left or over the lights for the tenth time you may well have forgotten which direction to start in. The information has been wiped because it is just too much and you are overloaded.

Interruptions can be just as bad. Imagine you have just read through a complex recipe. You may be muttering the ingredients under your breath as you start to get them all out. Your daughter comes into the kitchen to ask where you put her school bag. By the time you have told her where it is you need to reread the list of ingredients because you can no longer remember what they are.

Sometimes we need to do more than just hold information (such as directions or an ingredients list) in our immediate memory and this is where working memory comes in. Working memory refers to the system we use when we need to manage or manipulate the information that is being held in short-term memory. A simple example would be if you were asked to repeat back a string of numbers (two, five, eight, four, nine, three, six) but instead of just repeating them in the order given you had to repeat them back in reverse order. A more complex example would be if a maths problem is read out aloud to you and you are asked to work it out in your head without the help of pen and paper. You must keep the number facts in mind while simultaneously having to remember what maths operation to apply and even call up maths facts stored in long-term memory.

The analogy with a whiteboard for both short-term and working memory gives us a very simple image of some complex activities which are happening in the brain. I am unable to describe this in terms of neuronal connections or electrical or chemical activities, but scientists have suggested a simple model of what they think is going on.

They suggest that working memory uses three areas of the brain. We have two short-term stores and the central executive.

One short-term store deals with auditory information and the other with visual/spatial information. The auditory information is processed in the left hemisphere of the brain while the visual/spatial is dealt with in an area of the right hemisphere. The central executive is in the frontal cortex, which is located in the forehead.

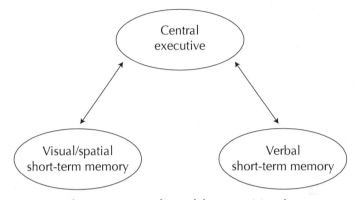

Figure 2.1 A simple model summarising the main components of working memory

We use the auditory store when we are 'mentally' holding on to verbal instructions, a list of numbers or a new name. We use it for holding on to meaning as we read. We rely on it as we repeat a long and previously unknown medical term. We use it when we are learning a modern language or simply retaining a sequence of sounds.

We use the visual/spatial store when we are carrying out activities such as keeping our place while reading, sequencing letters for spelling and learning pictorial scripts such as Chinese. School children use it when they are copying off the board or from other notes.

The central executive is the coordinator. It uses information from the two short-term stores and it can also 'pull up', integrate and use information from long-term memory. To return to the mental maths problem mentioned earlier, you will need to use your long- and short-term memory if you are to be able to work out the answer. The following problem will illustrate the point. Read it once, then turn the page over so that you can no longer see it.

> A family goes on a 160-mile journey. They drive for three hours, stop for half an hour and then drive for a further one hour before they reach their destination. What is their average speed while driving?

This is a simple bit of maths but (unless it is written in front of you) it requires you to keep the key bits of information in your working memory while drawing on your long-term memory about how to work out an average and how to divide.

How much information can the working memory deal with?

On average adults can successfully hold on to seven 'bits' of information in their working memory while they need to use them. Seven is average and the range is plus or minus two. The 'bits' of information may be seven numbers or even seven ideas. Obviously, if it is seven ideas then the memory capacity is much larger than if it is seven letters or numbers or names.

Just to complicate things we can help ourselves by using specific strategies to aid our short-term and working memory. If, for example, you were asked to remember the following 12 words you would find it much easier if you were able to place them into categories. Read the list of words, cover them and see how many you can recall:

shetland, collie, terrier, arab, labrador, tabbie, welsh, tom, dartmoor, ginger, dalmation, siamese.

Now read this same list of items and see if you don't find this easier:

- collie, terrier, labrador, dalmation
- tom, tabbie, ginger, siamese
- shetland, arab, welsh, dartmoor.

Working memory is also closely connected with 'efficiency' in processing. For example, if you are asked to multiply 246 by 7 in your head your ability to do this will be affected not only by your working memory capacity but also by how well you know your times tables and number bonds. If you are fluent with times table facts then the strain on your working memory will be less.

Working memory is similarly connected with concentration and attention. If your ability to pay attention is weak then whatever your working memory capacity, unless you make a great effort to attend, you are likely to have difficulty with the 246 times 7 task. Your mind may wander off in the middle.

What about children?

Let's start with capacity. Children's working memory improves with age. From the age of three until the child reaches adolescence memory capacity increases steadily. We would not expect a four-year-old to be able to remember more than a couple of items, but by around 14 years we would expect them to be able to remember up to seven items plus or minus two, like an adult.

At around seven years of age children become aware of the need to use rehearsal strategies to aid memory and at this age also they shift towards preferring to remember information in terms of verbal characteristics. In part, the increase in working memory capacity with age reflects a child's improving capacity to pay attention and to process information more efficiently.

However, as with adults, there are individual differences, and within any particular age group we will find that there is a wide variation in the working memory capacity of individual children.

Working memory and the classroom

The impact of having a poor working memory relative to the peer group is significant, and this is because the school day involves many activities and interactions which require a child to use working memory.

First there is listening. Much of what goes on in the classroom is verbally mediated; most teachers use verbal instruction to teach as well as to manage their class. They give instructions about when, where and how to line up for playtime or to pack away books or start to change for PE. As well as these many and varied moment-to-moment directions most teachers teach through talk and discussion.

A teacher might say, 'Get out your blue textbooks, turn to page 49. Get out your green exercise books; put a margin on the left and the date on the right. Now start the first comprehension exercise on page 49, and don't forget before you start, please can you hand in yesterday's homework.' The child with poor working memory is likely to be thoroughly overloaded. Once he has given in the homework, he probably cannot remember which page to go to. He might ask or copy a friend. He may be so used to forgetting instructions that he switches off and waits to be told again.

Not only may it be difficult to follow instructions but the child may also have difficulty in dealing with multistep problems, particularly if too much information has to be held in mind while going along.

Talking as well as listening can be impacted. Some children seem to interrupt, or simply give up contributing to the class, nervous that if they put their hand up and then have to wait to speak they will have forgotten what they wanted to say by the time the teacher asks them.

The child with poor visual/spatial short-term memory is going to find it hard to copy off the board and may frequently lose his place.

So we see that many things that happen in the classroom, which on the surface appear quite normal and manageable, may, in fact, be placing an impossible memory load on those children with poor memory. This effectively reduces their learning opportunities and means that they are getting rather less out of education than their peers.

How does working memory capacity affect educational progress?
Literacy and maths skills
Thanks to the work carried out by Professor Susan Gathercole and her colleagues (see Further Reading) we now know that working memory is extremely important in that it is a very strong predictor of educational progress. Children with good working memory have been found to show excellent reading skill and also to do well on maths tests.

Children with poor verbal working memory have been found to have difficulty with literacy. Children with weak visual/spatial working memory have been found to have difficulty with maths.

We now know that children as young as four or five years old who are identified as having poor working memory are very much at risk of having difficulty in mastering literacy and maths skills.

What is going on?
Limited working memory means that a child has a short window of opportunity to commit new information into a long-term store.

Learning/memorising tasks are affected
First there is early reading which requires the child to learn to match letter sounds to letter names. Then as he progresses through school there are other things to be learnt but which have little intrinsic meaning to help aid his memory. Days of the week, months of the year, times tables, French vocabulary and spellings are all a challenge. Children with poor

working memory capacity will find that they need to go over the material to be stored many times before it is fully captured and reliably stored into long-term memory.

Activities which require the child to multitask or retain a sequence of actions can prove difficult

Writing can be hard. There is just so much to keep in mind; which letters to use, how to form them, what to say. By the time the child has worked out the letters that go into the word he may well have forgotten the sentence he wanted to write.

Activities involving several sequential steps (which are not all familiar), such as a dance sequence or a science experiment, may also be impacted.

So we see that for children with poor working memory many tasks are significantly more onerous than for those who have good memory and that memory overload in both formal and informal learning situations can lead them to forget crucial information. This in turn leads them to fail in many tasks.

How can parents tell if their child has a good, average or poor working memory?

There are various standardised tests that can be given to establish working memory capacity, but these are not available for parents as they are for professional use only. However, if your child has an educational assessment at any time, this will most probably include a working memory test. Meanwhile here are things which parents might have become aware of.

The child with poor *auditory working memory* is likely to show many of the following traits. These will be evident both at home and in the classroom.

He is a poor listener, so he will be likely to:

- find it hard to follow and retain a set of instructions, particularly if the instructions are long or complex

- return empty handed after being sent on a mission to fetch something, or come back asking what it was he was meant to be doing

- find it hard to wait his turn in conversation. He may often interrupt, particularly if he thinks he is going to forget what he wants to say or to ask

- fail to put up his hand in class if he thinks that by the time he is asked for his view or his answer it will have popped out of his head

- find himself in trouble in school but may not be clear just what it is he has done wrong.

It takes him longer than most to learn names and lists, especially if they have little intrinsic meaning, so you may notice that he finds it difficult to:

- pick up the names of people he has just met

- learn and retain the days of the week or the months of the year

- learn and retain new spellings

- learn and retain the vocabulary of a modern language.

The child with poor *visual working memory* is likely to:

- have difficulty copying information from one source to another

- have difficulty in recognising written symbols.

He may fail to complete (or copy inaccurately) any homework or notes that have to be copied from the board. The child with poor working memory may also:

- have difficulty in maintaining attention during some activities. He may, for example, give up halfway through a family game of cards

- give up on multistep activities at school if he cannot remember what to do next

- not complete what he is doing if it involves a sequence of actions

- put his bag by the front door ready for school only to walk right past it two minutes later

- walk out of school at the end of the day leaving his coat or his school bag or his musical instrument behind

- fail to give his parents important notices from school. These are the ones which parents may find crumpled up in the bottom of his bag weeks later.

Just to complicate things there can be other reasons for some of these behaviours. The child with ADHD may also appear to have poor working memory capacity, though when focused and prompted a good number can demonstrate an excellent working memory capacity.

Can working memory be improved?

Now that it has been established that a poor working memory is a grave disadvantage, the race has been on to find a way of remediating the situation. What every parent (and teacher) wants to know is just how working memory can be improved. Like so many educational issues and problems there are really no quick remedies or magic bullets.

Some improvements have been found as a result of memory strategy training and also direct practice on memory tasks. There are also a number of commercial programmes which have been developed and which are being studied. Results are being recorded and monitored. The issues are first whether any improvement in working memory is maintained, and second whether improvements shown on the training material will transfer to other areas of life. When large-scale studies have collated results there has been no clear demonstration that any one programme can successfully do either, though there are individual cases where great improvements have been noted. These programmes are listed in the resources section.

Anecdotally, I find it interesting that after assessing more than 2000 pupils and students the one who came up with the highest score on tests of working memory was a bright and competitive ten-year-old with a significant visual impairment. She could not rely on vision to help her learning and remembering. I have speculated that she might have managed, through determination and concentration, to maximise her working memory for what she had heard. She may have developed specific techniques and strategies, but whatever she had done she had really managed to develop a capacity well above the average.

How can we help children with weak working memory?

A key problem for children with poor working memory is that it is so easy to become 'overloaded'. Once overload occurs then things are forgotten, the thread is broken, and it is difficult for the children to remain on track and on task. Learning opportunities are lost.

There are two approaches to helping these children. First, parents and teachers need to behave in a way which minimises overload, and second, children need to learn strategies, tricks and methods to prevent overload from being a disaster.

Let's start with interactions

The most helpful way for parents or teachers to talk with the child for whom information often seems to go in through one ear and straight out of the other is to wait until the child is listening before giving an instruction or starting to talk. Then give instructions slowly and in short, simple sentences to reduce the memory load. Pause between sentences to make sure the child has time to process the information. Keep language structure simple.

Be prepared to repeat instructions calmly, slowly and without irritation. Saying things faster and louder can be counterproductive. It simply makes the child feel inadequate and he may panic or switch off. Many children who have difficulty in taking things in will play for time by saying 'pardon' or 'what'. This does not mean they have not heard. It means they have had difficulty in taking it in and understanding. They need a little extra time to process what they have heard before having to continue to listen. So asking you to say it again gives them a bit of a breathing space. Sometimes, however, asking for repetitions can become a habit, so asking the child to try and remember what you have said before you repeat it can be useful – some would say vital! Asking the child to repeat what you have said is also a good way of checking that instructions have been absorbed.

Often the child who finds it hard to listen has a great visual or kinaesthetic memory. Think of ways in which you can tap into this. Accompany verbal instruction with a gesture, a picture or other form of visual aide-memoire.

Key points for interaction:

- Wait until you know he is listening before giving an instruction or starting to talk.

- Give instructions clearly in short bites.

- Allow time for him to process what you say before you continue.

- Do not talk too fast.

- Use language which can be easily processed, i.e. simple sentence structure.

- Repeat instructions calmly, slowly and without irritation.

- When he starts a new task after listening to instructions, check that he has processed what he has to do and can carry it out.

- If necessary, give a written list of what needs to be remembered (use pictures for a pre-reader).

Clear communication can also be enhanced by using visual aids:

- Use memory aids such as wall charts, posters, useful spellings, dictionaries, cubes, counters and number lines. These may all help with homework and are not just helpful for the classroom.

- Accompany verbal instructions with a picture or some other form of visual aid.

For children who have poor working memory for visual information which leads to difficulty in copying from the board or from text it is important that they are not forced to copy down important things such as homework. If, as they are likely to do, they miss a line or other key facts, they are left at sea, unable to figure out what they are meant to be doing.

If possible, negotiate with their teacher to ensure that they get a good copy of notes or homework. The interactive whiteboard should be a help here. It is now so easy for the teacher to transfer anything she writes on the board onto the computer, and this can either be printed or made available for the pupil to access from home.

As a last resort maybe a neat, fast-writing friend could have his or her work photocopied or perhaps the teacher could write it out for your child.

Rote learning

As I mentioned earlier in this chapter the learning of times tables, spellings, French vocabulary and other information that has no intrinsic meaning can be particularly hard. It helps to learn a little at a time and to space practice carefully. Gradually increase the time between each practice period. Start small – maybe revisit newly learnt material after one hour, then two, then four, then half a day, then a day, etc. Make sure that it is securely learnt before introducing more material. The secret is little and often. The more meaning that can be introduced into the material to be learnt the easier it will be.

Routine and systems

Establishing daily routines can help the child with a poor working memory. If actions can become automated then there is less to keep in mind at rushed periods such as getting out of the house for school.

Self-awareness and strategies

The child with a poor working memory may not be aware that he is any different from the child sitting next to him. It is just part of his experience of the world.

Parents have a role to play in helping their child to develop self-awareness about their strengths and difficulties. It is important to help children to understand that, while they may be bright and intelligent, they do not always take in, process and remember what has been said or what they have seen as easily as some other pupils. They can, however, learn to compensate by using helpful strategies.

Children seem to become aware of the need to use strategies by the time that they are around seven or eight. They may not be very good at articulating what they are doing but you can work with them as they go through school to ensure that they are using effective techniques. In the early days playing memory games can help to make a child aware of the need to use strategies to aid memory. Games such as Pelmanism or 'my aunt went shopping and bought…' can be useful (see the games section in the appendices for an explanation).

The first simple strategy a child can use is to repeat things in his head or under his breath. As children mature and as the demands made on them increase then the use of strategies will broaden. You can encourage your child to:

- use repetition. Say it again, write it down, revisit the information, cover it and check it

- take simple notes as his teacher speaks. If this is difficult then it could be a picture or anything that can act as a memory jog later

- create spider diagrams. If the listener writes key words they will later act as a good prompt to aid recall of what has been listened to

- recap information at the end of a lesson. Immediate recall of key points is valuable particularly if they are then written down

- keep a little notebook to hand and jot down important information (bits of paper are so easy to lose)

- record important information on a voice recorder and write it down later

- use an electronic organiser or phone alarm as a reminder

- develop effective study skills. No time and effort must be wasted on learning inefficiently (see Chapter 24, Habits, Strategies and Study Skills)

- ask for information to be repeated. Help him to gain the confidence to do this.

Independent study can be marvellous for the pupil who has spent years struggling in class. What a relief to find that you are studying subjects that you love and that play to your strengths and where you no longer have to struggle to follow and recall all that you are told verbally.

KEY POINTS

⇨ Working memory is our mental capacity to hold and manipulate information in mind in the short term (seconds rather than minutes).

⇨ It is limited in capacity; on average an adult can 'hold on to' seven bits of information (plus or minus two).

⇨ Working memory develops from the age of three or four until full capacity is reached at around 14 years.

⇨ Working memory capacity is linked to school attainment and the early acquisition of basic skills. Poor working memory can have a negative impact on reading and maths skills.

⇨ Pupils with poor working memory are easily overloaded. It can be hard for them to follow long or complex instructions and they may all too easily 'switch off'.

⇨ Working memory capacity is linked with concentration and attention as well as with knowledge and experience.

⇨ The child with below average working memory capacity can be supported through modification of the learning environment and through clear, thoughtful adult communication both at home and in school.

⇨ Children can learn useful techniques and strategies to help their immediate memory.

⇨ Some memory training programmes have been found to help particular children, but the jury is still out on how much impact they have in the long term.

Chapter 3

DYSLEXIA

The staff at Tom's nursery school loved him. He was a bright and sociable little boy who was constantly engaged in one activity or another. He got on well with the other children; he was cooperative and able to look after himself. He may have asked a lot of questions but staff enjoyed his friendly interaction; they were, however, surprised that this apparently quick and able child did not recognise the names above the coat pegs and that his drawings of people never included arms. Despite this everyone assumed that he would do well when he moved on to his primary school. This was not to be the case. Tom struggled with literacy and was eventually identified as being dyslexic when he was eight years old.

I imagine we have all read about people with dyslexia who are incredibly successful, Albert Einstein and Richard Branson being two well-known examples. There is some evidence that the dyslexic brain does have compensations. The dyslexic entrepreneur may be bad with small details yet have vision and an amazing grasp of the big picture. There are many people with dyslexia who are excellent artists, sportsmen and scientists.

The young person with dyslexia does, however, have to navigate and survive school before he can burst onto the world and follow his own interests and talents. Each child will take a different journey and will need appropriate support and encouragement. Parents have a vital role to play.

We live in a print-filled world. Fluent reading and writing is expected to be the norm, not the exception, and yet for our dyslexic children every school day will present difficulties and challenges. The child with extreme dyslexia may struggle to read even at secondary level. The child with mild dyslexia may read well but very slowly; small reading inaccuracies may affect his understanding of text.

This chapter looks at the kind of difficulties typically experienced by dyslexic children at different ages and stages of development and will consider how parents can help. The problems encountered by a seven-year-old will of course be different to those of a 10-, 15- or 20-year-old.

The chapter looks at particular ages and stages, ranging from nursery to 18 plus. At the end you will find individual case studies to illustrate particular aspects of dyslexia. These stories also help to show how the needs of the dyslexic learner change as they progress through school.

The sections of the chapter are not mutually exclusive but you may want to skip bits that you think are not relevant to you. But before that, a little background information should be useful.

The story so far

Back in the 1980s, which is when Tom started primary school, there was growing acceptance and understanding of the label dyslexia but at that time there were still many people (teachers included) who held the view that it was a middle-class invention to explain away dim children.

Things have moved on. Dyslexia was recognised under the Disability Act in 1995, and in 2009 Sir Jim Rose published a government report entitled *Identifying and Teaching Children and Young People with Dyslexia and Literacy Difficulties.* Dyslexia is also specifically mentioned in the 2010 Equality Act, which means that schools now have a duty to make reasonable adjustments to ensure that those affected by dyslexia are not disadvantaged compared to their peers. Despite this, adequate help is not always forthcoming, and the parents of children who are struggling to read and spell can feel concerned, frustrated and at times helpless. It is not always easy for them to know how to progress or what to do to help the child who is having difficulty.

Over time there have been many definitions of dyslexia. What they have in common is the idea that dyslexia is a difficulty with reading and spelling. 'Dys' means difficulty and 'lexia' means words. The Rose report agreed on the following broad (and somewhat circular) definition: 'Dyslexia is a learning difficulty that primarily affects the skills involved in accurate and fluent word reading and spelling.'

It is difficult to be more precise because it is genuinely difficult to pin down. No two people with dyslexia have exactly identical profiles of strengths and difficulties. Reading, writing and spelling are complex skills that involve many different processes, which means that there are many places where things can go wrong.

The one thing that all people with dyslexia have in common is difficulty with reading and spelling. The majority of such people have associated difficulty with aspects of language. A number of them have difficulty with visual analysis of print but by no means all. Some also have both language and visual difficulty. Brain scans show atypical electrical activity in certain areas of the dyslexic brain when reading is happening (compared with the non-dyslexic reader) but this varies from one dyslexic brain to another. Dyslexic people are not all alike.

If this all sounds a bit woolly there is some firm ground out there, and there are things which we can say with certainty about dyslexia:

- The characteristic features of dyslexia are difficulties in phonological awareness, verbal memory and verbal processing speed (these are explained further on in this chapter).

- Dyslexia occurs across the full range of intellectual ability.

- Dyslexia is on a continuum ranging from mild to severe. There are no established cut-off points.

- Co-existing difficulties may be seen in relation to language, motor coordination, mental maths, concentration and personal organisation. Of course, many non-dyslexic children also have these difficulties.

- It is only by looking at a child's response to good teaching and intervention that we can establish the severity of the difficulty.

- Dyslexia is neurological in origin.

- There is a genetic basis and it tends to run in families.

It is estimated that about 10 per cent of the population experience a degree of dyslexia. The earlier we can identify and support children who are at risk of difficulty the better.

Reception class through to the end of the infant phase

So how can we identify difficulties and support four- to seven-year-olds during this period?

There are two ways in which the young reader starts to make sense of the words on a page. She either has to learn to sound out each word or she has to learn to recognise the whole word visually. Both approaches play a part and most children rely on a combination of both to get off to a successful start. The dyslexic reader, however, has difficulty with one or both of these systems.

The sounding-out approach to reading requires good phonological awareness, and whole-word recognition requires good visual memory.

There are, however, a number of additional cognitive and information processing weaknesses which have also been found to occur alongside poor literacy skills.

These trademark problems which are described below are often evident from an early age – certainly before the child is in school. If many of these are evident before school then it is prudent to consider the young child to be at risk of future difficulty. If they are evident and your child is already in school and perhaps not finding it easy to take off with early reading activities then now is the time to start planning and making sure that good help is in place. Tom and Pippa, whose stories are at the end of the chapter, are good examples of the early difficulties found.

The areas of cognitive and information processing which are linked to poor literacy skills are detailed below.

Phonological awareness

Children cannot 'crack the code' of reading until they have gained the ability to identify and distinguish all those small sounds which build into words. To do this they need good phonological awareness. They need to be able to hear and to tell the difference between the sounds made by the different letters of the alphabet. They need to be able to tell if two words rhyme or sound different. They need to be able to hear and distinguish the first, middle and end sounds within a word. The ability to do all of this is called phonological awareness, and children need to have developed the ability to make these distinctions fluently before they are expected to match spoken sounds onto written letters and before they are expected to blend letter sounds together and to segment the sounds in words; in other words, before they are expected to learn to read and spell.

Reading is not the only activity that suffers if phonological skills and awareness are weak. Children with poor phonological awareness are likely to:

- transpose sounds in words, for example saying par cark instead of car park

- have difficulty or lack interest in learning nursery rhymes and in playing other word games such as I spy if letter sounds (not names) are used

- mispronounce words more frequently than other children of their age.

Working memory

We know that children who have a poor working memory have considerable difficulty in learning to read. The chapter on working memory elaborates on the reasons for this. Young children with poor working memory are likely to:

- struggle to remember the names of people and places
- struggle to find the words they want to use
- say 'the thingy' or 'the whatsit' or just point when they cannot call up the word they need
- find it hard to remember instructions or requests
- forget what has been said as though things went in one ear and out of the other, and so need to have things repeated.

Sequencing

The child with poor sequencing will be likely to have difficulty in learning and retaining sequenced information such as days of the week, months of the year or the alphabet.

Visual processing

If visual processing is a problem the child will be likely to:

- lose their place when reading
- forget words from line to line – if he reads a word on one line and meets it again within a few moments he is quite capable of failing to recognise it
- transpose letters, for example reading was as saw and no as on.

Children who are showing some or all of these difficulties are definitely in need of support. If in addition there are problems with attention and concentration and if there is a history of dyslexia in the family then they should really be taken seriously. The important thing to remember is that these children can and will learn but it may take longer and need much repetition and rehearsal.

What can we do to help these young children?

Parents can work on:

- phonological skills – check the games section in the appendices for appropriate activities to help your child to start to hear and discriminate the small speech sounds which go to make up language

- reading – share books and read to him on a daily basis and ensure that a love of books is fostered. It is important that books do not become something associated with difficulty and failure

- using a paired reading technique – reading together with your voices in unison. You will find full details in the chapter on reading. This takes away much of the struggle and is a godsend to parent and child

- playing plenty of table-top games such as snap, Pelmanism, matching games and all games relevant to pre-reading skills (see the games section in the appendices).

The secret of success is that learning should be little and often, with plenty of reinforcement and practice and lots of fun – always start with what he can do and move forwards gently, ensuring that any new activities are set at a level that he can manage. Success is important. Set small, achievable targets and celebrate success.

Many dyslexic children will perform really well one day and struggle the next. This is a reality and it is not because they are being lazy or not trying. Do not extend or overdo practice on a good day. Just praise him and stop at the normal time.

Literacy teaching should be:

- highly structured and systematic

- multisensory.

This means that dyslexic readers need to follow a programme which teaches them small step by small step in a logical and systematic way. Even learning the sounds of the letters of the alphabet will be better learnt in a specific sequence. These children are unlikely to suddenly 'get it' and take off. They will need to learn brick by brick. Programmes such as Toe by Toe are structured and well designed (see the Chapter 14 section in Useful Resources, Organisations and Websites).

New learning should be introduced through different mediums. If, for example, your child is learning a new letter sound, make sure that he hears it, says it, feels it (draws it in the air or in sand, or traces it on sand paper, or copies it in pasta shells). Learning is better reinforced if more than one sense can be engaged (see Chapter 1, Information Processing). If you are teaching at home, follow a specific programme.

You may be wondering if you should get any help for your child from a teacher who has a qualification to teach children with dyslexia. This may depend on your pocket, how easily you manage to engage in games and activities with your child and your time constraints. If you have work commitments and/or a large demanding family, it may be particularly difficult to find time.

However, if you can work with your child on a very regular basis in a calm and enjoyable way and he is progressing, you do not need to look for outside help. If you have any doubts, do all you can to find a dyslexia specialist to help.

It is important not to allow your own feelings of anxiety or frustration to transmit to your child. It is all too easy to put a struggling reader off reading and for their confidence to evaporate.

Working with school

If you have concerns, talk with your child's teacher and see if they have picked up any problems. Become familiar with the school reading programme and find out the policy if a child needs additional help. Find out if your child's class teacher is making any allowances for your child in class. If necessary, ask to talk to the school special educational needs coordinator. Find out exactly how your child is coping with school, and if you have serious concerns, follow things up.

By the time that children have had their seventh birthday they should be well on their way to being independent readers. Many dyslexic pupils are still struggling. They may be starting to feel that they are different or stupid. Supporting them in learning to read is now a priority. Please do not panic but take it seriously. Talk it through at home and make a plan of action. Any help must be fun, systematic and daily.

The junior school years

So how can we recognise and help the older primary school child (those aged seven to eleven)? By this time you will know for certain if your child is finding it hard to learn to read and to spell and you may be wondering if this might be dyslexia. You may not be sure because he may be different from other children who you know have been identified, or you may know of other children in your child's class who are struggling more than he is. Dyslexic children are not all exactly alike, so just because he is not like others does not mean he may not experience a difficulty.

Dyslexia is not a single entity. The pattern of difficulties which children experience can be varied. The severity of the difficulty can also range considerably from mild to severe. Even a mild difficulty can need attention and it is important that children with mild dyslexia get support too.

Dyslexia can also co-exist with other areas of specific learning difficulty. He may, for example, have elements of difficulty more generally associated with dyspraxia, dyscalculia or ADHD. Children are individuals.

The stories about Pippa, Ethan and Chloe at the end of this chapter show that the composition and degree of difficulty which individual children experience can be very varied.

What difficulties are the seven- to eleven-year-old children with dyslexia likely to experience?

The obvious difficulties will be poor reading and poor spelling. These may be serious or quite mild.

- Children who are struggling with reading are likely to have difficulty in all subjects because of insufficiently well-developed basic skills. By this stage there is an assumption that children can read simple instructions and write independently.

- Some children are reading well but having difficulty with written work. Spelling may be odd and unreliable. It may vary from day to day and from line to line.

- Writing may look spiky and the margin may travel across the page. The child may find the process of writing hard work.

- Homework may not be recorded accurately or in full, causing difficulty at home when the child does not know what he is meant to be doing.

There may be difficulties with verbal expression and short-term/working memory. The dyslexic child:

- will often have difficulty with word finding and with self-expression. Maybe he starts his sentences over and over while he searches for the next words that he needs. Maybe he uses a lot of words such as 'thingy' and 'whatsits'

- may find it hard to follow instructions

- may have difficulty in completing tasks because he has forgotten what to do next

- may find French a challenge. The child may perceive it as yet another mysterious and irregular set of words to be learnt. Many children with dyslexia love Latin; it is phonically regular and follows predictable rules.

Although many dyslexic children are good with numbers and quick to get maths concepts they are likely to have some quite specific difficulties. They may:

- lose track while working through multistep calculations due to poor working memory. Many dyslexic mathematicians prefer to work fast and become frustrated if they have to set out and record each step involved in problem solving

- find it hard to learn and retain their number bonds and times tables

- have difficulty reading questions or problems.

There may be some issues relating to vision. The child may:

- suffer from headaches after reading

- sometimes see the words moving or letters looking blurred or double (this is rare but can happen for some children)

- have difficulty in copying off the board

- find that his eyes are sensitive to light

- prefer to read through a transparent coloured overlay.

There may also be some behavioural issues:

- An unsupported dyslexic child may be coping by becoming the class clown, being teacher's pet or opting out and presenting challenging behaviour.

- The child who is really 'good' in school may take out his frustrations and unhappiness at home. This is a much safer environment, and kicking the cat, winding up a sibling or just annoying a parent may provide the much-needed outlet.

You may be worried that the bright child you know at home is performing at a very average level in school. Some bright children with mild dyslexic difficulties may seem to be bumping along. As far as the teacher is concerned they may appear to be an average pupil doing just fine. But the reality may be that he is a very bright but 'mildly' dyslexic child who has to work particularly hard to cope and to keep up. Parents may have noticed that there is a discrepancy between what their child is doing in school and the way they see him at home. Parents can often feel that if they say anything they look like 'pushy parents' who think their child is a genius.

No child will have difficulty with everything on the list, but if your child ticks over half of these items it does sound as though he needs some help. Do not be put off by a teacher who tells you not to worry and that it will all come good given time. I think that you do need to worry. Your child really does need to have mastered basic literacy skills and to have become a reader by the time he starts secondary school at 11. It is almost impossible for children to make up lost ground once they embark on Key Stage 3. There is just too much going on and so often they are putting enormous efforts into covering up their difficulties and making sure that they appear to be coping. By this stage your child will still need extra support but of a more sophisticated nature. If your child is seriously behind with reading at age seven, eight or nine it is a priority and all stops must be pulled out to ensure that he becomes a reader. He will never have these years again – make the most of them, whatever it takes.

What can you do to help?

At this stage an educational psychologist's assessment could clarify the nature and extent of his difficulty and could provide you with a profile of his strengths and difficulties (see the chapter on assessment). More importantly, it could help pinpoint the areas on which to focus help. With or without an EP assessment you could build on the suggestions made for the younger child and also follow these general principles:

- Follow a well-structured multisensory reading and spelling programme.

- Little and often is the rule and this applies to reading as well as to learning new spellings.

- Allow time for reinforcement. Although he may be very quick to learn some things this does not include spelling and reading. Make sure that anything learnt which comes into the difficult category is practised again and again, starting with short time intervals. The chapter on working memory explains why this is necessary and helpful.

- Do not push things if he is tired or having a bad day.

- Try and stick to a daily routine so reading becomes an automatic part of the day and does not have to be renegotiated every time.

- Make sure he has enough sleep.

More specifically where literacy skills are concerned:

- Look for specialist help if you possibly can, unless you are certain that you can help on a daily basis in a way that does not exacerbate the difficulty.

- If you are working with him, follow a small-step learning approach to spelling and introduce spelling rules.

- Encourage him to complete written work on a laptop. Learning to touch type has been very liberating for many children. Although children can often write extremely fast with just two fingers I do advocate learning to touch type. It is a valuable life skill.

- Introduce study skills (see Chapter 24, Habits, Strategies and Study Skills).

- Refer to the chapters on reading, spelling and writing for more specific thoughts.

Foster his motivation:

- Above all keep a light touch. He is not going to be motivated or take personal responsibility for his learning if he hates every minute of extra help.

- To help with motivation involve him in setting targets for what he is going to learn or achieve over the next few weeks. It is important to do all you can to get him involved in his learning. Some children let extra help wash over them. Read the chapter on motivation.

- Encourage his enjoyment of books and his experience of reading and make sure his vocabulary is building.

- Read with him copiously. Use a paired reading technique when necessary.

- Give him story CDs to listen to alongside the written version.

- Pay attention to his vocabulary and make a conscious effort to enlarge it. Children who read are picking up new words fast. Non-readers can get left behind.

Dealing with poor working memory (he is the one for whom things seem to go in one ear and out of the other and the one who sets off upstairs to find three items for you and returns five minutes later asking what he was meant to get):

- Limit the length of instructions and give him time to process what has been said or asked.

- Get him to repeat instructions as a way of ensuring that he has taken them in.

- Read the chapter on working memory to find ways of supporting the child with a poor working memory.

Help him to stay confident and happy:

- Do all you can to ensure that he maintains confidence in himself. Can you find something that he is good at and allow him to excel, even if it means preventing his younger sibling from competing with him?

- Remember that the child who is dyslexic will be having a tough time in school. He needs emotional support as well as practical help.

- Allow him activities that help him let off steam and get rid of frustrations when he gets home from school.

Family life:

- Enlist the help and support of other members of the family and make sure that you and your spouse are in agreement about what to do.

- Think through how you are going to give this child additional help in a way that does not adversely affect, or disrupt, family life.

What about homework?

This can be a dilemma for parents. If you leave him to his own devices he may produce two lines of careless-looking work. It's hard to allow this to happen, as you know the response it will evoke when he hands it in at school. So, do you sit over him while all concerned get uptight and frustrated, do you insist that he spends three times as long as the other pupils in his class to get it done properly, or do you do half of it yourself or leave well alone? So many parents I have talked with have faced this problem. Here are some suggestions:

- Help him by reading any relevant texts.

- Write out or get him to copy out a list of the words he may need to use for different subjects so that he can have them easily to hand while he works.

- Act as a scribe but try and do so without passing judgement on the content. Just write what he dictates and leave him to have ownership of what he has to say.

- Discuss the problem with his class teacher and let her know the work she is setting is often beyond him. Explain your dilemma. Ask if she could differentiate his work (differentiation means modifying the work set to ensure that it is at a level which he can manage). Would she accept less quantity or be happy for you to scribe part or all of his work for him?

- If this particular teacher expects her pupils to copy homework instructions from the board or from dictation chances are your child will fail to do so accurately or completely. Ask her if she can find a way to ensure that he knows what he has to do. For example, can she provide photocopied instructions?

- Encourage the use of dictionaries, spell checks and computer-aided learning.

All these learning and performance aids are helpful if introduced to the right child at the right time. You will find useful information in the resources section.

Above all, remember that if your child is struggling with basic skills during these precious school years it is essential to do all you can to ensure that he is helped to get his reading, spelling and writing to a good functional level before he moves into secondary school.

Recognising and supporting the pupil in secondary school

Many pupils will have been identified as having a specific learning difficulty before they finish their primary education but others may go undetected. Those who have not been identified tend to be children who are particularly bright and who have managed to stay under the radar. If there is a dyslexic difficulty it is unlikely to be very serious or it would/ should have already been picked up. Even if it is mild it should not be ignored; it still has an impact.

The information processing difficulties which underpin dyslexia do not seem to change or disappear; however, the teenager with dyslexia will experience a different set of problems at this stage of his education. He will therefore need to be armed with a new set of strategies for coping.

Teenage pupils want and are expected to work independently and to take responsibility for their studies. It can be hard for the dyslexic teenager who must yearn to get on with things on his own but who still needs some help. Many dyslexic pupils will have had years of one-to-one work focusing on phonics and multisensory-structured spelling programmes. Whatever level they have achieved it is time to let them off the hook and to help focus on acquiring really good study skills. (Study skills are discussed in Chapter 24, Habits, Strategies and Study Skills.)

Problems that may be encountered by the secondary school child with dyslexia

- There is likely to be a continued discrepancy between ability and the standard of work being produced.

- He may have continued problems with spelling – even easy and common words get misspelt or can be spelt differently on the same page.

- Reading may be at a good level but is likely to be slow compared with the good reader. The dyslexic pupil may have to stop and 'sound out' words he does not recognise. This process can interfere with comprehension and the pupil may have to reread texts. The first reading may be to work out all the words and the second to get the meaning. He may also get stuck on unfamiliar words not already encountered.

- He may have difficulty in verbal and written expression. This may be due to a more restricted vocabulary (lack of reading) as well as difficulty in mentally accessing words as and when needed. These students may also prefer to use words that are easy to spell even if they are aware that they do not contain the exact nuance they wish to convey. Sentences may be rather convoluted.

- Note taking is challenging, and at the worst end of the spectrum some students will be unable to read their own notes due to poor handwriting and spelling.

- Poor working memory will continue to make it hard for him to absorb lengthy instructions.

- Planning, organising and sequencing difficulties are likely to result in messy folders, lost bits of paper and problems with essay planning and developing logical arguments.

- Talking in groups or in public may make him self-conscious. Poor working memory and difficulty in accessing the words he needs may make some students shy of talking in large groups.

Helping the dyslexic teenager

Depending on the level of difficulty any of the suggestions for younger children may still be appropriate. In addition:

- Study skills. He should have started to learn good study skills but it can be important to update these as the demands of the curriculum change. Studying for GCSE requires certain skills, but the A-level student will have to develop a more sophisticated set of learning strategies and habits and a booster course will be a good help with this (see Chapter 24, Habits, Strategies and Study Skills).

- Planning and organising. Help to make sure that his workspace is well organised and that there is a place for books and files. Make sure that he has the right files for the different subjects.

- Time management. Discuss ways in which he can be helped to stay on top of weekly assignments and homework as well as preparing for exams and keeping to deadlines. A visual timetable with dates marked in when work should be completed may reduce the last-minute scramble to get things done. Both a weekly as well as a yearly timetable can be helpful in planning when and how to get work completed without last-minute panic.

- Other aide-memoires. Some older children find it helpful to use an electronic alarm to remind them what they should be doing. This is so easy to set up today. It could be the diary on the computer or a message on a mobile phone.

- Technology. This may be the time for the severely dyslexic student to use a word recognition program. There are a number of very helpful programs available.

- Ensure that he has access to his own computer. He can use the spell check, and poor grammatical sentences will be flagged up. Typed work also looks neat and is easy to read.

- An electronic dictionary will be helpful.

- Encourage good self-expression. Give time for conversations.

Liaison with school:

- Parents will need to have continued liaison with school. It is useful to have a key contact such as the school special educational needs coordinator now that your child has a number of subject teachers, and this key contact should ensure that all who teach him are aware of his difficulties and of how to support him.

- Discuss whether your child could have a specific member of staff to support him and to act as his advocate.

- You could also discuss the possibility of dropping a subject such as French (usually of great difficulty for the dyslexic pupil) to free up some additional study time.

Finally:

- Do not forget that your child has to work especially hard to keep up. He needs encouragement and praise for the things he is doing well.

What about the dyslexic undergraduate?

Even those pupils who have quite marked difficulties can find their way into higher education. Generally they are following a course which suits their strengths and have been able to drop the topics which they found hardest. Those students who have come back to see me for a final assessment have generally done so to see if their needs are such that they might qualify for additional time for exams and whether their local education authority might provide them with the technological facilities which would enhance their learning. They might, for example, be provided with a laptop and printer.

There are always a number of students whose dyslexia is not uncovered until they are in higher education. These students are by definition intellectually able. They have managed to cope in secondary school and acquire the necessary grades to gain entry to university. But once at university the new and more complex demands which are made of them in an unfamiliar environment may mean that they find it difficult to keep up. It may be the slow speed at which they can extract information from source material or their inability to make good notes in lectures or just the lack of imposed structure on their time which results in a performance which is disappointing and which does not reflect their enthusiasm, commitment and ability. These students can also be helped.

What can parents do to support their undergraduate child?

This is the time when your child should really be finding his wings and flying the nest. Hard as it may seem, parents must cut the ties and let him manage on his own. However, the last task for parents is to ensure that he:

- has developed some good strategies for time management. He will no longer have a school timetable and teachers handing out detention if he fails to hand in work. This can be a hard transition. He needs to plan in time for essays and for revision. Essays may not be evenly spaced through the year and he needs to know how to cope with this

- can organise his work environment. He will need an uncluttered work surface, storage for files, shelving for books. He needs a systematic and reliable system for keeping notes

- has learnt appropriate study skills to meet the new demands made by his university course

- has the technological aids and computing hardware that will help with his studies.

This means that parents must find a way of helping instil good work habits. An appropriate course on study skills for the undergraduate can be exceptionally helpful. There are also several excellent books which can be used, although it is always so much more difficult to learn from a book without a tutor.

Finally, it is important that the dyslexic undergraduate makes use of the facilities available at his university. I recommend that these students contact their university special needs department. In recent years universities have started to take the needs of their dyslexic students much more seriously and there is expertise available to help them. If they make themselves known to the university special needs department, they can find out what is available and whether they wish to avail themselves of what is on offer.

Although this is the time when parents need to stand back and let their child go, some new undergraduates may need a bit of parental encouragement to make sure that they do make use of specific facilities. The sheer volume of things which the student is now adjusting to as well as a degree of embarrassment may be a barrier to seeking support. Ideally, parents will find a way of monitoring things but in a 'hands-off' way.

CASE STUDIES
Each story has been selected to illustrate a particular point.

Anthony's story

Many parents of young children who are identified with dyslexia are anxious to know what will happen next. Of course, it is hard to make predictions when there are so many unknowns ahead. However, it can be reassuring to hear about other children who have managed to get through school and who have achieved well. Anthony's story is an optimistic story and illustrates what can be achieved when there is good parental involvement, positive support from school and appropriate specialist teaching help.

Anthony was seven when I first met him. His reading was well below the level expected for a child of his age. He could barely read words such as 'the', 'up' and 'into' and certainly could not manage anything longer. He had difficulty in distinguishing the sounds within words, which is the all-important prerequisite for learning to read and spell. Anthony had experienced an intermittent hearing loss (glue ear), which could well have had an impact on the development of his phonological awareness.

Anthony's writing was slow and laborious. He was able to write a few regular words such as 'cat', 'fish' and 'hand' but tended to miss out letters such as the 'm' in jump. Anthony had not built up any bank of words that he could recognise by sight.

Perhaps not surprisingly Anthony had become afraid of going to school despite a wonderful teacher and despite the fact that he had many friends and was popular with his peer group.

Assessment revealed that Anthony had a very poor working memory for both auditory and visual stimuli and he had difficulty with the tests, which sampled his visual/spatial skills and his hand–eye coordination.

He experienced specific learning difficulties which were primarily dyslexic in nature but with additional coordination difficulties. The combination of poor phonological skills as well as poor auditory and visual memory suggested that he was going to have ongoing difficulty.

Anthony urgently needed regular specialist teaching on a one-to-one basis. He needed to follow a multisensory teaching programme which was very structured and cumulative. The programme would need to cover reading, spelling and writing. He needed daily help at home too.

He needed to develop his phonological skills as well as focusing on how words look and building a sight vocabulary to help him on his way. Anthony was a candidate for paired reading.

Anthony's mother and I discussed appropriate spelling techniques, the learning of times tables and how to ensure that it was kept fun, all of which are discussed in the relevant chapters later in this book. It was really important that any extra help or work should be done on a little-and-often basis. There was much for them to be getting on with.

Eighteen months later Anthony's reading had progressed but was still well behind his peers. He had become much better at decoding words but it was still a slow process, and his spelling had only made a few months' progress. His ability to read individual words was now age equivalent to seven years, but sounding out words such as 'photograph' and 'comforting' was laborious work.

The very best thing was his attitude. He was now able to say 'I am dyslexic' rather than 'I am stupid' and was aware of the many things that he could do.

A key concern was that during the following year the school curriculum would 'speed up'. Most children of his age would have mastered the basic skills and therefore it was likely that there would be a growing gap between Anthony's level of achievement and that of his peers. We wondered whether he might need a change of school and whether he would need either a specialist school or one which was a little less academic. His mother decided he should stay where he was, and on the plus side the teaching staff were superbly responsive to his needs.

This was a good decision. At the age of 11 there had been a huge improvement in his reading fluency and comprehension. He also seemed more confident and had a real twinkle in his eye and a good sense of humour. His reading accuracy was still two years behind his chronological age but his reading comprehension was at a 13-year-old level. He still appreciated having stories read to him and that was how his mother was helping to make sure he was accessing age-appropriate information.

The key recommendations at this point were:

» the implementation of a small-step learning approach to his spelling. This meant learning a few words at a time and practising them on a daily basis until he had become fluent and achieved 100 per cent accuracy at speed and was able to do this on several consecutive days before moving on to learning new words (see Chapter 15, Tips for Spelling)

» the use of a voice recorder that he could keep in his pocket in order to take down important information such as homework. (This was to avoid having to copy it from the board or from the teacher's dictation, both requiring him to use skills which he found particularly hard.) This turned out to be a great success. Fortunately his class teacher embraced the idea and helped to facilitate it

» undertaking a touch typing course. Many children experiencing dyslexic difficulties, especially those with poor handwriting, find that the use of a laptop is really liberating. Word processing improves the presentation, speed of writing and general organisation, but it is important to be competent before taking a laptop into the classroom

» support with study skills – this was now very important.

By his mid-teens Anthony's reading accuracy had progressed to a 13-year-old level. (This is a level of reading ability which is sufficient to enable a student to access most texts presented in secondary school without too much difficulty.) Many of his reading errors were the misreadings so typical of students with dyslexia; for example, he would miss out one letter or insert another. This sometimes changed the sense of what he was reading, thus making it an effortful process. His spelling lagged but had now progressed as far as a 10–11-year-old level. This is no mean feat when we consider that he was required to spell words such as 'strength' and 'doubt'. His errors were not serious – 'beginning' spelt as 'begining' and 'excitement' spelt as 'excitment'. They were certainly not such that it would impede the reader.

Anthony had dropped French (always a difficult subject for dyslexic pupils), which gave him five spare classes each week, and this allowed for his specialist teaching and gave him time to keep up with the subjects that were difficult. Anthony was finding school very tiring. Although he was superficially confident, this was shaky.

As with many dyslexic students Anthony needed help with his planning and organising. He needed help remembering to remember. He needed strategies to help him to remember to hand in homework, to take the right books to school. Effective aide-memoires were discussed. The most simple is a timetable, which is easy to see at a glance and shows what equipment is needed when. A small notebook, which can live in a pocket and in which all-important information can be stored, avoids the paper chase of trying to find where information has been recorded.

Anthony needed continued help with his study skills.

By the time that Anthony was ready to embark on a degree course he was a 'well-compensated' dyslexic student. He was reading at a good level but it remained an effort and was slow. His spelling was at a 13-year-old level. His personal organisation was weak and he found it hard to settle down to work. Anthony was aware of his challenges but by this stage had found ways of dealing with them.

He had showed great determination to overcome the educational barriers which he encountered through school, and his success provides us with a clear illustration of the importance of long-term support and help from home and school.

But this isn't quite the end of the story and we can give the final word to a recently graduated Anthony. He told me that as he has matured he has discovered a great love of literature. Reading, he explained, has enriched his life. An initial passion for history has led him to open up to many wider interests. His message to parents and to young struggling readers is that 'people with dyslexia can also have a rich and rewarding relationship with books'.

Pippa's story

This provides us with an example of the importance and value of early intervention and of parent involvement. Pippa was nearly six years old when her mother first made contact. She was concerned about Pippa's slow progress with reading.

Pippa had always appeared to be a very bright and alert child, curious, busy and engaged. But now, having started school, reading was becoming an issue. She found it hard to sound out words and she often transposed letters in words, for example reading no as on, or was as saw. She would read a word on one line and then fail to recognise it on another just a few moments later. Pippa had never enjoyed playing I spy or learning nursery rhymes. She was finding it hard to learn the days of the week. Poor attention and concentration were also an issue.

At this stage in the chapter you will recognise how the difficulties which Pippa's mother described reflect characteristics which we know are associated with dyslexia. The question was what to do. Pippa needed to:

» develop her phonological skills and awareness. This could be done following a programme such as Sound Linkage (see Further Reading) or through playing games that would improve her listening and sound analysis skills. A full list of appropriate games can be found in the appendix on games and activities for parents and children to play. The chapter on reading also lists helpful resources

» build a sight vocabulary which would give her rapid recognition of words and avoid the need to sound out. The chapter on reading gives greater detail about the best way to do this

» maintain a love of books and stories and to see these as a source of pleasure. The importance of reading aloud to and with Pippa was emphasised

The huge importance of making any joint activities fun and engaging was stressed. Anything which Pippa was asked to do in the realms of reading and writing was to be pitched at a level where she could succeed and they should have fun. Pippa's mother said that she would keep in touch.

A year or so later there was still concern about Pippa's slow progress with reading. By now seven years old, Pippa had also been having extra help in school for several months and her progress did not match her lively mind and high level of motivation. We arranged an assessment.

Pippa was very bubbly and threw herself into the test activities with an almost constant smile. She turned out to be extremely bright. Assessment of her reading showed that it was a little below the expected level for her age but considerably below the level we might have expected in view of her supportive family and excellently targeted extra help. Her phonological skills were weak and she did not always process what she heard very well. Her attention was variable but her short-term memory good. On the plus side, she was a great communicator and loved writing, which she did willingly and with enthusiasm.

It seemed that she had mild dyslexic difficulties and it was important for her to have as much reading practice as possible. It takes 'normal' readers at least two years to progress from the initial learning of letter names and sounds to fluent reading. It takes children with dyslexia considerably longer, particularly when you consider that they are unlikely to 'practise' on their own and read for pleasure (in the early days). The reading section covers reading in greater detail.

Paired reading is a great way of making the daily reading practice motivating and fun; it can be so frustrating for parent and child when the reading practice is slow and the same word is misread line after line. Parents who care deeply about progress can feel agonising despair. So if this sounds familiar, paired reading is for you (see Chapter 14, Tips for Reading).

Pippa also needed to follow a spelling programme (see Chapter 15, Tips for Spelling) and she was both bright enough and sufficiently motivated to think about using a spelling aid. These can be helpful to many children but probably not until they are eight or nine years old. The Franklin spell check is one such aid (see the Chapter 15 section in Useful Resources, Organisations and Websites).

Pippa came for her last assessment soon after entry to secondary school. She was loving school. Her reading accuracy and comprehension were excellent. She loved creative writing and excelled.

However, the 'mild' dyslexic difficulties evident earlier were still having an impact on some aspects of her life. Her spelling lagged behind. She struggled to organise thoughts and sentences in a logical and comprehensive order when having to do more structured written work. She found the school day extremely tiring. French vocabulary was a challenge. She had to work hard to absorb and retain classroom instructions.

We will never know how Pippa would have done if her mother had ignored her initial concerns and had not sought advice about helping Pippa. I have, however, assessed enough children at intervals of a few years to know that there is a definite trend. The children who have parents who get involved and ensure that their child has regular, calm, consistent and appropriate help do better, without a shadow of doubt, than the children whose parents have not taken or acted on the advice given and have not managed to give this kind of input. Pippa's difficulties were definitely at the milder end of the spectrum, and by the time she was 12 her reading was good but she still experienced residual difficulty with spelling.

Chloe and Ethan's stories

These two are polar opposites and show us that dyslexia is not a single entity and that children can have very different strengths and difficulties. We will start with Chloe. What is unusual about Chloe is that she has excellent language skills and very good phonological awareness but nevertheless has found learning to read a very slow and laborious process.

There are some children for whom literacy skills present a challenge, but who do not have a phonological deficit and have no apparent difficulty with language-based activities. Their reading difficulties appear to be due to visual weaknesses. Visual memory is weak. Memory for sequences is poor. The child whose reading difficulties seem to stem mainly from poor visual processing may lose his place easily and fail to recognise a word on one line which he has just learnt to read on the line above.

Chloe proved to be one of these children. She was a very articulate small child. She would sit and chat from an early age, play games and make intricate models. Unlike many young children she never showed any ability to pick out logos or names of shops or products. (Many young children will quickly recognise the sign for things such as McDonald's.) Chloe became unhappy in her reception year at school. She had difficulty with the early reading activities. Her teacher complained that she was disruptive when she was doing reading tasks.

Chloe made little progress over the following year or so and by Year 2 still had minimal reading and writing skills. An educational psychologist's assessment showed her to be verbally able. Her phonological skills were excellent, but her working memory for both auditory and visual information was poor. Chloe was not a 'classic phonological deficit' dyslexic child, but she did have poor visual processing, visual sequencing and visual memory. She could be described more accurately as a 'visual' dyslexic child.

Chloe's eyes were checked by a behavioural orthoptist but the assessment did not reveal any visual difficulty with acuity or with other important aspects of vision such as tracking and convergence.

At this point much effort was made at home and at school to launch her as a reader. She read on a regular basis with parents and had small-group support in school. Progress was slow, but by the age of ten she was reading for pleasure. She tended to select easy books that were suitable for younger children.

Her parents continued to read extensively to her to ensure that she was able to access age-appropriate stories and information. Chloe's spelling remained delayed for her age, but a passion for wildlife which developed some time before her 11th birthday gave her the motivational boost that she needed to read extensively. She also liked to make notes and this made her much more aware of how words should be spelt. In the long term the prognosis looked good. By the time she was 12 she was reading well though not fast, and her spelling remained variable. She coped fine with spelling tests but would misspell the same words when she was focused on the content of her written work.

It is worth asking your child if she sees words or letters move on the line. Subtle visual difficulties (beyond long and short sight) can make reading hard. This may not be detected by a standard optician's assessment, which only assesses long and short sight. An assessment from a behavioural orthoptist can be helpful. It might be necessary to implement eye exercises. The use of coloured overlays or glasses has been found to help some people. (See Chapter 10, Visual Processing Difficulty.)

Ethan came for assessment at the age of nine. Until that point there had been no concerns regarding his progress but suddenly he had become unhappy about school and was struggling with work. It was quickly apparent when he read to me that he either knew a word or did not know it. When he did not know a word he had no strategies available to work out what it might say. He made no attempt to sound it out and did not even seem to know the sound made by the initial letter. Ethan had an excellent visual memory. It seemed that he had managed to build up an extensive sight vocabulary, which had compensated for his lack of phonological awareness and knowledge. Ethan had memorised enough words by sight to get by, but books were getting harder and had a more extensive vocabulary. Work in school was also getting more difficult and sophisticated. His strategy for dealing with reading could no longer carry him through and he needed to be taken back to basics and to learn about letter sounds and how to decode (sound out) and encode (spell) unfamiliar words. Chloe's very good visual memory was unusual, but again it emphasises the fact that no two children are ever identical in the way they learn and in the strategies they use.

Tom's story

You will remember that we first met Tom at the start of this chapter. Even before he started in reception class he was showing many signs that he was going to have difficulty in learning to read. These could have been picked up and his entry to school could have been managed better as a result. His early days in school were not very positive and he was frequently in trouble.

Trouble started almost the moment that Tom began school just before his fifth birthday. He found it hard to stay sitting and had little interest in reading and writing. His teacher found him difficult and frequently excluded him from the classroom. One classroom assistant decided he was lazy because, she asserted, he would learn if she got cross with him. Tom, it was later discovered, was dyslexic and showed many signs of ADHD.

Although it was not until he was eight years old that a formal identification was made, there had been plenty of signs that he was going to have problems in acquiring literacy skills. These signs were apparent well before he started reception class.

First, Tom came from a family where there were several known dyslexic members. We know that there is a genetic basis to specific learning difficulty.

He had the kind of language-based 'word finding' difficulties that are typical of many people with dyslexia. He would often say 'thingy' or 'whatsit'. He had difficulty in remembering people's names.

His phonological awareness was poor:

» He had no interest in games such as I spy or in learning nursery rhymes or children's songs – all of which require good phonological skills.

There were signs that his auditory working memory was not great:

» He had difficulty in following instructions and these often needed to be repeated or broken down into small steps.

» He had a tendency to interrupt when he wanted to tell his parents something. If he couldn't get it out right away he would forget what he had wanted to say.

Finally, at nursery school, there were signs that his visual memory and visual analysis were weak:

> » He had difficulty in recognising his name on the coat pegs.

> » His pictures or paintings of people always missed arms.

> » He was not able to recognise or match number symbols to their spoken name.

> » He had little interest in constructing puzzles.

These issues in relation to visual analysis, visual memory, working memory and word finding are all very much associated with dyslexia, and coupled with Tom's very poor attention should/could have set warning bells ringing.

As it turned out, Tom did have huge difficulty with reading. An educational assessment at the age of eight indicated significant dyslexic difficulties.

Despite the extra help he had both at school and at home he started secondary school with literacy skills that were well below his chronological age. His reading was slow and laboured; it was insufficiently good to enable him to cope with the texts he would be presented with. He was resistant to writing, and when he did settle to writing tasks his spelling mistakes made it difficult to read.

Soon after starting secondary school Tom was assessed by his local authority and it was decided that his educational needs would warrant a statement of special educational need (now known as an education, health and care (EHC) plan). This meant that he had a few periods of specialist teaching and the help of a classroom assistant for several classes each week, which went some way to enabling him to access the curriculum.

Staff at his comprehensive school were enlightened and supportive. They found, for example, that, despite his weak skills, his behaviour and involvement with learning were much better when they moved him into the top group for English literature, which he enjoyed. His science teachers realised that the work he handed in did not represent his understanding of the subject and were able to accommodate his weaknesses. He was allowed to give up modern languages.

Tom was also fortunate that he had great social skills; he was also a good all-rounder at sports. He enjoyed and was good at art. Teachers liked him and he had many friends, so the overall experience of school was positive. Tom was able to remain in education and to continue into higher education due to his strong practical and artistic abilities. Despite continued difficulty with both reading and writing/spelling, he emerged from university with a degree in one of the subjects within the field of art, design and media.

Tom now runs his own business. He explained that he is able to read tolerably well and to write and spell with some ability. He is quite proud of his spelling. He plays and wins games of online scrabble with bright and literate friends. He says that this process has taught him a great deal about spelling and about how letters generally go together. The instant feedback regarding words which are incorrectly spelt has improved his spelling.

Tom also explained that his literacy skills have improved as a by-product of running a business. He is no longer reading to learn to read or spelling in order to learn to spell. He has to read, write and spell to achieve a larger goal and one that he is immensely motivated to achieve. He needs to make his business work, and to do this he has to read and to write – accurately.

There is surely a message here about the great importance of motivation and the need for pupils to be prepared to open themselves up to learning. It is so easy for those pupils whose difficulties are marked rather than mild to become jaded. So much of their energy goes into appeasing teachers and finding ways to do as little as possible to get by without losing face or self-esteem.

This is a challenge to all of us who parent or teach a seriously dyslexic child.

KEY POINTS

⇨ Dyslexia is a learning difficulty that primarily affects the skills involved in accurate and fluent word reading and spelling. It is neurological in origin. There is a genetic basis and it tends to run in families. It is estimated that around 10 per cent of children are affected.

⇨ Dyslexia is on a spectrum and can be mild or severe. There are no established cut-off points. It is only by looking at a child's response to good teaching and intervention that we can establish the severity of the difficulty.

⇨ The characteristic features of dyslexia are difficulties in phonological awareness, working memory and verbal processing speed. Co-existing difficulties may be seen in relation to language, motor coordination, mental maths, concentration and personal organisation.

⇨ No two people with dyslexia have exactly identical profiles of strengths and difficulties. Reading, writing and spelling are complex skills which involve many different processes. This means that there are many places where things can go wrong.

⇨ Dyslexia can affect pupils of all intellectual abilities.

⇨ The earlier we can identify and support children who are at risk of difficulty the better.

⇨ Early help should encompass work on phonological skills and awareness. A learning programme should be multisensory, highly structured and systematic.

⇨ Specialist help should be fun as well as provided little and often.

⇨ Dyslexia does not fully disappear. The type of difficulties which dyslexic children experience in school will change depending on their age and the stage of education they have reached as well as the severity of the difficulty.

⇨ At each stage they will need to learn compensatory strategies as well as work to enhance basic skills.

⇨ Parents have a crucial role to play and can do a great deal to support their dyslexic child.

Chapter 4

DYSPRAXIA

Abigail, who was 13 years old, was unable to get on with her peer group, and confrontations were constantly occurring. The girls in her class were complaining about her. Her work was slipshod and she appeared to make no effort. She was uncooperative and rude to school staff. At home Abigail's parents were also at their wits' end. She had become more and more angry. She had actually bitten, slapped and fought with her younger brother the previous holidays. She refused to engage with her family and was continually unpleasant to them all.

Abigail's behaviour left no one in any doubt that something had to be done. Challenging behaviour can often bring a message. Abigail's distress was evident and needed investigation. What followed was the identification of dyspraxia and the implementation of some effective support. Abigail's story is taken up again at the end of this chapter.

What exactly do we mean by dyspraxia? As with the other specific learning difficulties, providing a good, clear definition is not easy. At its simplest dyspraxia refers to difficulty with motor coordination. 'Dys' means difficulty and 'praxia' means doing. In years gone by the term 'clumsy child syndrome' was used for some of these children, but more recently additional terms have come into the mix. Some people prefer to use the term developmental coordination disorder (DCD), while others refer to a non-verbal learning difficulty.

Typically the dyspraxic child will have difficulty in both planning and executing a sequence of coordinated movements. He might, for example, wish to cross the room but despite seeing what route he will take he will bump into a chair or a table. He might aim to walk in a straight line down a passage way but actually meander, with arms or shoulders brushing against the wall. If a dyspraxic child is asked to walk on the outside edge of his feet he will be very likely to curl his hands inward. If he is asked to stand with his eyes shut and to make a big arc with his arm ending up with his finger on his nose he is likely to miss the nose by a wide margin. The dyspraxic child may find it almost impossible to stand on one foot with both eyes closed. Another telltale sign is associated movements of mouth and tongue. When a dyspraxic child is writing he is likely to hold his pen tightly and you may notice that as he writes his tongue comes out and/or he may open his mouth and make movements which almost echo the hand movement.

Some children who are dyspraxic also (but not necessarily) experience sensory integration impairment. These children can be easily overwhelmed by too much stimuli, so if the environment is very noisy or busy they find it hard to cope. Others may also (but not necessarily) have difficulty with their proprioception. They have poor body awareness and need constantly to fidget to feel sufficient physical stimulation and know where their body is in space. Others may have poor core stability. These latter children will tire easily and will find it genuinely hard work to sit upright at a desk even before they have to hold a pencil and perform a task with it.

As you can see from the description above, dyspraxia is at root a physical coordination difficulty, but where it gets more complicated is that it goes way beyond a degree of clumsiness. As well as affecting the coordination of movements, it can also affect perception and thought processes, so while the younger child may be struggling to get his teeth cleaned in the right sequence, the teenager may be struggling to plan and organise his written work, his timetable or his school bag.

Although by their teenage years many dyspraxic teenagers will have largely overcome their physical difficulties with coordination, they are likely to continue to experience difficulty in the organising, planning, sequencing and execution of day-to-day activities or mental processes. They may also have some difficulty with concentration and attention.

There can be social implications. The dyspraxic pupil may be socially gauche. He may not pick up on social cues; he may not read body language or interpret gestures and facial expressions.

To add to the confusion there is a considerable degree of 'co-occurrence' or overlap with other areas of specific learning difficulty. While there are a good number of pupils who experience dyspraxia with no other area of difficulty, there are a larger number who show signs of dyspraxia and dyslexia or dyspraxia and ADHD, or even a combination of all three. And, as you may have noticed, the poor social skills which may also accompany dyspraxia share characteristics with autism spectrum disorder (ASD).

It is important to stress that dyspraxia can be 'mild' or 'severe'. Like all the other specific learning difficulties it is on a continuum. A 'diagnosis' of dyspraxia does not mean that your child will experience all the difficulties described in this chapter. As with other specific learning difficulties, it will not go away. The dyspraxic child will find strategies to help live with his areas of weakness, and as an adult he has a greater opportunity to focus on the things which he is particularly good at.

If you feel you are now more confused about dyspraxia than before starting the chapter I hope that the following sections will bring more clarity.

Dyspraxia in infancy

When children are very young, parents are most probably not aware of anything untoward, but looking back they may remember that their child had certain tendencies. He might have been:

- hyperactive – all limbs going, or hypoactive (under-active)
- slow to achieve independent sitting
- late to walk.

He may also have had:

- sleep problems. He might have been overly or under-demanding
- feeding problems.

The underlying cause of these tendencies is a high level of neurological immaturity. As babies and young children develop, the neural pathways of the brain should become more refined and efficient. Imagine that the brain is a wood full of trees; you are a messenger and you need to take a message through the wood from one side to the other. The first few times you may try different routes, but over time you find the fastest way through and the path you take becomes well used. Each time you go through the wood you can do it faster and more efficiently. You know the way and the ground is smoother, so the message gets there faster. Our neural pathways are analogous to this. Dyspraxic brains continue to take the long route and to muddle their way through.

The nursery, reception and infant stage child (aged four to seven years)

As children get a little older it may be more evident that, compared with their peers, some areas of development are happening rather slowly or with comparative difficulty.

- *Fine motor skills.* You may notice that your child's manual dexterity is weak. He may be having difficulty in dealing with buttons, zips and laces. He may find it hard to use scissors and cutlery. Colouring in and pencil control may be weak. He may dislike having to write.

- *Gross motor skills.* The dyspraxic child can appear clumsy and uncoordinated. Activities such as catching and throwing are difficult for him. He is likely to be slow to learn to ride a bike. He may trip and fall easily or bump into things. He may be unaware of external dangers such as high walls and busy roads. He may have difficulty in disassociating movements; a deliberate movement with one part of the body may be accompanied by an involuntary movement with another associated part of the body. For example, as he writes he may move his tongue. As he walks he may scrunch up his hands.

- *Self-help skills.* The manual dexterity and sequencing needed for some activities may be a real challenge. Teeth cleaning is a good example where he needs, but finds it hard, to do things in the right order. First he must take the top off the toothpaste, then wet the brush, put paste on the brush, rub teeth, rinse mouth, rinse brush and put it away. Getting clothes on in the right order can also be a challenge. Vests can end up on top of sweaters and pants over trousers. Clothes may often be inside out.

- *Visual/spatial ability.* He may have no interest or skill with puzzles and construction toys. He may experience confusion with left and right.

- *Eating skills.* He may also be a messy eater. Quite apart from difficulty using a spoon he may find it hard to chew and swallow with ease.

- *Verbal dyspraxia.* This refers to difficulty with the use and coordination of mouth and tongue muscles. Speech may be 'slushy' because clear annunciation is hard.

What impact will this have in school?

The young child with dyspraxia is likely to find it a struggle to sit still for long at a desk or table. His posture will be poor and he will find it difficult to learn to write neatly. He may find the playground too boisterous and have no interest in games that seem rough. He may find himself in trouble for being slow to dress or to find his equipment. It may take him more time than others to learn classroom routines. The child with dyspraxia is likely to be viewed by the teacher as immature, particularly if they are a boy.

How can parents help?

At this stage the most important thing is to give the child the chance to develop his physical strength, coordination, stamina and fine motor skills. These are all attributes which are needed in the classroom, particularly when the curriculum becomes more formal and when sitting still and demonstrating skill with a pencil is required.

A physiotherapist or occupational therapist's assessment can identify specific areas of weakness and may lead to a course of treatment. Positive changes are generally very quickly apparent. For families with a garden and adequate space, a climbing frame and trampoline can provide opportunities for developing physical skills. For those without such facilities, regular trips to the playground will be valuable.

There are other ways in which the child with dyspraxia can be helped and which will ease their way through the early years of school. Parents can:

- provide clothes with elasticised waist bands and avoid dressing him in clothes with buttons and zips (particularly helpful when changing for PE or gym). Make it easy to know which way round things should go. Get baggy clothes that are comfy and easy to get into

- label all his equipment and clothes.

For the child who is finding it hard to settle in and to make friends:

- plan and organise some play dates. Think about activities which the invited child will enjoy

- be prepared to direct proceedings and do not leave them to their own devices for long.

Parents should liaise with school staff with regard to his particular needs. Make sure that school staff are aware of difficulties and talk with them about any areas where you think that allowances should be made. For example:

- He may need plenty of extra time to complete desk work.

- He may need directions and instructions given bit by bit and not more than two or three at a time.

- It may be helpful to have modified equipment; for example, for some children, a sloped desk, special pen and/or wobbly cushion can help. An occupational therapist (OT) can advise on this.

- He should not get into trouble if he is slow to complete self-help activities such as changing for PE lessons.

Dyspraxia in the junior school (7–11 years)

By the time the dyspraxic child has moved from infant to junior (age seven to eleven) the following difficulties may be familiar.

- *Fine motor skills.* He may really dislike having to write. It is likely to be hard work and he may be finding it a struggle to produce what is expected. His books are likely to look messy.

- *Gross motor skills.* These are also still poor. He may have little interest in ball games such as football or netball. He may not be good at team games so may often find that he is not picked by his peer group to be on their side. He may drop things and seem clumsy. Dance or PE classes may be hard.

- *Self-help skills.* Dressing is still slow and arduous. He may find that he is last to be ready for PE or for games. He may find himself in trouble for being slow or for getting things the wrong way round. He may find it difficult to follow school routines.

- *Organisation and sequencing.* He may find it hard to follow class instructions about getting books out, bags ready or coats on the back of chairs, etc. It may be difficult to follow class and playground rules. He may have little sense of time. He may not know which day of the week it is or whether it is a school day or weekend. He may find it really difficult to respond to sequential instructions.

- *Visual/spatial ability.* Copying off the board may be a challenge. Aspects of maths are difficult (see Chapter 5, Dyscalculia and Other Maths Difficulties, and Chapter 18, Tips for Maths). He may find it impossible to keep numbers within the small boxes or squares in his maths exercise book. As he gets older maps and diagrams may be hard to follow.

- *Social interaction.* This may be immature. He may have difficulty in reading body language and may not react appropriately to facial expressions. He may sometimes overdo things, be too rough, mistime a joke or just be a little 'off centre' and socially gauche. He can be that irritating child who just doesn't know when enough is enough. He may be easily distressed and emotional.

How will this impact in the classroom?

The classroom can be a tough place for dyspraxic pupils. They are likely to produce messy work and to be poorly organised, and are often last to be dressed after PE. They may be slow to copy off the board and may find that important information has been removed before they have managed to get it down. They may find it hard to get along with their peers and they probably hate organised team sports. From day one these children are likely to get criticism rather than praise. If they are male their teacher may also be of the opinion that their lack of ability to sit still, to hold a pen and to write neatly is just a boy/girl difference and that it will be fine in the long run.

Seeking support and advice

I would urge you not to be complacent. If he is struggling to manage the demands of school, if he is tired out when he comes home and if he 'hates' writing, do seek professional advice. A clear analysis of exactly what his physical immaturities consist of can be helpful, particularly if they lead to an individual treatment programme. With the right help (from an OT or physiotherapist), young children can make dramatic improvements to their coordination, strength and stamina. This in turn will make school easier to cope with.

The knowledge and skill of the OTs and physiotherapists with whom I have worked never fails to impress me but it also makes me aware that we have different areas of expertise. They know about the physical and organisational difficulties experienced by children with dyspraxia and are good at knowing what physical programme will be helpful and what physical modifications may be used in the classroom. The job of the educational psychologist is to look at the educational implications and to help parents and teachers to make a plan of action that will help the child concerned. Very often the most pressing need is to ensure that life is made easier and happier for the dyspraxic child.

How can parents help?

With or without a formal assessment there are ways in which parents can help.

There are six absolutely essential strands to supporting all dyspraxic pupils.

1. Physical development

Paying attention to the development of physical skills and coordination. This has already been discussed.

2. Facilitating writing and ensuring that he can use a computer

As far as possible try and see that writing tasks are made as easy as possible. This can range from being a scribe for him to ensuring that as he gets older he learns to touch type and has access to a laptop computer in the classroom. Copying presents particular difficulty and it is important that any information which he is expected to copy from the board is also presented in another form. For example, is it possible for the teacher to provide notes or could the work of a fast, neat writer be photocopied for him?

3. Study skills

Ensure that he develops effective study skills. Make sure that number bonds and times tables are learnt really well. He is likely to need help to structure written work.

4. Personal organisation

Help him to develop good strategies to keep organised and on top of daily requirements.

- Maintain a regular routine during term time.
- Make sure his clothes are put out the evening before school. Lay them out so that they are easy to put on.
- Break tasks down into small component parts. Help him to sequence these.
- Help him to develop strategies for remembering what he needs to take to school or how to keep his kit organised. Checklists are useful.
- Put up a list of what he needs to take to school for each day of the week.
- Get him to pack and put out his school bag in the evening ready for the following day.
- Encourage him to stop, think and check that he is organised and has what he needs at particular moments.

5. Moral support

Parents are a strong source of moral support, although for some young people it might eventually be necessary to consider external help in the form of counselling or therapy.

Parents can:

- give descriptive praise. When he has behaved in a way that you like or want to encourage, make sure that, in addition to saying 'well done' or 'that was great', you actually describe the behaviour that you liked so that he is specifically aware of what is required. For example, 'I was really happy to see that you had your school bag ready and packed and by the door; that really helps us in the morning' (or whatever!)

- talk with him about his strengths and abilities while working with him to find ways of dealing with the weaker areas

- ensure that he continues to enjoy and engage in the activities at which he excels, particularly those where he is not in competition with siblings.

6. Liaise with his class teacher or other member of school staff with regard to his needs

Make sure that school staff are aware of difficulties and can avoid giving unnecessary criticism as well as looking out for and commenting on his good efforts. Pupils who experience dyspraxic difficulties may often appear careless, lazy and disorganised and can find it hard to demonstrate their ability on the page. All too often their work does not receive praise and they find themselves in trouble for being disorganised. It is therefore very helpful if individual teachers can be encouraged to:

- mark for content rather than presentation

- give sufficient time to copy from the board (or provide a copy of the notes)

- provide typed notes where possible

- give sufficient additional time to finish tests and exams

- break complex tasks into achievable chunks

- recognise when effort has been taken even if the results may be messy or slow

- modify homework where appropriate.

If he has difficulty in paying attention it would help if his teacher can:

- think about seating and have him in the front where he can see and hear easily and where the teacher can check that he has absorbed new information

- give him a warning when important information is about to be given

- provide a positive comment when he is attentive. This may help him to increase his self-awareness and ability to monitor his attention.

Dyspraxia in the secondary school (11–18 years)

Unfortunately for many children, their dyspraxic difficulties do not emerge until their teens. Many of them have had years of confusion and stress in unsympathetic classrooms and on playing fields. They may be very bright children who are seen as average pupils bumping along. At best they cope reasonably happily with all that is demanded of them. At worst they can become alienated by complaints about their untidy physical appearance and their difficulty in getting to the right place at the right time with the right equipment. They can appear lazy. Their teachers find them confusing. How is it that they can give the best and most articulate oral answer in class and then hand in five lines of messy, brief and simplistic written work?

It is not, however, just the newly emerged dyspraxic pupils who can find the teenage years a struggle. Even those whose difficulties have been identified previously can find it hard to manage the new demands of a bigger school where there is a greater emphasis on personal organisation and responsibility and where they must change classrooms for different subjects. These are the pupils who often struggle around school weighed down by a vast bag into which they have put all their school textbooks so that they are sure they will arrive in class with what they need. They are the ones who arrive late in class because they have not yet learnt their way around the large new school and have ended up in the wrong place.

As the years go by it is not unusual for parents to be found pulling their hair out as they wonder if they are going to have to drive forgotten books, musical instruments or games kit into school for ever or whether they should continue to help with organisational issues until their child leaves home.

Signs of dyspraxia

If you are wondering if your teenage child might be dyspraxic these are the things to look out for:

- *Fine motor skills.* Handwriting is still a challenge. He will have difficulty with hand–eye coordination and thus in using tools and equipment in DT or science classes. Clumsiness may be less evident.

- *Gross motor skills.* He may be better at games now but will probably prefer a sport that does not involve being in a team, for example swimming, riding or throwing the javelin or discus. Many dyspraxic teenagers love skiing; their balance may be good and less coordination is needed. He may be sensitive to external stimulation, for example different levels of light, sound and heat intensity. He may tire easily. He will find it hard to follow dance sequences.

- *Self-help skills.* He may look very untidy with shirt tails hanging out, cuffs chewed and ink stains on fingers. He may find it hard to get dressed quickly.

- *Visual/spatial ability.* He will probably have difficulty copying from the board or other source; he may find it hard to interpret diagrams, maps and charts where position is relevant. He may have difficulty finding his way around and take longer than others to memorise different locations.

- *Organisation and sequencing.* He may find it hard to get the right books to the right classroom. Science experiments may be a challenge because of the necessity to sequence the actions and the need for precise measurements and good hand control. Story or essay writing can be hard. Not only is there a handwriting challenge, but the material needs to be organised, planned and sequenced.

- *Social and emotional.* The pupil whose difficulties have not been recognised may, by secondary school, have become an unhappy loner. General lack of recognition for the efforts he has made may have made him uncooperative and 'bolshy'. His social skills are still awkward and he may not go with the flow.

What can parents do to support their dyspraxic teenager?

As before the key strands to help include:

- access to a laptop and the opportunity to learn to touch type. He will need to be able to use a laptop for exams and may also qualify for additional time

- study skills help/tuition

- providing and ensuring he is 'trained' to use computer software programs which support organisation, mind mapping or note taking, for example *Inspiration* and *MindGenius*

- help to develop strategies to aid organisational challenges

- counselling or therapy (as indicated)

- a key member of school staff to liaise with, particularly if they run into any problems or difficulties.

By their teens children are, in my view, less likely to benefit from physical therapy and indeed many of them no longer show obvious signs of clumsiness, though they may never be someone with whom you would find it easy to make a bed or fold a sheet.

There are, however, other important things to focus on and for which parents can still give good support.

Work environment

First of all, attention needs to be given to the child or young person's work area. A work environment should be created that he likes and can feel comfortable in. Files, notebooks and so forth need to be organised so that they are easy to find. Bookshelves, cabinets and drawers need to be situated in the right place.

Time management

He should try and avoid having to rush to deadlines by creating his own. When he makes a list of things he needs to do, whether this is shopping or completing a piece of important coursework, these should be categorised into activities which are 'urgent' and activities which are 'important'. Sometimes important activities are also urgent, particularly if these are left to the last minute! It would also be worth dividing out activities which will take just a few moments from those which are going to take a significant amount of time. It is important for him to decide which are his 'boulders' – these are the important and time-consuming activities. Boulders should be timetabled into his daily or weekly schedule. If a slot is created in which to complete his boulders, then he will be able to fit in the other less urgent or less time-consuming activities around them.

Timetables and lists

A weekly/termly/yearly timetable, which can be seen at a glance, may help him to pace his assignments. He will probably have to draw up his own, but perhaps he can use an appropriate spreadsheet. If he can see how many weeks he has before the end of term or number of days before work needs to be handed in or exams are due to take place, it will help him to pace the work that he does. It may also help him to see the year as a shorter rather than a longer period! He will then be able to write up his own deadlines, which will help with weekly planning. I would suggest that each evening he looks at his 'to do' list, deletes the things that have been done and then produces a new list for things to be completed the following day.

Memory aids

Various ways of helping him to remember what he is meant to be doing include using notebooks and lists. For example, a timetable of the week written up clearly and colour coded could be a help. The lists must, of course, be somewhere where he can see them so that he will not leave without checking them. Another useful item would be a small notebook that he can take everywhere with him. It can help tremendously to jot down everything that needs to be remembered in one place so no time is lost in looking for lots of bits of paper. A tape recorder can also be useful, as long as it is easily available and he can record on to it things which he needs to remember. An electronic organiser or mobile phone can be used as an alarm when specific things need to be remembered. Certainly an electronic organiser could produce a list of things that he has to do each day and remind him of coursework and when this needs to be handed in. Many children find that a mobile phone is a great place to store information (and it's handy for photographing information on the whiteboard). And finally, don't forget the humble sticky label.

Breaking down complex tasks

This continues to be a vital process for dyspraxic pupils. A complex task can feel overwhelming, but if it can be divided into small sequential steps it can be made to feel much more manageable. Help may need to be given here. If he could do this easily on his own he would most probably have done it. Tasks for analysis range from how to structure an essay to how to set about cooking a two-course meal. It may be a higher-order thinking skill or something far more practical and physical.

Opportunities to shine

The dyspraxic teenager needs to feel that he has areas of expertise and competence in order to keep confidence and self-esteem high. It is important to try and find something which he loves to do. It might be debating or discus throwing. It might be taking part in a choir or acting.

Routine

Maintaining a routine during term time is helpful. It is important that these young people do not get too tired, and a routine also helps to reduce memory load. If the same actions are performed regularly then it is not so necessary to have to think and plan and remember.

Encouragement

Parents are important encouragers and it is important for pupils and students to feel that their parents believe in them. Children should not be defined by their difficulties and by what they cannot do easily.

CASE STUDIES

In this section we will meet Callum, Dylan, Luca, Ruby and Abigail. We will also hear the comments of parents. These stories have been selected to show the ways in which dyspraxia can affect pupils. Dyspraxia is perhaps the most invidious of the specific learning difficulties because the underlying difficulties are *not* easily visible and yet the dyspraxic behaviours which we *can* see are those which often annoy and alienate. It is the dyspraxic child who has ink on his fingers and shirt tails, whose books are messy and who is likely to wander into class late and disorganised. These are the behaviours for which children are blamed. They are not behaviours which elicit sympathy and support. Dyspraxia needs to be recognised and dyspraxic children really do need the support and encouragement of parents, teachers and family. They are all too often criticised for the very things which they find difficult.

Callum's story

Callum's moderate difficulties were picked up early by his vigilant mother. His story illustrates the importance of parental involvement with learning. He is keeping up well, but left to his own devices he would probably be drifting.

Callum's mother first talked with me about him when he was in nursery. She was worried about his poor coordination and poor fine motor skills. She was also a little worried about his tendency to prefer to play with the girls – he shied away from any rough and tumble 'boys' activities.

At this stage the most important thing was to give Callum the best opportunity to develop his physical strength, coordination and fine motor skills. An occupational therapist's assessment identified several specific areas of weakness and he attended a course of treatment. Positive changes were very quickly apparent. At this point the family moved to a house with a larger garden where they were able to put a climbing frame and trampoline into the garden. These daily activities were very good for his physical development.

Thanks to his improved strength and coordination as well as parental support he coped well with Key Stage 1. His handwriting was not brilliant but there were no very serious concerns. Generally Callum seemed to be doing well in school, though he did have a tendency to daydream. Callum's parents were keeping a close eye on things. They noted that he needed more 'pushing' and organising than his older sisters.

By the time Callum was nine years old his parents decided to have an educational psychologist's assessment and to ascertain the extent of his difficulties and to what degree it was reasonable to push him. His test results showed a classic 'dyspraxic' pattern of strengths and difficulties in relation to how he processed information. His verbal reasoning was very good, as was his non-verbal reasoning, with the exception of the test which sampled his ability to deal with visual/spatial information and hand–eye coordination.

He read beautifully and was well ahead of his chronological age, but his handwriting was laboured and slow. Maths was patchy. His number sense was good but he had difficulty with some maths concepts, particularly those which involved shape and orientation.

Background information revealed that a degree of dyspraxia may have been 'in the family'. A cousin had been identified with similar difficulties and there was also an aunt who was poorly coordinated (though no assessments had ever been done). Callum was not a good ball sports player and preferred solo sports such as judo and swimming. His organisational skills were poor and he needed reminders and help at home to keep on top of things. His parents were concerned about his rather variable concentration. Despite all this he was generally doing well in school.

Three years later Callum was achieving well academically and enjoying his first year of secondary school. His parents had, however, needed to give him more help than his sisters. He had needed considerable support with exam revision and with general organisation. At times his father found his laissez-faire attitude, his lack of organisation, his tendency to daydream and his inability to get stuck into his homework fast and efficiently highly frustrating.

It can be hard for parents to continue to empathise with the child who is given help but apparently does not seem to care what marks he gets. We do need, however, to bear in mind that a specific difficulty is just that. It is a difficulty that the child is generally acutely aware of; he knows all about his shortcomings. His apparent lack of motivation and lack of interest in whether he does well or not may be his way of covering his own confusion and anxiety. Try and remember that he does have a specific difficulty. This is not an excuse but it is an explanation. Nagging will only alienate.

Patchy performance can also be hard for parents to deal with. It is also important to remember that it is genuinely hard for the dyspraxic pupil to maintain a high level of hard work. Many dyspraxic pupils will, like Callum, pull out the stops and do well in exams but will not show this level of application on a daily basis. This, again, is more frequently a genuine difficulty rather than laziness.

Specific learning difficulties do not go away. They change with age and stage, and at each stage strategies need to be found to enable the dyspraxic pupil to minimise the impact. Callum's parents have continued to monitor his progress and get involved as and when it seems necessary, but the good news is that a further two years down the line he is self-motivated and doing well at school. He is a popular, happy and confident student and plays a full role within the school community.

Dylan's story

I have included this short vignette of Dylan to make the point that while many dyspraxic pupils find it really difficult to remain organised they can, if sufficiently motivated, manage to pull off some spectacular one-off events. Parents should not conclude that the day-to-day failures to stay on track can easily be avoided.

Dylan started out with significant reading difficulties, but now in his teens his difficulties were primarily 'dyspraxic' in nature. Despite chaotic organisation and the usual dyspraxic issues he coped well emotionally. He was well supported in his comprehensive school where the staff clearly appreciated him. He was creative and had the opportunity to make a film, which was good for his self-esteem. He also loved music and put together a performance with several bands. For a boy whose day-to-day organisation left all who knew him wringing their hands, this was no mean feat. This is another confusing issue for parents and teachers. If he can organise a concert why can he not organise his books? The answer is that organising books or other aspects of life on a day-to-day basis requires constant vigilance, which he finds almost impossible. The concert was a one-off and he was hugely motivated. He had much riding on it. He could make a monumental effort just this once but it would not have been sustainable. Dylan continued to need support to develop good habits in relation to time management and to keeping his work environment under control. Many of the suggestions in Chapter 23, Tips for Confident Learners, were very relevant for him.

Luca's story

Luca's story demonstrates that a 'diagnosis' of dyspraxia is not enough, on its own, to bring about change. Parents, pupil and teachers all need to accept that there are difficulties and that it will take patience and effort to find ways around them.

Luca first came for assessment at the age of 13. It was clear that he was bright, he had an open and outgoing manner and was fun to meet. All the information gathered about him pointed to a 'diagnosis' of dyspraxia. His test profile was classic – he excelled on some tests and was below average on others. Feedback from school also indicated typically dyspraxic difficulties; Luca was verbally able – school staff commented on his exceptional verbal input to lessons but were confused that this was not reflected in his written work, which was poor in comparison. His personal organisation was described as a disaster. He struggled with aspects of maths – equations baffled him.

Luca came from a very high-achieving family. It was assumed that he would do well and he was keenly aware of the comparisons made between him and his bright, academically successful sister who was just a year or so older than him. The identification of a specific learning difficulty was not readily accepted by Luca or his parents; in fact, it was not really acknowledged or accepted at all. Everyone would have been happier if an external explanation for Luca's uneven academic progress had been found and no helpful provision was made for support on the home front. Over the next two years Luca received help from school staff with study skills and self-organisation.

Luca was 15 when I was asked to see him again. He did not appear to have benefited from the help given. He had not implemented suggested strategies and his academic success was patchy. Luca was clearly unhappy about his lack of success, but rather than accept the help given and risk failure he had apparently decided it was safer not to make an effort.

At the time of this second assessment Luca was again open, outgoing and wryly entertaining at his own expense. He was quick to shrug off his difficulties with a 'take me or leave me' approach to life. However, with a little more scratching it seemed that behind his well-developed defences there lurked a boy who was both sad and at times angry about his inability to get into a sports team, his confusion with aspects of maths and his difficulties in getting good marks for written work.

Luca, it seemed to me, was a pupil who needed help to accept and admit to his difficulties before he was going to find ways of dealing with them. Luca needed support from home as well as school. He needed to have his parents assure him that whatever his difficulties they admired his strengths and still valued him as a person. Without this support he was happier to laugh off his shortcomings than to tackle them. To tackle them would have exposed him to the risk of failure.

Luca very much needed to see that accepting support, putting in effort and trying to implement tried and tested strategies would lead to greater success, but until he was prepared to take that risk he was really rather stuck.

Ruby's story

Ruby's story illustrates the difficulties and anxiety that can ensue if pupils do not feel that their difficulties are recognised and supported by school staff. Her story also gives us insight into how much effort is required if one is to stay on track and to keep organised.

Ruby was 16 when I saw her. An assessment carried out previously by a colleague had said that she was 'experiencing difficulties indicative of dyspraxia'. Her school had been told but nothing much came of it. She had coped quite well with her primary years but things had really come to a head as she completed her GCSEs. By her first A-level year her parents were worried about her unhappiness and concerned to know what more they could do for her.

She struggled with many daily activities. She was bright and incredibly conscientious about her work but agonisingly slow. Her homework was taking her until midnight each night so she was exhausted in the morning, when it took her hours to manage to do her dressing, washing and prepare for the day. Her time keeping was appalling, and the combination of difficulties meant that she was constantly late for school. The school staff felt that this was a 'lifestyle' choice and were unsympathetic to her problems. The situation was compounded by the fact that Ruby was, through her efforts and hard work, achieving excellent academic results which seemed to be taken as evidence (by school staff) that she had no difficulty.

Ruby's assessment told the same dyspraxic story. Her verbal ability was significantly above average, but in contrast her ability to deal with spatial information and her hand–eye coordination were weak. Her literacy skills were excellent, but writing was slow and felt really uncomfortable. She pressed so hard on the page she was giving herself blisters. She had difficulty structuring her ideas for formal work but her creative writing really flowed.

Ruby was a very articulate girl and was able to express her views about her difficulties with insight and clarity. She talked about her significant difficulty in dealing with all practical work – handling materials in the lab or using precision instruments; of her need to plan and to make long sequenced lists in order to overcome her poor organisation; of her difficulty in dealing with more than one thing at a time in the classroom – for example, being required to listen to the teacher and to copy off the board simultaneously; of her poor time keeping; of feeling socially 'different'; and of being excluded and humiliated by both peers and teachers alike.

There was no magic wand to turn life around for Ruby, but I had hoped that a clearly written report outlining the nature of Ruby's difficulties with suggestions for how school staff could help to make things easier for her might make a significant difference. Sadly they continued to take the view that Ruby should pull herself together.

There is not a great deal that parents can do under these circumstances. Ruby's parents had taken the updated report with recommendations into school and asked that all relevant staff could read it. A meeting had been held which was attended by parents and key staff. It had been the hope of Ruby's parents that with the clear evidence that Ruby experienced dyspraxia a plan could be made for supporting her to deal with all that she was finding so stressful. They were not sympathetically received, and the outcome of this meeting left them feeling isolated and very much on their own. The only option left for parents who find themselves in this position is to consider changing schools.

By this time Ruby had become intensely anxious. She was setting herself high academic standards and was determined to follow a demanding professional career, and to do this she needed the top grades. The difficulties which she was having to overcome on a daily basis were huge, and the fact that these difficulties were not recognised meant that her mental health was suffering.

Ruby's family were really concerned but were always there for her. They provided as much practical and emotional support as they could, and with their help Ruby achieved the A-levels she needed to get onto the university course of her choice.

Ruby is not an isolated case. There are many other pupils who have spent years during which they are told off for careless work, for being untidy, for being disorganised and for appearing not to make an effort. Many of these pupils will eventually rebel or become increasingly demoralised. This should not be ignored and, for many, counselling or psychotherapy is a good way forward.

Ruby's parents are not alone in finding that they needed to give significantly more support for their teenage child than they might have expected. Once children move to secondary school many parents sigh with relief and are able to let the child take responsibility for homework, for keeping organised and managing school life. Not so with the dyspraxic pupil.

Over the years I have taken many phone calls from the parents of the dyspraxic children whom I have previously assessed. They have had to give much unconditional love and have had to work hard to ensure that school bags were ready and remembered, homework was handed in on time and that the show stayed on the road. It can be lonely and frustrating. Why is it, they have asked, that my 15-year-old needs all this support and help? Should I be giving it? Staff at his A-level college cannot understand why I am still involved. When should I give up?

I know that others share my view that parents should ignore critical friends, relations and school staff and keep giving the necessary help. Unless the detractor has had the hands-on experience of parenting a child with a dyspraxic difficulty, he or she cannot make critical judgements about what is needed. If without parental support a child is not going to cope or to achieve academically to the level for which they have the ability, then there really is no option. He is not going to get a second chance. As well as continued help with organisation, there are other things which parents can do.

Abigail's story

Abigail's story is a success story. It, too, demonstrates the importance of unwavering parental support and shows what self-confidence this can give. Abigail's parents and school staff implemented all the strategies which we know are of benefit to the dyspraxic pupil.

Abigail herself must also take much credit for working hard to manage her difficulties.

We met Abigail at the beginning of the chapter. She was 13 years old and she had been at her all girls' boarding school for a little over a year; the head mistress had written to say that if Abigail's behaviour and work did not improve dramatically she would be asking Abigail's parents to take her out of school at the end of term.

Difficult behaviour so often brings a message. What was Abigail trying to let us know so loudly and clearly? Abigail's test profile along with her general strengths and weaknesses was strongly indicative of dyspraxia. She did well on the verbal tests (in fact her verbal IQ was way above average), she was highly articulate and her comprehension and verbal reasoning were excellent. In contrast, she scored average and below on tests which sampled her visual/spatial skills.

Abigail's reading was advanced and she achieved test scores that hit the test ceiling, i.e. her reading accuracy, comprehension and spelling scores were all age equivalent to more than 17 years.

Her handwriting was poor. She wrote slowly for her age at a speed of ten words a minute. (As a rather rough rule of thumb, to achieve an average speed a child must write at an average number of words per minute equal to his age plus one.) Letters tended to squash into one another or to have huge gaps between them, and words went up and down off the line in waves. She squashed words in together at the end of the line and the presentation was generally very messy and untidy. It was immediately clear that this bright and articulate pupil was having considerable difficulty in conveying what was in her head onto the page.

Discussion with Abigail's parents revealed that she was not well coordinated and thoroughly disliked team games, particularly those which involved a ball. Her catching and throwing was poor and she was still unable to ride a bike. Abigail's social skills were not good. She was one of those children who would stand too close; she did not pick up on the more subtle aspects of communication and could be tactless or inappropriate in her responses to others.

Despite being able to give a good oral response in class she was not able to achieve well with her written work and was consequently frequently admonished for brief and messy work. She appeared careless and lazy. She had no friends and was unable to get on easily with her peer group. With no opportunity to go home at 4pm and get away from it all, Abigail was with other children, in a classroom or dormitory, literally 24/7. The strain was huge, and eventually her challenging behaviour meant that things could not be left to drift.

The first thing which we needed to do was to make sure that the staff in her school were made aware of her difficulties and of how hard Abigail was finding life both in and out of the classroom. A meeting at school with key staff was all that was needed to start to bring about change. They were very receptive and quickly took up the challenge of seeing Abigail as a child with a difficulty which they could help to ameliorate, rather than seeing her as a difficult child. A case conference was called so all those who taught Abigail could understand the nature of her difficulty. There are five key things which can be a lifeline for children with dyspraxia:

1. *Typing:* completing work on a laptop can be liberating. Writing is so much faster and the end result is neat and legible. Suddenly there are no more comments about scruffy, untidy and illegible work, and there is no need to focus on letter formation at the cost of content.

2. *Counselling:* for those children who, like Abigail, have been suffering for some time and who have consequently become depressed, angry, confused or have simply opted out, counselling provides a much-needed safe place to explore the issues.

3. *Occupational therapy:* this helps to improve coordination, strength and balance, and for the older child it may cover personal organisation.

4. *Help with organisation:* chaotic organisation and time keeping is pretty much synonymous with dyspraxia, so guidance and support to improve self-organisation is an important part of the mix. It can be helpful to break activities down into a clear sequence of actions which the child can work through. Aide-memoires for remembering what to do when and what is required can help.

5. *Help with study skills:* this too is vital. For the pupil who struggles to sequence and structure her ideas on paper it is essential to develop effective strategies to help.

These were put in place for Abigail, and in addition things were arranged so that she could sleep on her own and not in a dormitory. There was an immediate improvement in the situation, and by the end of term there was no mention of her having to leave.

Abigail completed school successfully and went on to take a degree followed by a professional qualification. I spoke with her parents to find out how things had worked out over the intervening years.

Abigail's father explained that by the time they had sought an educational psychologist's assessment they were at their wits' end with worry. The 'diagnosis' of dyspraxia came as a huge relief and removed the worry that somehow her difficulties might have been their fault. Now they knew the nature of the problem they could get on with helping her and this really 'turned her life around'.

Abigail's father was emphatic that once the difficulty is identified parents must set up a military campaign of support and must ensure that it all happens. He underlined the fact that parents should not leave it to others; they must 'wade in', even if they are not in the front line. He acknowledged the very positive role of school staff, of Abigail's counsellor who worked with her throughout school and of the head of pastoral care, of the teacher who taught her to touch type and of the brilliant nutritionist who helped them work out a diet to help with concentration levels (slow-release foods and strict avoidance of all additives – for further information see the resources section).

The family discovered that they had many relations with similar dyspraxic difficulties, both physical and social. They explained that Abigail continues to find it difficult to live with others and that she does not suffer fools gladly. They described the high level of support she needed as she coped with her postgraduate training. They are deeply proud of what she has achieved. There is no doubt that their unwavering support has been a vital ingredient in her success.

Abigail was also kind enough to talk to me and she will have the last word in this chapter. We talked about the significant challenges which dyspraxia had created for her and about the ways in which she had overcome these. It was fascinating to hear her say that it was the small changes which teachers, parents or employers made which had ultimately had the greatest impact on her ability to cope. Why is it, she said, that it can be so hard for schools to get their head around this?

Abigail emphasised that:

» having permission to take a laptop into class had enabled her to survive in an educational setting

» being really, really well taught in school about how to structure her written work had been imperative and indeed it had taken her right through her degree. She emphasised how much the 'how to structure writing' had been drummed home

» the time spent learning to touch type (it took most of one of her summer holidays) had been well worthwhile

» the organisational strategies she was taught alongside the touch typing were vital; for example, how to print off written work, how to store it in a ring binder and make proper use of dividers (this may all sound simple, but it is interesting to hear again what a difference it can make to day-to-day survival)

» the time, help and support given by her parents had been wonderful.

Although for Abigail the social aspects of school were 'awful', her message for others is that 'it does get better'. Relationships improve. She maintains that at school she was socially immature for her age. Although by the sixth form she felt more integrated, it is only since the age of 22 years that she has begun to feel that she is truly on the 'same level' as her peer group.

Abigail is aware that she needs to plan well. She cannot leave things to the last minute. She is also aware that she can easily lose sight of the big picture and get lost in the detail. When she is working on a big project she makes regular use of reminders to help.

Abigail has considerable confidence in being open about her difficulties. She had learnt how to explain to others that she is dyspraxic and has generally found this to be helpful. She explained things to relevant staff when she started university and she has explained at work.

She has worked immensely hard to minimise any difficulties caused by dyspraxia. Small bits of clumsiness can cause havoc, so she thinks around situations to try and ensure that life goes smoothly. For example, she never puts a cup of coffee in the middle of her desk where the downsides to spilling it are so high. Because she tries so hard to avoid such problems she explained that she can feel very angry at herself when something does go wrong. She hoped that her supreme effort would have made it all go away.

KEY POINTS

⇨ The young child with dyspraxia has immature physical responses and is poorly coordinated. He or she will benefit from specialist help from an appropriate practitioner such as a physiotherapist or occupational therapist.

⇨ Difficulties with physical coordination often diminish with age but the difficulty with planning, organising and time keeping tend to remain and impact on higher-order thinking skills.

⇨ All dyspraxic pupils need help with written communication and copying. There are likely to be occasions when it is appropriate for parents or others to scribe for the pupil. All pupils should learn to type and to use a laptop. Not only does this ensure good presentation but also for many pupils it liberates their thought processes and enables them to communicate fluently.

⇨ As the dyspraxic pupil progresses into secondary school it is important that he develops effective study skills. Good strategies for structuring written work are paramount (see Chapter 24, Habits, Strategies and Study Skills).

⇨ The dyspraxic teenager needs strategies to support all aspects of planning and organising, from belongings through to essay writing.

⇨ Dyspraxia can lead to significant anxiety, stress and mental health issues. A further challenge can be exhaustion from the extreme effort of trying to 'keep up'. However, we have seen from case studies that if difficulties are recognised and accommodated it is possible to cope successfully.

⇨ Good, ongoing, positive parental support can make a world of difference. Parental support will almost inevitably be needed well past the age that many other children are functioning independently.

Chapter 5

DYSCALCULIA AND OTHER MATHS DIFFICULTIES

Maths involves a range of complex mental processes. Violet's poor number sense made it hard for her to carry out simple computations; Peter's poor visual/spatial skills affected his ability to understand graphs, tables, fractions and place value; and Leonard's poor working memory meant that he struggled to learn times tables and often lost track midway through a multistep calculation.

By the end of primary school our children are expected to be fluent and familiar with a vast range of mathematical concepts and techniques. They need to manage numbers to count, add, subtract, divide and multiply. They should be fluent in dealing with all kinds of measurements covering weight, length, volume, space and time. They will have started to handle data and read graphs, diagrams and tables. They will be able to manage coordinates. They should be able to change fractions to decimal points; they will have started geometry, algebra and equations.

For some children this does not happen easily. Of course, it is all too easy for children to fall behind. Maths is cumulative. It is like a wall going up brick by brick. Each new concept or method taught will depend on a firm foundation below. If a child is away or has difficulty understanding on a day when an important new brick is introduced he may then start to struggle. Some children find certain teachers easier to follow than others; maybe the teaching style does not play to their strengths. Children can all too rapidly start to feel inadequate and anxious. Once this happens they may decide they are 'bad' at maths and that they cannot do it. Mathematical anxiety and low confidence can be a huge impediment to progress. But for some children, difficulty with maths is more than a missed lesson or a dip in confidence.

In this chapter we will look at the impact of specific maths difficulties. Difficulties with maths can usefully be seen to cluster into three rather separate groups. These are not necessarily mutually exclusive and a pupil may have difficulty in one, two or all three areas.

Maths uses three fundamentally important cognitive skills and abilities:

- a sense of number

- spatial awareness, pattern recognition and sequencing skills

- memory; both long-term and working memory.

A problem in any one of these three areas may lead to difficulties. It is important to ascertain whether difficulties are due to poor number sense, poor visual/spatial skills or poor working memory because this will impact quite specifically on the way the child learns maths and this in turn will inform the best way of helping him. We will go over each of these and look at the way they each contribute to our mathematical understanding and performance. Of course, we need to remember that these areas of difficulty are not mutually exclusive and some children may have difficulty in all areas, but for the purpose of analysing difficulties it is useful to separate them out.

A sense of number

The basis to all mathematics is number. As a species we appear to be 'hard wired' to grasp number. Experiments with young babies have shown that they have a sense of quantity and can discriminate between groups of three, four or five items. Indeed, it has also been demonstrated that some other species also have an appreciation of number and can visually discriminate between groups containing different numbers of items. The following story about a farmer and a crow illustrates this point:

> The crow was destroying his crop and the farmer wished to shoot it. The crow was often to be seen sitting on a wire which crossed the farmyard. When the farmer walked across the yard with his gun the crow would fly off and did not return until it had seen the farmer safely back into the house. He decided to trick the crow. He asked a friend to cross the yard with him. Once the two men had crossed the yard the farmer remained hidden in the barn (positioned so that he could shoot the bird when it came back) and his friend returned to the house. The crow was not fooled and stayed away until it had seen the farmer return to the farmhouse. The farmer then enlisted help from a second friend and the three men crossed the yard together with two of them returning to the house. Once again the crow was not fooled. It was not until six men left the house and five returned that the crow was unable to discriminate between the size of each group.

I have included this story because this capacity to discriminate and understand number, which comes so easily to most people, is of such central importance to our numerical abilities and our ability to understand

and manipulate quantities. Yet there are some individuals who do not have a natural grasp of numbers. These are the pupils whose maths difficulties are dyscalculic in kind and for whom it is so hard to acquire arithmetic skills. We will return to them later in the chapter.

Spatial skills and awareness

Next are spatial awareness, pattern recognition and sequencing. So much of all that is encompassed in maths is about patterns and relationships. An ability to recognise patterns and to see spatial relationships underpins much mathematical understanding. This is true whether we are thinking of times tables, fractions or even the simple fact that where a number is positioned on the page can make a difference to its value. For example, 3 is different from 0.3 or 300 or 3000.

Spatial awareness certainly seems to play a very important role in many aspects of maths. Data from many hundreds of children that I have seen shows a strong correlation between the ability to complete tests which sample spatial awareness with their ability to manage sums involving decimals, fractions and geometry, as well as their ability to read graphs and maps and do coordinates. Decimals are easily understood if you have a clear idea that the position of a number relative to the decimal point provides vital information about the value of the number; 300.00 is very different from 00.030. Fractions also rely on a good grasp or feel for what fraction of a whole the numbers mean. Some children readily grasp that if you cut a cake into three equal parts you can call each slice one third; others struggle even when they have concrete materials in front of them. Learning to write one third as a one over a three can be confusing and the child may find it just as compelling to write three over one. It is easy to understand that difficulty with geometry will be another casualty of poor spatial awareness. Geometry is all about space and shape and relationships.

Poor spatial awareness is strongly associated with dyspraxia. It is both the dyspraxic pupils and those with poor visual processing and poor visual memory who are likely to have the difficulties described above.

Memory

We rely on long-term memory to enable us to recall what procedure or calculation we should apply to what problem. We use our long-term memory to bring up number facts and times table facts.

Working memory is used extensively while pupils are engaged in maths calculations. Working memory refers to the mental system which enables us to hold onto information over a short period of time (seconds and minutes, not hours) while managing or manipulating the facts or figures. Pupils with weak working memory find many aspects of maths a challenge. The information which they need to keep up on the mental whiteboard will often get wiped off before they have finished using it.

Pupils with poor working memory are also likely to have found it hard to learn and retain their times tables and number bonds (see Chapter 2, Working Memory). This means that they are likely to run into difficulty in multistep calculations; if, for example, they have to stop to work out eight times eight part way through a long calculation, they may well lose track of why they had to work it out in the first place.

Poor working memory is strongly associated with dyslexia and with ADHD. Thus many pupils experiencing these areas of specific learning difficulty will experience the difficulties described above.

What is dyscalculia?

Now let us return to dyscalculia. What exactly is it? There is general consensus that it is a specific learning difficulty that affects a person's ability to acquire arithmetical skills. The dyscalculic pupil or adult has an inability to conceptualise numbers, number relationships (arithmetical facts) and the outcomes of numerical operations (estimating the answer to numerical problems before actually calculating). They also struggle to recognise symbols and to comprehend quantitative information. Dyscalculia is thought to be neurological in origin.

This can have a devastating impact on many day-to-day activities and most certainly makes maths lessons in school a potentially miserable experience.

Although there is considerably more awareness of dyscalculia and it is officially recognised, the study of this specific difficulty is in its infancy compared with our study and knowledge of dyslexia or dyspraxia. We are, however, slowly making inroads and much more is now known about the most effective teaching methods.

As with other areas of specific learning difficulty, many of those affected are of high intelligence and their difficulties may be mild or extreme. Having very poor number sense will impact on all aspects of maths but it does not mean that a child or adult will have difficulties in any other field.

It is important to stress that many children have difficulty with maths but *not* all of them are dyscalculic. A key sign of dyscalculia is an inability to subitise. This term refers to our ability to enumerate a small quantity of things without having to count them. This is something which most people can do quite naturally. How can you check this? Scatter a few counters, not more than five, and ask the pupil to say how many there are. Can he answer immediately or does he have to point and count?

Other signs are:

- difficulty in counting on from a number
- difficulty in counting backwards
- difficulty in counting from one decade into the next. For example, a child with dyscalculia may count out 38, 39, 41, 42 or go 39, 31…
- an inability to estimate whether a numerical answer is reasonable
- a tendency not to notice patterns
- problems with all aspects of money
- difficulty in learning to read a clock to tell the time.

The good news is that children with dyscalculia can be helped to gain a level of understanding and to master maths procedures. They will need a good teacher and it will require effort, structure, discipline and appropriate concrete materials. What they need is to work from the basics and to progress at their own speed.

What comes so naturally to the vast majority must be carefully taught to the dyscalculic pupil. The aim is to help them to develop some form of understanding through experience and also to master basic procedures so that, even if understanding is wobbly, they can carry out some procedures accurately.

The dyscalculic pupil will need support to understand and explore number patterns and relationships. He will need to be carefully taught about number facts and about the basic computations. He will need to learn about base 10. He will need to be taught about the way in which the processes involved in addition, subtraction, multiplication and division relate to each other. He will need to be helped to generalise from facts: $3 + 4 = 7$; $30 + 40 = 70$; $300 + 400 = 700$.

In order to do this successfully he will need practical experiences using concrete materials such as beads, counters and Cuisenaire rods. This needs to be coupled with the over-learning of maths procedures.

He will need time to learn. He will need to be encouraged to talk about what he has learnt. He needs to learn appropriate maths vocabulary to support his understanding. He should be encouraged to estimate. He will need to develop fluency with times tables and number bonds.

He will need regular involvement in practical activities relating to money, weight and measurement. He can be encouraged to help with shopping, counting change and measuring out cooking ingredients.

Ultimately, the aim should be to ensure that our dyscalculic children have sufficient maths skills to cope with all the day-to-day activities which involve maths, for example using money, reading times tables, buying ingredients, measuring fabric and so forth.

Tutoring for dyscalculic pupils should aim to:

- help them make up for the missing concepts
- connect these to their mathematical needs
- help them develop the prerequisite skills for maths learning.

There are several excellent books which elaborate on the best way to plan and to teach pupils with dyscalculic difficulties, and recommendations are made in the Further Reading section at the end of the book.

Difficulties associated with poor spatial awareness, dyspraxia and weak visual processing

Those pupils (and adults) who are showing signs of dyspraxia and/or the associated difficulty with hand–eye coordination and in dealing with spatial information will often have very particular or specific weaknesses with maths. While their number sense, mental maths and ability to understand maths concepts may be excellent, they are likely to have difficulty in dealing with maths activities which involve orientation.

Dyspraxic pupils may frequently confuse left and right; their sense of direction is poor and they may have a lack of awareness of themselves in relation to objects around them. These difficulties go hand in hand with many of the processes that come within the remit of maths. Such pupils frequently experience some difficulty with:

- interpretation of visual data such as graphs, coordinates and times tables
- interpretation of written numbers when the position is of critical importance. The position of a number in relation to the decimal point is important in telling us the value of that number, i.e. 3 has

a very different value depending on whether it is placed in the hundreds or thousands column

- fractions. The value of a fraction depends on which number is above and which below. For those children who have poor spatial awareness it is not obvious or immediately apparent how the position of a number will affect its value. I have noticed how some children will use 1 over 2 or 2 over 1 interchangeably

- telling the time from a non-digital clock/watch. This really is hard; two hands moving at different speeds and in a particular direction!

Geometry can also be hard. The recognition of shapes whatever their orientation will be difficult, and for the pupil who has poor working memory for visual information there will be additional challenges. Sophie explained how hard it is to copy shapes from the board. She also explained that in addition she cannot follow what her teacher is saying at the same time as copying either text, formulas or any other kind of maths information. Unfortunately, her teacher tends to talk and explain while expecting them to copy and it is just impossible for her to copy and listen simultaneously. Despite her having perfectly good number skills, maths has become one of Sophie's least favourite subjects.

The dyspraxic pupil also tends to have poor hand–eye coordination. Handwriting is often untidy and uneven and frequently the squares in maths exercise books are unnecessarily small. The combination is not good. It is really hard for the child to keep his written numbers within the small squared places provided. The page looks a mess and is almost impossible to read.

Then there is adding and subtracting in columns. We must work from the unit and then to the tens and so to the hundreds – in other words from right to left. We must subtract the bottom from the top. This does not come naturally to some pupils and it has not been unusual to observe children taking the top number from the bottom number or starting their addition from the left-hand column. The wrong answer which comes out at the end of one of these misguided calculations may make perfect sense and be 'correct' when we understand what the child has been doing.

All forms of division and long multiplication can suffer from the same type of error, which is so very easy for some pupils to make, and maybe the numbers get misaligned because of untidy writing.

What can you do to help at home?

The first thing which may help is to provide hands-on practical experience of shape and pattern in order to improve these underlying skills. These are most probably the children who never enjoyed playing with puzzles (it didn't come easily to them and it's not fun doing things which are difficult) and may not have spent long on Lego or other construction toys. You will probably have to 'play' or engage with them to get it going. Help them to be systematic and to sort or order in a way which is consistent. It may be that they need help to find all the outside edges of a puzzle or that they need help with construction games or activities (see Chapter 18, Tips for Maths, for more ideas).

It is important to attach language to these activities as well as to maths challenges. It can be particularly helpful to 'talk' through a problem. Turning thoughts into language and language into maths does seem to work. I have come across many children who, when confused or needing to think carefully, will start a commentary about what they are doing. The inner voice can guide thinking, planning and doing. It also helps us to keep on track.

Using the right vocabulary is also an aid. It is important to develop a good understanding of the words we use to denote position, shape and orientation and to use them. Words such as column, row, top, bottom, diagonal, cube and hexagon need to be well embedded into understanding.

It can help to talk and describe graphs, coordinates or times tables. It means that we are forced to slow down and turn the information that we are looking at into words. The act of doing so can help understanding.

We can use the voice to support visual memory too. You might have the child look at an illustration of a particular shape, then cover it over (or turn it face down) and see if he can reproduce it accurately or if he misremembers details. If he has difficulty with recall, let him look at the illustration again, but this time ask him to describe its salient features. Then cover it or turn it over and ask him to reproduce it. Chances are that the second effort will be an improvement on the first.

From a purely practical point of view, use larger squared paper. For the pupil with untidy writing it is hard to squeeze numbers into the tiny squares that we find in some maths exercise books.

Maths, dyslexia and poor working memory

There is another group of pupils who are likely to have difficulty with certain aspects of maths, and these are the pupils who may well be dyslexic and who most definitely have poor working memory.

These pupils may be very good with numbers; they may have an excellent grasp of maths concepts and can be brilliant with shape and space. They may have a good intuitive understanding and at times may seem to arrive at the correct answer to a maths problem with little idea of how they got there. In other words, they may be good natural mathematicians but their weak working memory can cause problems.

Working memory is the memory system that we use in order to 'hold on' to and manipulate information in the very short term (a full description is given in the chapter on working memory).

Poor working memory can cause a number of difficulties:

- It is hard to mentally 'keep hold of' information and facts while working out a multistep problem. If, for example, the pupil has to multiply 7×8 as part of a maths problem it is likely that once he has managed this he will have forgotten why he needed the answer.

- Mental maths can be a struggle. If a maths problem is read out the child with poor working memory is likely to have forgotten the first part of the problem before the full question is finished. Fascinatingly though, I have often noticed that if the good mathematician with a poor working memory can work out the sum rapidly enough he can manage some very challenging problems. But if he has to stop and think, he is sunk. He rarely has a clue how he managed.

- Some children find it hard to record their 'workings out' because it interferes with their thinking and problem-solving process. This can also be quite an issue as many teachers require that they see how the process has been completed.

Poor working memory is also associated with difficulty in:

- learning and recalling number facts such as times tables and number bonds. It is hard to explain why this should be so, but rote learning information, which has no immediate meaning, until it is fully embedded and, perhaps more importantly, can be recalled with ease, is a challenge for those with poor working memory. These number facts can be memorised but will need to be rehearsed over and over until they finally stick

- sequencing numbers correctly. Rosemary's dyslexic son called her to ask for his account number. Both Rosemary and her son find it hard to read and record a sequence of numbers correctly. They are both capable of misreading a number without noticing. Neither of them will take in and remember more than a few numbers at a time and neither of them is any good at writing them down in the order they have been spoken. He was calling from an area with poor reception and Rosemary recalled with hilarity the number of attempts they had to make before they were satisfied that the correct numbers had been transmitted and recorded. Sadly this can lead to numerous 'careless' mistakes.

Poor working memory is very strongly associated with dyslexia and it is likely that many of the children who have the difficulties described above will also have difficulty with aspects of literacy. This may mean that they:

- have difficulty in reading written maths problems
- muddle maths symbols.

Both of these problems are a real frustration for the fundamentally good mathematician. Their success at maths can be immensely important in relation to their self-esteem. It can be the area in which they can show that they are able and in which they experience success. It is doubly important that they are supported to find ways around this and to overcome the impact of poor working memory and poor literacy skills.

How can we help these pupils?

Parents can ensure that times tables and number bonds are well learnt. It is helpful for these children to have number facts at their fingertips. No mental space is wasted in struggling to remember 5×6 midway through a computation.

Practice should be little and often. The unfair fact is that it is the dyslexic pupils who have greatest difficulty with this type of rote learning, but the following ideas may help:

- Use a sound recording device. Let the child read the chosen times table onto a recording device as follows: '1 × 4 = (pause) 4' and so on. The pause is so that when he replays the recording, he can beat himself giving the answer.
- Create your own Kumon maths system. Draw up a page of sums. These will be chosen in the light of the child's level of ability and the areas that need attention. They might all be one type of sum

or they might be a mixture. Run these through a photocopier so there are a good number of identical pages. Your child can practise this sheet of sums on a daily basis until he has become fluent and achieves 100 per cent accuracy at speed. He should achieve this level of success on several consecutive days before moving on to a new page of sums. For motivation the child can keep a record of his accuracy and speed; he will be working to beat his previous performance and this has been found to be motivating and fun.

There are other ways of lightening the load for these children. For example:

- See if he might be allowed to use a calculator when 'how to' solve a problem or what process to use is of importance rather than the actual number crunching. This helps to avoid silly errors that happen because of poor working memory. It is all too easy for the child with a weak working memory to lose track when working through a multistep calculation. Quick and accurate number crunching can improve accuracy as well as helping some children to become more confident about problem solving.

- Make sure that he is fluent with maths language and that it is well understood.

There are alternative strategies for helping children to internalise number facts, which range from poems and ditties to patterns and systems. For example:

'I *ate* and I *ate* and was *sick* on the *floor*' can help to get $8 \times 8 = 64$ stuck in memory.

The ten times table follows a pattern, as does the five times table, both of which are easy to recognise. Where things are more complicated there are other strategies. The following method can help with the nine times table.

- $5 \times 9 = 45$ 1 from 5 is 4. 4 and 5 makes 9. Answer 45.

- $6 \times 9 = 54$ 1 from 6 is 5. 5 and 4 makes 9. Answer 54.

- $7 \times 9 = 63$ 1 from 7 is 6. 6 and 3 makes 9. Answer 63.

General principles

The following three teaching principles are relevant for all children who are experiencing difficulty regardless of whether they are primarily dyscalculic or have poor spatial skills or poor working memory:

1. Try and help your child to feel relaxed and ready to open his mental 'doors' to new learning, revision and reinforcement. We all make mistakes, this is part of learning and he doesn't have to fall to pieces if things do not go right immediately. Keep it light and try to keep activities fun. Can you inject some humour into the situation? It can be difficult for parents to be the ones to motivate and inspire; sometimes it takes an outsider to succeed.

2. We all learn best if new things can hook onto our existing knowledge or understanding. Can you find a way of linking new learning onto something which he already knows? If he has to learn new and difficult vocabulary, such as circumference or radius, make a story or enjoy exploring the word and expanding on it. For example, play with the word circumference – expand the meaning through circumnavigate, circus and circle.

3. Put experience first. All children and pupils must have hands-on experience and concrete examples in order to fully understand theoretical maths concepts.

CASE STUDIES

Violet's story

Violet's difficulties were around her lack of number sense. She really seemed to have no feel for numbers and no ability to deal with simple calculations in her mind. She was, however, doing reasonably well when she was given a paper and pencil test and was able to apply the maths procedures which she had been carefully taught.

Violet was eight when she was referred for assessment because she had 'gaps in her maths knowledge'; she was said to be struggling and highly anxious. She could not remember her number bonds and could not sequence numbers easily. In school she panicked if she was asked a question in class and would 'pick an answer out of the air'. She was also having difficulty in learning to tell the time.

Due to a long waiting list Violet could not be assessed for some months. During this time Violet received specialist teaching in school and support with maths homework at home. Violet was said to have made very good progress but her parents thought that it was worthwhile keeping the assessment appointment to see whether there might be any underlying difficulties.

Violet proved to be bright and to have excellent literacy skills; as far as maths was concerned she did indeed seem to have made progress and her score on the paper and pencil tests was only very slightly below the average for a child of her age. She had mastered the basic maths processes and she could add and subtract numbers in columns. She had learnt how to carry over and had no problem in adding 587 and 315.

So far this was excellent, but when she was asked to complete a simple addition of two single digits in her head she became very flustered and anxious and had to use her fingers. Further investigation confirmed that although Violet had learnt how to cope with the paper and pencil tests following a well-drilled procedure she had little intuitive understanding of numbers. She had little ability to form mental images with which to deal with computation and was unable to deal with very simple maths questions presented orally. It was like an unknown foreign language to her.

The improvements which her parents had noticed were due to the good and supportive teaching which she had received and which had taught her 'how to' complete the procedures on paper. Violet presented with a significant underlying difficulty in maths, which was due to a poor intuitive understanding of numbers. Although she was able to apply and carry out an arithmetic procedure, her lack of ability to estimate meant that she would not have known if her answer was way off the mark or whether it was approximately correct.

Violet needed continued specialist support and well-targeted teaching to help her to gain a more fundamental understanding and feel for numbers as well as continuing to learn how to apply appropriate procedures.

At home, although it was important that her parents should encourage her to rote learn her number bonds and times tables, she also needed as much practical experience as possible to help her to become familiar with underlying ideas and concepts. She needed to be encouraged to get involved in practical activities relating to money, weight, measurement and so forth, for example helping with cooking, shopping and counting change. She also needed to be encouraged to estimate what the answer might be before working it out. Maths problems needed to be made fun.

Peter's story

Peter had poor spatial awareness and this had affected his ability to deal with certain maths activities. Peter's story demonstrates very clearly how specific this kind of difficulty can be. He was intellectually able in every other way but struggled with visual data requiring any kind of analysis.

Peter had just finished a degree when he came for assessment. He had seen the assessment report completed for his younger brother and, encouraged by his parents, he decided that he would like to find out if there was any explanation for the great difficulty which he had always experienced with some aspects of maths. He asked if I would carry out an assessment. He explained that he had always experienced problems with shape, space, sequencing and ordering. He had problems map reading and generally analysing visual data. He wanted to know if there might be any ways in which he could be helped to read statistical data presented diagrammatically in a more effective way.

As I suspected he turned out to have excellent verbal skills but his scores on all the tests which sampled his visual/perceptual skills and his non-verbal reasoning were well below average.

Peter had absolutely no difficulty with the mathematics that involved straight computation. It was interesting to see that he was successful with problems such as calculating the average and solving multistep problems where only numbers were involved. He did, however, have difficulty with other questions where he was required to order fractions, deal with mixed decimals, find out a perimeter, interpret pictorial information and interpret a graph.

Dealing with these latter maths problems certainly correlates with perceptual organisation in that they both require the ability to understand how one item relates to another; they also need good spatial awareness and the ability to order and recognise patterns.

Peter was pleased to hear that his difficulties were quite specific and that they seemed to be due to poor visual/perceptual processing and poor visual/spatial analysis (not lack of general ability). We discussed ways in which he might be able to make life easier for himself when dealing with the kind of data he found difficult.

We discussed the importance and value of talking through maths problems in a logical and step-by-step way. Talking through and labelling is very powerful in terms of helping to understand. I thought that he would benefit from a few sessions with a maths specialist who could help to break down the key elements of the data that he found hard and work with him to build his understanding step by step.

I also suggested that if he were interested and wanted further analysis and advice then he should consider getting an occupational therapist's assessment. This would provide a more detailed look at his visual/perceptual skills. I suggested that any work on visual/perceptual organisation should include direct work looking at the type of information that he was finding it hard to interpret.

Leonard's story

Leonard's story illustrates the complexity of the mental processes used in maths. The three distinctions which I have made with regard to number sense, working memory and visual/spatial analysis are useful in terms of assessing where difficulties seem to be happening, but in reality there are many children, like Leonard, who experience difficulties across the board.

Leonard was 11 when he came for assessment. It had previously been suggested that he was experiencing 'mild' dyslexia. By the time I met him his reading was going along well, though spelling was still delayed and was lagging a couple of years behind his chronological age. What was really concerning his parents was his continued difficulty with maths, and this led them to wonder if he might be experiencing dyscalculia.

Leonard's assessment showed that despite good ability he had something of a 'full house' where maths difficulties were concerned. He had a poor working memory, he had visual/spatial processing difficulties and to cap it off he had really poor number sense.

Leonard struggled with the mental maths test. A series of maths problems were read to him. He had to process the language involved in each question, turn it into a number problem and work out the answer in his head. Not only did Leonard find it hard to memorise the question but he also struggled with the number operations required.

The written maths test was also a challenge for Leonard. Although he could complete sums involving the four basic operations (addition, subtraction, multiplication and division), he had little 'feel' for whether numbers were big or small or what answer a sum was likely to have. For example, when he multiplied 24 by 5 he made the answer 1200 but had no sense that this was not very likely.

Leonard also had difficulty with the sums that can be particularly difficult for the pupil with poor visual/spatial skills. He could not manage fractions and had difficulty with squared numbers.

Leonard needed to have continued support for his maths; this needed to be systematic and as slow as necessary to ensure that all the basic skills became fully embedded. The late Dorian Yeo, who was a pioneer and expert in dyscalculia, always maintained that people with dyscalculia *will* learn and *can* succeed, but at a much slower pace.

Leonard also needed as much practical experience as possible to help him become familiar with underlying ideas and concepts. He also needed to get involved in all home activities that involved numbers, measurements and money. He needed encouragement to try to estimate answers before working them out. He also needed to engage in maths games and activities.

KEY POINTS

⇨ Maths is a vast topic and uses many different mental processes.

⇨ The acquisition of maths knowledge is cumulative. New concepts and skills must be built on firm foundations.

⇨ It is easy for difficulties to occur; many children lose confidence and feel that they are bad at maths. This may lead to anxiety, which is itself a cause of poor maths performance.

⇨ Maths requires/uses three important cognitive skills and functions: number sense, recognition of pattern and good working memory.

⇨ Difficulties can occur in one, two or all three areas.

⇨ It is helpful to understand where difficulties occur because this will help to facilitate well targeted support and specialist learning.

⇨ Pupils lacking an innate sense of number will lack arithmetic skills and may be described as dyscalculic.

⇨ An indicator of dyscalculia is the inability to look at a small number of objects and to say how many there are.

⇨ Dyscalculia is neurological in origin.

⇨ Dyscalculic pupils can be helped through systematic teaching which goes at their pace.

⇨ Maths also involves the recognition of patterns and relationships.

⇨ Poor visual/spatial skills can affect a pupil's ability to readily 'see' and understand these patterns and relationships.

⇨ The dyspraxic pupil is likely to experience difficulty with visual/spatial skills and this will impact on his maths ability.

⇨ Poor working memory can also impact on maths operations. A pupil may have good number sense and good ability to recognise pattern but if he has difficulty with working memory he may lose his way in multistep calculations and he may find it hard to learn and retain number bonds and times tables.

⇨ Many dyslexic pupils have poor working memory and they are also likely to misread or muddle maths symbols and find it hard to sequence numbers correctly.

Chapter 6

ATTENTION DEFICIT DISORDER WITH OR WITHOUT HYPERACTIVITY – ADHD

Phoebe's early development was full of promise. She was talking at a very young age and her development seemed to be well in advance of other children of her age. Phoebe's parents had no reason to think that school would present any difficulties. However, once she started school, problems cropped up. She was fidgety, her concentration was poor and she had difficulty in listening and absorbing information in class. There was nothing about her school performance to suggest to her teachers that she was an able child. Parental concern mounted when it became apparent that she was also having difficulty with reading and maths.

What is ADHD?

For many people the first image that comes to mind is of a hyperactive and disobedient child who is constantly on the go. While some children are exceptionally active and indeed may be difficult to discipline and to manage, there are many others, particularly girls, whose dreamy behaviour will go largely unnoticed but whose ability to maintain and control attention is very weak. What they have in common is considerable difficulty in paying and controlling attention. Like other areas of specific learning difficulty, ADHD is on a spectrum and not all pupils who need support and help are racing uncontrollably around causing mayhem in their wake.

As parents and teachers we need to be concerned for all children whose ADHD behaviour impairs their ability to thrive and cope with school both academically and/or socially.

In this chapter we look at the way in which ADHD is identified, the impact it has in the classroom, the impact at home, management issues and ways in which these pupils can be supported.

Over the past 10–15 years our knowledge and understanding of ADHD has grown enormously. It has, however, been a controversial topic, and within the field of education there have been sceptics and detractors. The sceptics have argued that ADHD is a social construct used as an excuse for difficult behaviour.

There is now a growing consensus of opinion, including those in the medical profession, that the behaviours associated with ADHD are at one end of a normal spectrum. It has been suggested that back when we were hunter gatherers this behaviour conferred survival advantages. The child who is quickly distracted from what he is doing by a movement at the other end of the garden might have saved our lives by alerting us to predator danger out in the wild.

Difficulties in identifying and defining ADHD have arisen because the whole concept is rather 'woolly'. Unlike measles or mumps where we can see clear symptoms indicative of a specific disease, ADHD is defined at a behavioural level. It is 'identified' or 'diagnosed' through observation of the child's behaviour. If the child exhibits a range of inattentive, impulsive/hyperactive behaviours then (in the absence of any other explanations) he might be deemed to have a version of ADHD. This is certainly not so clear-cut and clinical as the diagnosis of measles.

Despite the sceptics it is now widely accepted that ADHD is a valid construct. Neuroscientists and psychologists have produced evidence to indicate a genetic and physiological basis for this condition. Their work, which looks at the chemical, electrical and structural brain differences which might underpin ADHD, has shown up an imbalance in the brain's neurotransmitter chemicals noradrenalin and dopamine.

Through their investigation we now know that the pre-frontal lobes of the brain are a necessary part of our cognitive executive function and that it is this executive system which regulates attention control as well as impulsivity, planning ahead, working memory, task switching and aspects of social awareness.

How can we set about identifying ADHD?

The most commonly used guidelines which professionals refer to in order to identify ADHD come from the fifth edition of the *Diagnostic and Statistical Manual of Mental Disorders* (DSM-5) which is published by the American Psychiatric Association.

The DSM-5 provides guidance for 'diagnosis' which is based on the presence and intensity of certain behaviours. These fall into two distinct categories:

- inattentive

- hyperactive-impulsive.

These two categories are not mutually exclusive and a child may also show signs of combined inattention and hyperactive-impulsive. These guidelines do not make any differentiation for different ages; the checklist is thus relevant for children (or indeed people) of any age.

Indicators of *poor attention* can be:

- making careless mistakes, for example in school work

- being forgetful

- losing things

- having difficulty at sticking to tasks that are tedious or time consuming

- having difficulty listening to or carrying out instructions

- often changing activities or tasks

- having difficulty with personal organisation

- having a short attention span

- being easily distracted by extraneous noises and activities.

Many parents tell me that their child cannot have an ADHD problem because when he is interested in something he will focus for hours and can be totally absorbed. This is the confusing thing. Children with ADHD are often 'all on' or 'all off'. When he is absorbed you may have noticed that it can be really difficult to get his attention at all; he can seem oblivious to the outside world. This is as much a difficulty with attention control as lack of focus. We will discuss this further on in the chapter.

As you go through this list you may also be thinking that many of us and our children are forgetful, lose things and can be easily distracted. What is so special about this? Well, this is one reason that 'diagnosing' ADHD can be difficult. We have to try and ascertain whether these behaviours are out of the usual range for a child of that particular age. It is necessary to find out how often the behaviour happens and how extreme it is. To do this professionals such as doctors and psychologists must rely very largely on what parents or teachers report. This brings a further difficulty. Parental judgements about how forgetful a child is tend to be very subjective. Different families may have very different 'norms'. What is tolerated in one household might cause despair in another. The same difficulties arise as we look at levels of hyperactivity and impulsivity.

Indicators of *hyperactivity-impulsivity* can be:

- having difficulty sitting still, especially in calm or quiet surroundings
- constant fidgeting or having a permanently tapping leg or hand
- difficulty in settling to tasks
- being constantly on the go physically, rushing about and rarely settling to more sedentary activities, and behaving as though 'driven by a motor'
- talking excessively
- finding it hard to wait his turn
- acting without thinking
- interrupting conversations
- breaking rules
- having little or no sense of danger; for example, do you find that you take hold of his hand as you approach a main road because you know that if he stops thinking he will walk right into the traffic, even when he is ten years old?

Because these same indicators can be applied to children of all ages we must be careful to judge the 'normality' of a child's behaviour against that of his peer group. Many of these descriptions of hyperactive and impulsive behaviour would be normal for a toddler but not for a nine-year-old, so we see that it is important to compare like with like and to take age into consideration.

A positive response to six or more items in one of these two groups may form the basis of a diagnosis of ADHD. In addition these behaviours must have been present for more than six months (generally they have been evident for as long as parents can remember) and should not just be evident in one situation, i.e. at school or at grandma's house.

The proportion of positive responses in these two different categories will indicate whether the child is mainly ADHD inattentive, ADHD hyperactive-impulsive or ADHD combined.

Does ADHD often co-occur with other specific learning difficulties?

It seems that the child with ADHD is very likely to experience a further co-occurring difficulty. Studies completed in the past ten years show a marked overlap with dyslexia, dyspraxia and autism spectrum disorder (ASD). The overlap is significant and is in excess of 50 per cent. I have also checked my own database. Out of a sample of 400 children I found that 68 (17%) had appeared to show clear signs of ADHD, and that out of these 68 pupils 59 of them had co-existing areas of specific learning difficulty. Or to put it another way, only nine of them had no additional difficulties.

Who can or will make a diagnosis of ADHD?

For a definitive 'diagnosis' of ADHD and advice regarding medication and management your child will need to be assessed by an appropriate psychiatrist or specialist doctor.

Many other professionals such as educational and clinical psychologists will also be alert to the possibility that ADHD might be a contributory factor to a child's poor progress and can discuss with parents whether they wish to take this further and seek a 'diagnosis' from an appropriate medical practitioner. Below I describe the ways in which Freddie and Lily behaved when they came for assessment.

Freddie's story

Freddie, who was aged nine, arrived with his mother for assessment. He came right in without so much as a glance in my direction, let alone a 'hello'. As his mother and I exchanged greetings he rushed through the door, crossed the waiting room and turned the carriage clock around. 'Is this your flat?' he said. This was followed rapidly by, 'Do you live here? I like the sofas. Why does your clock tell the wrong time?'

Freddie was observant and quick but he had limited focus on anything which was not of immediate interest to him. Although the main reason for Freddie's assessment was concern about his slow progress with reading it did not take long for me to start to wonder whether he might also experience a degree of ADHD.

We sat down so that I could talk Freddie and his mother through the assessment procedure. Within minutes Freddie was up and had gone to look out of the window. I asked him a direct question, which he ignored, and his mother answered for him. She did not suggest that he should come back, sit down and pay attention. This is not how most children of his age behave in this situation.

During the assessment Freddie:

» fidgeted throughout the verbal tests and was happiest if he could stand up while he talked. He swayed from one leg to the other and then twirled around. He moved onto the sofa and then he lay on it. All the while he gave good and appropriate answers

» was able to sit at the desk and focus when he had materials to handle and manipulate, though he made squeaky noises and chatted to himself

» showed that his vigilance on the paper and pencil test where constant attention is required was very poor

» struggled with a five-minute writing task. It took time and rather a lot of discussion to decide what topic he would write about. He started, and after a minute said he was going to change to one of the other topics we discussed. He asked if he could have a rubber. He commented on a noise out in the road. After five minutes he had completed very little

» made 'careless' errors despite being good at maths; he muddled the plus, minus, division and multiplication signs.

» often interrupted what we were doing to comment on things that caught his attention. It might have been a plane passing by or the very distant hum of a drill in the road below. Even the faint sound of my neighbour's vacuum cleaner was a distraction.

Even in this one-to-one situation it was hard work for me to keep Freddie on task. He was fun, engaging, lively and intelligent, but it was a real struggle for him to stay tuned in long enough to show what he could do.

After a couple of hours we were both exhausted. It was time for me to talk to Freddie's parents; he had brought his Game Boy to keep him occupied while he waited. Within seconds he was so deeply engrossed in play that he seemed oblivious to anything further said to him by either his mother or myself. When we returned after the parent consultation he was fast asleep.

Lily's story

Lily was aged seven when she was brought to me for assessment because of concerns about her very slow educational progress and her difficulty in keeping up with the rest of the class.

Unlike Freddie, who exhibited behaviour that was a combination of inattentive with impulsive/hyperactive, Lily was mainly inattentive. As soon as we started working together I knew that it was going to take more than the usual two hours for her to complete the various tests. She was slow to answer questions and often needed to be given encouragement to elaborate. The untimed tests seemed to take an age. It was difficult to tell if she was on task or whether her mind had gone off somewhere else. There were moments when Lily was desperate to talk to me about something totally unrelated to what we were doing.

Lily was anxious. I think it is reasonable to surmise that this was due to her inability to stay focused in class, which must have frequently left her feeling adrift and uncertain about what she was meant to be doing.

How prevalent is ADHD?

The number of children 'diagnosed' with ADHD has increased dramatically over the past 10–20 years both here and in the USA, though numbers in the UK are well below those in the USA as a proportion of the population. In the USA it is estimated that between 5 and 10 per cent of school children experience ADHD, though some people think it is considerably higher. In the UK the diagnosis rate is nearer 3 to 4 per cent for boys and 1 per cent for girls. One reason for this is that different cut-off points are being applied to the spectrum of ADHD behaviours each side of the Atlantic.

How can we account for this overall increase? Is it due to a change in the diagnostic criteria? Are we more aware of it and therefore on the lookout for it? Is it something in the environment causing brain changes? Are we over-diagnosing or misdiagnosing ADHD? These questions do matter, not least because so many of these children are subsequently 'medicated' over long periods of time.

There are no easy answers to these questions, and while we wait for the next definitive research paper to clarify things we are still faced with the day-to-day practicality of helping the child (as well as the parents and teachers of the child) whose poor concentration and attention is impacting on his education, his learning, his behaviour and his interactions with his peer group.

What impact does ADHD have in the primary school classroom?

It does not take much imagination to see that children like Freddie are going to find the classroom full of distractions and that our dreamers, like Lily, are going to find it hard to stay on track. These behaviours which make up ADHD can have a marked impact on their learning and educational progress. Although the level of impact will depend on the severity of the problem, the child's age and school experiences, it is likely that the ADHD child will:

- often be off task; he will not be doing what he is meant to be doing. He may be gazing out of the window and ignoring the task in hand. He may be sharpening his pencil as a diversion or chatting with his neighbour

- produce work that is below the expected standard. He may have forgotten the instructions or may not have been able to focus for long enough to finish

- lose or forget his homework instructions before he gets home. He may forget that he has work to hand in

- have difficulty working independently and need someone on his tail making sure he has got it done

- find it hard to absorb instructions. Because of this he may not be sure about what he is meant to be doing

- interrupt due to difficulty in waiting his turn

- be slow to learn classroom routines.

Written work is likely to be a struggle. Writing is a complex activity. It involves holding and sequencing ideas in the head, and remembering vocabulary, punctuation, grammar and spelling. The physical process of writing (letter formation, pencil grip) also takes up mental as well as physical energy. It is easy to lose track or become single minded in relation to the content, thus ignoring layout, punctuation and spelling. So we see that the process of transferring thoughts onto the page is complex and full of challenges. The ADHD child may find writing an enormously taxing and difficult task.

- It may often be incomplete.

- There may be numerous careless errors and words may be repeated or left out. Easy words may be misspelt; there may be a lack of attention to detail and several grammatical errors.

- Note taking and copying off the board may prove hard and result in inaccuracies.

- The structuring of written work may become increasingly difficult as the demands are more.

It is not just written work which can be a struggle; maths can also be affected by careless errors and misreading of signs.

Much that happens in the classroom is verbally mediated. The ADHD pupil is not an effective listener because he is likely to daydream or find that his attention is caught by some extraneous noise or activity. He will therefore:

- miss out on instructions

- lose the thread of what is being taught and consequently zone out. At best he will sit quietly, but at worst he may then talk to someone else or generally disrupt the class.

Some children with ADHD have poor working memory. This means that they have difficulty in holding information or instructions in their mind over the very short term. They can be quickly 'overloaded' with information and then forget what they have been told or have just read or learnt. Others have a perfectly good working memory, but if their mind is drifting off elsewhere when the teacher talks they may not tune in immediately and may have missed out vital information.

It is easy to see how the child with ADHD may quickly be labelled as a behaviour problem. As well as chatting in class, interrupting his neighbour or constantly asking to sharpen a pencil or get a drink, he is also the one who fidgets in the dinner queue, plays with the hair of the girl in front in story time, has his eyes closed in the school photo and spends all of his class assembly production waving to his mother in the audience.

The inattentive child may not be a behaviour problem but she will also fail to thrive. She may be dreaming in the back of the class unaware of what she is meant to be doing. If she keeps her head down and does not cause a nuisance she may be happily ignored. The half-finished or inaccurate work she hands in may be taken as an indication of lack of ability. She may never be quite sure about what is expected. This state of affairs can last for many years and may never be picked up. The inattentive but conscientious child may become highly anxious, worried and even depressed by her poor performance and difficulty in keeping on track regarding what is expected.

For many ADHD children impulsivity is a real issue. The impulsive child will blurt out answers without putting his hand up. He will be in trouble for acting inappropriately on the spur of the moment. He may hit out at someone in the lunch queue; he may rush out into the road to fetch a stray ball but without checking the traffic. He may make hasty decisions without any thought of weighing up the evidence. Any one of his impulsive actions is likely to get him into trouble.

Like the other specific learning difficulties, ADHD is on a spectrum. At the extreme end of the spectrum it is only too clear when there is a problem and it is generally the overly active children who are most readily identified. It is less obvious where the cut-off point is in terms of identifying a problem. If a child has difficulty in one or more areas of learning and poor concentration is a contributory factor, then we may consider it to be a problem. If a child is underperforming then it is a problem. If poor attention leads to behavioural difficulties then we may also view it as a problem.

What impact does ADHD have in the secondary school?

Many of the difficulties experienced in the primary school and which are described above will continue to be an issue in secondary school. Even those pupils who have no co-occurring learning difficulties can fail to thrive. Where work is concerned it is likely that he will:

- produce work that is below the expected standard. He may have forgotten the instructions or may not have been able to focus for long enough to finish

- forget assignments – he may intend to complete work but forget

- fail to allocate appropriate time to complete tasks

- fail to complete work

- fail to keep deadlines

- have considerable difficulty with written work. Many pupils with ADHD are verbally fluent and articulate but find it extremely hard to deal with the complexities of written work, particularly when it needs to be well structured

- have difficulty with revision

- experience difficulty with time keeping.

Behavioural issues can also continue to be a problem. Many ADHD children find themselves involved in 'incidents' and have little understanding of the consequences. They are often the ones who get 'caught' while their more 'savvy' peers have long since left the scene of the crime.

Social interaction is often poor. He may appear to have poor social skills but this may be more to do with not caring than actually having the type of difficulty generally associated with ASD. He may be quick to anger, and impatient.

For some children, the unwanted attention that they get as a result of their behaviour can lead to feelings of alienation and anger. If things escalate, the situation may become very distressing for all concerned.

What impact does ADHD have at home?

The ADHD child can be exhausting whether he is 3 or 13. Grandparents may be critical of the way that parents are handling the child. Friends may prefer not to have him round to their home. Friends may also 'tut, tut' when the parent appears to be overly fussy. 'For goodness sake, why are you taking his hand to cross the road?' Whether it is justified or not he is going to take the blame for many things which go wrong.

Your ADHD child may feel like the cuckoo in the nest. You will want to protect him when he does something impulsive. You may know that he didn't mean to do it and that it just happened. While you want to protect him from the irritations and unkindness of other people, he is simultaneously capable of sending you utterly mad. Why did he forget his homework – again? Why, after absolutely promising that he would go straight to his room and do his homework, do you find him reading a book under his bed? Should he be getting so much more attention than his siblings? You know it is not fair but if you do not 'stay on his case' you know things will not get done.

ADHD behaviour can influence family life. The fallout due to the ADHD child (who ignores requests, who is not ready at the door when you want to leave, who does not have the right school bag with him, who has lost his school blazer and so on and so on) can affect siblings as well as parents. It's no fun for anyone when everyday events, such as leaving for school, end up as a screaming match and stressful rush. Siblings may resent the time and attention the ADHD child manages to gain. They may find it unfair that they are expected to behave well and get little credit for this. They may find it unreasonable that they have to assist parents in managing the difficult brother or sister.

There is one further issue which gets no mention in the diagnostic criteria and this is perception of time. Typically the child (and adult) who experiences ADHD has difficulty with time keeping. The younger child may find it hard to get a sense of the days of the week. He may find it hard to discriminate between weekdays and the weekend. He doesn't seem to have a natural internalised sense of the sequence of daily events. As the ADHD child gets older it will become more apparent that he has little sense of how long things take and can make quite unrealistic plans about what can be fitted into what time frame. This will impact on scheduling a work programme, on travel plans and general day-to-day organisation. He finds it hard to understand why others can get so frustrated with his general tardiness and difficulty in meeting at the appointed time.

While your ADHD child is likely to be the one who is more difficult to discipline or control he may also be the very person you would choose as your companion on an adventure. This may make it more difficult for you to be rigorously strict and consistent in the way that you respond to him. If, in addition to ADHD, he also experiences dyslexia or dyspraxia, there are going to be times when your heart will be wrung right out on his behalf. Parents, particularly mothers, find it immensely difficult not to make exceptions for the child with areas of specific learning difficulty. I cannot stress enough the need to provide clear boundaries with regard to what is acceptable behaviour. Parents often need to give themselves permission to set expectations and to expect compliance.

Managing ADHD: What can parents do?

Managing children with a significant degree of ADHD can, over the years, be highly stressful and exhausting for parents. It can put a strain on relationships within the whole family. There are no quick fixes, and support will need to be consistent and ongoing. In this section I aim to look at parent and family needs as well as those of the child with ADHD. There are three broad approaches to management:

- medication
- behavioural issues
- diet and lifestyle issues.

These are not mutually exclusive, and it has been found that a combination of good behaviour management along with medication can achieve the most effective results, although for many parents a trip to the psychiatrist or doctor and the decision to put their child on daily medication may be the last resort. Nevertheless I am starting the section on management with an overview of some of the issues relating to medication.

To medicate or not to medicate?

The most widely prescribed medications for ADHD are the stimulants methylphenidate (Ritalin, Equasym XL, Medikinet XL, Concerta XL, Matoride XL, Xenidate XL), dexamfetamine (Dexedrine) and lisisdexamfetamine (Elvanse). The impact of these drugs is to increase dopamine levels in the brain, which has the effect of increasing attention and concentration. They can be prescribed in either a long- or short-acting form. The short-acting form lasts for approximately three hours and the long one for between six and 13 hours, depending on preparation.

Not everyone responds in just the same way to these drugs and there are known side-effects such as loss of appetite, headaches and insomnia. However, just as we do not all suffer from the long list of side-effects mentioned on the back of every packet of Paracetamol, not every child will suffer from the listed side-effects. However, they are serious enough to make parents think twice, and the decision is not going to be easy.

It is important that the dose is just right and it may take some adjustments to arrive at the optimum level. So you should be concerned if your prescribing doctor does not suggest regular reviews in the early days.

Medication is not a total panacea. It will increase attention and concentration, enabling the child to learn more effectively, but it will not 'cure' other learning difficulties or, for example, it will not miraculously improve his social skills, if this is an issue. Work will still need to be done to help remediate areas of difficulty; however, this should be easier to achieve with medication.

For many parents this is a very difficult decision. Concerns range from lack of clarity about the long-term effects of medication, the idea that a child should be regularly on brain-altering substances, down to a fear that medication might obliterate that spark of enthusiasm which is simultaneously so exhausting but also so endearing and engaging.

If, however, parents have got to the point where medication is an option, it is important that they make the decision with all the most up-to-date information available. It is important to weigh the medical facts against the level of difficulty that the child is experiencing in school – either with learning and/or behaviour. If you dislike the thought of medication do try not to allow your own subjective feelings to interfere with what will serve your child best.

For example, is your child's lack of concentration holding him back in school? Is his impulsivity getting him into trouble? Would medication give him a taste of what it feels like to succeed and to behave in a manner that receives praise? Medication can give a child an important window of opportunity to concentrate and learn. This is particularly important for the child who is struggling with an additional learning difficulty. The dyslexic child who is also ADHD may derive little benefit from his specialist one-on-one lessons if he is only 'tuned in' for a quarter of the lesson.

Do remember that your child is only seven, eight or nine years old once and any time spent in school when he is not learning is time wasted. It becomes increasingly difficult to catch up lost ground. This is particularly relevant for the child who is struggling to master basic skills. Medication will not enable him suddenly to read or do his maths but it will provide him with periods of concentration when he can apply himself.

I have talked with many children who are on medication and those with learning difficulties have been quick to say that overall they like the benefits, even if there are downsides and side-effects. A frequent observation is that now they can hear what their teacher says. By 'hear' what they mean is that they are able to listen and process the meaning. Without medication, when the teacher talks much of what she says is going in one ear and out of the other.

In a lovely letter to her doctor soon after she started medication, ten-year-old Lena told him how clear her head felt – like a bird in a blue sky. She explained that the tablets helped her to concentrate and that the experience of concentrating made her feel as though her eyes could burn through books. She was thrilled that she had completed a test and done all questions before many others had got even halfway. She told him that she had got a house point and that she could even listen to instructions in maths (not her favourite subject).

This is certainly a strong endorsement but it is vitally important that medication is also accompanied by a clear behaviour management plan or a programme of work. On its own it is of limited value.

If parents are struggling to decide whether to go down a medical route I often suggest that they give it a trial period. This only needs to be for a few days as the effect is immediate (and only lasts while it is in the bloodstream) and you will quickly tell if there are benefits. There is really nothing to lose and potentially much to gain.

If you do decide to go down the medication route remember that it does not have to be given 24/7. Some children take it on school days but not at weekends or during the school holidays. If it enables a child to learn an essential skill, to focus on what his teacher is saying and to benefit from education, I think that parents have an obligation to try it and to make an objective decision.

Behavioural issues

So, how can or should parents handle all this?

It is worth taking a moment to remember that he is not impulsive, forgetful or inattentive just for fun. ADHD is a genuine difficulty. He does need adults and siblings around who love him, enjoy him, encourage him and help his self-esteem. The difficulty can be getting the right balance between leniency and acceptance versus the consistent application of rules and maintenance of boundaries. It is wounding when friends or relations imply that if only you managed him better there would be no problem. It may look from the outside as though parents are just too lenient with this child and that what he needs is a proper dose of discipline, but the reality is that it can be extremely difficult and taxing to deal with.

That said, there are some ways of managing behaviour that are more successful than others. Parents need to be one step ahead and to work out their best strategy for managing (and helping the child to manage) ADHD behaviours.

Let's start from basics. Behaviour is learnt. We know that behaviour can be shaped and modified. The big issue with our ADHD children is that it takes them longer to establish new habits and routines. They do not internalise new behaviours so rapidly as their non-ADHD siblings, which means that parents have to be amazingly consistent. The other side of the coin is that once behaviour has been established it will be hard to unlearn.

Important aspects include the following:

- *Routine.* Establishing routines is helpful. If we follow a routine the behaviour involved becomes automatic (and does not need to be thought about or attended to) and this reduces the memory load. The difficulty for the child with ADHD is that he gets distracted in the middle of doing things; however, if he can do it while on automatic pilot then so much the better. Whether it is doing homework at a particular time or sorting his kit for the following day or putting the bag by the door ready for the next morning, if these behaviours can become automatic it will help him and you. He may need help initially but you can reduce the help little by little. If you are giving a sticker as a reward when the bag is by the door, make sure you keep your side of the bargain.

- *Deciding where you are going to concentrate effort.* If you want to change or shape his behaviour, take one thing at a time. Do not try and change six things at the same time. Once you have decided on your and his priority then establish a routine. Consistency is vital. Do involve your child in this process once he is old enough. Maybe he has a view on what he would like to change or learn.

- *Have clear and consistent expectations.* Be very clear (and realistic) in your expectations about what your child will do and how you expect him to behave. If you are trying to establish a routine, make sure that you have consistent expectations that it will happen. Do not make exceptions or he will simply learn that he can slide out of it. He is probably very good at getting what he wants from you, but if you have set the agenda, stick to it. If you change your mind he has learnt that nagging pays.

- *Stick to established rules.* You might, for example, have established a general household rule that the children do not take items from your desk. Today he has taken your Sellotape and is playing with it. You are busy, the other children are out, he is restless and you want him to wait for the next few minutes. It is keeping him occupied, so where's the harm? – you can make sure it goes back in its place. Unlike your other children who might be allowed the 'treat' of playing with the Sellotape just this once and who will have no difficulty in resisting at other times, your ADHD child just does not have this inbuilt restraint. Let him play today and he is significantly more likely to remove it again tomorrow. You will only have yourself to blame!

- *Do not issue empty threats.* Do not issue a threat which you cannot carry out. There is no point saying 'If you don't stop that we will leave you at home' if he knows perfectly well that you can't leave him at home. Any threat should be carried through if he fails to comply with whatever you are expecting him to do.

- *If you make a promise stick to it.* If you promise to do something nice or to give a reward for good behaviour, make sure that you do keep your side of the bargain.

- *Give good descriptive praise.* Give rapid and descriptive feedback. Make sure you notice when he is behaving in a way that you appreciate. Praise or thank him and make sure you describe the behaviour so he knows exactly what you are pleased with.

- *Keep negative comments to a minimum.* Many of our ADHD children find that they are living their lives to a constant sound track of negative comments, so it is hardly surprising if they screen it all out and decide that it's really not their problem, or simply become alienated.

Parental teamwork

The first step is for parents (and if necessary members of the wider family) to discuss the issues and have *an agreed plan of action.* It is no good if one parent tries to establish a rule or a routine if the other is unwilling to support or to reinforce it and generally undermines the situation. I just cannot emphasise enough the huge importance of parents working together.

If adults involved are 'on the same page' there will be less chance for him to play one off against the other (not an uncommon happening) and there should be more understanding and less criticism or blame when things are not going smoothly.

Children can be unbelievably divisive. If they sense the smallest disagreement between parents they are very adept at playing on it; once parents are frustrated and angry with each other the child is off the hook and out to play.

Tough love is important

The ADHD child can be charming, funny and brilliant company. He can be exasperating but it can be amusing. I know from many, many conversations with parents how much most parents love that slightly wicked child who will defy authority and is always willing to have a go or take a risk. It is very easy to feel that setting clear boundaries and imposing rules may squash his joie de vivre or extinguish his essential flame of life.

But if you, his parents, do not manage to help him to learn to live with himself, to stop and think before he acts, to take personal responsibility, to manage his time, to respect others and so on and so on, who will? Sooner or later as he grows up he will find that the consequences for many ADHD behaviours are considerably more serious and you will not be there to pick up the pieces or smooth over the situation. He may be thrown out of college. He may lose his job. He may break the law.

In the long term you will be more of a help to him if you impose structure, boundaries and clear consequences as he grows up than if you cheer him on and make excuses. He needs much help over time to learn to self-regulate his behaviour. The chapter on behaviour also covers these areas.

Diet and lifestyle issues

The jury is still out over whether diet can make a difference. Supplements such as Omega 3 fish oil has, in some studies, been found to have a beneficial impact; however, it has also been suggested that such supplements will not make any difference unless the person taking them has a deficit. Fish oil has generally had a good press, so there is nothing to lose by trying. Several studies have shown that children with ADHD tend to have low iron stores, but there is no conclusive evidence as to whether extra dietary iron makes much difference.

There are other logical and common-sense approaches too; eating sugary cereals for breakfast will boost energy in the short term but blood sugar levels will quickly drop, leaving the child feeling tired and below par. In contrast, eating foods which release energy slowly can help keep glucose levels and energy levels more stable over a longer time.

This is certainly something that parents can look into and perhaps take advice from a nutritionist. You may have read Abigail's story in the chapter on dyspraxia. She is adamant that a careful diet is important if she is to cope.

The homework challenge

ADHD and homework can be a nightmare cocktail. It can feel like a constant uphill struggle. The child may come home tired and possibly dispirited at the end of the day. He wants to eat something and then nags to watch TV or use his computer, 'just for a half hour'. He may tell you he has plenty of time to do his homework in the morning.

It is all too easy for one parent to end up taking all the responsibility for getting it done to a satisfactory level. She has had to nag him just to get started; she feels compelled to check the quality of the work and may have sat over him as it slowly gets completed. The other scenario is almost as bad. Let's take Edward; he is fiercely independent and just wants to get on with his homework on his own and resents any interference. The difficulty here is that he rushes through it making numerous careless mistakes and says that he has finished after five minutes. He may be happy with it but you know that it has not been done to an acceptable standard.

There are no easy answers but try the following ideas. Establish routines:

- same time every day
- same place every day – if necessary, where he can be supervised
- a clear workspace
- equipment organised ready and waiting at the start of homework
- specific shelves or drawers for files or books.

You and your child could work out a reward system to get each of these elements up and running. A reward system is where you agree to give a reward in exchange for something he does or achieves. For example, when he has managed to be sitting ready to start his homework at a prearranged time and place for one, two or three days in a row, then you could agree to give a reward. This might be anything from a sticker on a chart which he can trade for something he wants, it might be a tangible reward such as money or toy or it could be a visit to McDonald's or a trip to the cinema. Keep rewards as small as possible to bring about a behaviour change and be consistent in keeping your side of the bargain. Do not give a reward unless he has earned it.

You could also think of withdrawing a privilege if he fails to be in the right place with the right equipment ready to start.

For the daydreamers and procrastinators, set a time limit:

- Use an egg timer (one of the ones with sand which runs from one end to the other) or an electronic timer. When time is up he is not to do any more work.
- Give a reward if he starts promptly after the timer is set.
- Allow short breaks (factor this into the timing).

See if he is able to set his own goals (particularly the 'rusher'). Can he tell you what he would like to achieve? It might help to read the chapter on motivation.

- What mark would he like to get?
- What does he think his teacher is looking for?

Try and work out with him what kind of help he needs. Does he have difficulty in getting started? Is it hard to get his thoughts on the page? Where are the barriers to success? He might like you to work with him to:

- brainstorm ideas
- make a plan for written work
- act as a scribe for him while he thinks and plans

- challenge and ask questions
- check his work
- help him review his work.

The following aids might help him:

- computer
- Franklin spell check for anyone without a computer
- grammar check
- 'cheat sheets' with spelling, vocabulary and opening sentences to hand
- a list of things that need editing, such as headings and margins – all much easier to do for the child who is using a laptop.

What about the social and emotional needs of the ADHD child?

ADHD is often more of an issue or problem for parents and teachers than for the child himself. He can live with it, though the fallout can become a problem. Not all ADHD children have social difficulties but many do. Daniel was typical. His mother commented on his:

- reputation for being annoying
- tendency to make and then lose friends in quick succession
- lack of awareness of the mood of others
- incessant talking about subjects which interest him but bore his audience
- tendency to be the class clown to gain kudos from his peers
- confrontational manner with teachers, peers and friends.

From this description it is all too clear why Daniel had difficulty in keeping friends. Much of the behaviour which he had difficulty controlling was very annoying to others. Daniel was rarely, if ever, asked on play dates with other children in his school and this had always been the case.

Harvey is a little younger. He too gets himself into trouble as a result of his poor attention and impulsivity. School staff report that he is having relationship difficulty with his peers and can be very argumentative; he can be rather dismissive and he will upset others by the comments that he makes. He is seemingly unaware of the consequences of what he says and how he behaves.

So what can parents realistically do? One avenue is to put in social skills training or other forms of counselling to help the ADHD child develop more effective and positive ways of interacting with his peers. It is possible that, if the school has a counsellor, he or she could fill this role. Alternatively, some form of meditation or mindfulness training might help him to be more reflective and to gain more control of the behaviours which get him into trouble or which are a direct result of his distress and anger.

Social skills training can have a transforming impact and made a significant difference for Daniel. Daniel kindly talked to me about his experience of this help. He explained that it is a step-by-step guide about how to behave and what to do in different situations. He has learnt to think about whether the other person is bored. He has learnt to notice the other person's reactions. If he sees eyes rolling he knows it's time to switch topic. He has learnt to ask himself, 'Would I be interested?' He has learnt how to react if someone is rude or mean to him. He knows he should zone out, walk away or think about something else. He has learnt about appropriate body language, for example the importance of not looking afraid and of when to ignore others. He has learnt how to give eye contact, stand up straight and look confident. He has learnt how to deal with situations such as if a member of his team scores an own goal. He has had to learn the importance of not getting cross or going on and on about it.

The great result is that he now has friends. They are coming over to his house; he is being invited out and is 'hanging out' with his peer group. His mother was delighted to get home from work one evening and find her kitchen full of happy, chatty, enthusiastic and kind boys. It seems that it doesn't take much to change the way others react to us.

Another avenue is that parents discuss their concerns with a relevant person in school with a view to getting a school mentor the child can relate to in an easy and informal way. This should be someone he could meet with on a regular basis and who could talk through any issues that might arise. A mentor could/should be able to represent the ADHD child in relation to other staff. A mentor could also ensure that if behaviour is inappropriate it is dealt with sensitively and supportively. It should not be addressed publicly and in such a way that it might provide other pupils with an opportunity to tease or bully. The ADHD child needs help to build strategies to enhance his social interactions. Parents can provide suggestions as to how he might do better (rather than criticism for what he has done).

If things have got particularly bad for the ADHD child and he has become acutely anxious or depressed as a result, then psychotherapy or cognitive behaviour therapy would be indicated.

There is an overlap between some of the social difficulties experienced by the child with ADHD and the child with ASD and/or the child with dyspraxia. All three can find it hard to socialise smoothly and effectively. It is possible that the ADHD child experiences an element of ASD and/or dyspraxia, but with some unpicking it may be clear that the underlying causes of the social difficulties are quite different.

Parents and siblings

We have looked at managing the child and supporting him in relation to homework and social interactions, but what of the parents and siblings? Parenting an ADHD child can be challenging (though many other children are also a challenge). However, try and look after yourself.

- Do not expect miracles.
- Do not forget to enjoy the things he is good at and take pride in his strengths.
- Set achievable targets for him and yourself and make sure you acknowledge successes.
- Celebrate small achievements.
- Build in time for a break, perhaps a night off from supervising homework.
- Enlist help from babysitters or family so parents can have time together without their children.
- Remember to take time out if you become frustrated.

Try and ensure that siblings do not miss out because the ADHD child takes up an unfair amount of time and attention. Give siblings a special once-a-week slot when they can have the undivided attention of one or other parent. Allow them to choose the activity that ensues. Make sure that their 'special' hour is entirely theirs and you do not take phone calls or allow other distractions.

Do not feel guilty if you are less than perfect.

Will it get better?

About half of the children who show signs of ADHD in childhood will continue to show features into adulthood. For the other half many of the difficulties are resolved during adolescence. This is the time that structural and chemical changes are happening in the frontal lobes of the brain. However, your very fidgety and 'ants in the pants' primary school child may turn into a teenager who can sit but who has a limb which is constantly on the go. His internal restlessness may still be there but may manifest itself differently.

For the individual for whom ADHD remains into adulthood, it is important that he learns to understand his 'condition'. He needs to listen to his strengths and adapt to his weaknesses. Any girlfriends or boyfriends or spouses need to be able to understand how he functions. Why does he need, really need, to let off steam playing sports five times a week? Why does he find it so hard to get home on time?

It has not been unusual for one or other parent of a child who is 'diagnosed' with ADHD to realise that they too have been struggling with the same difficulties throughout their life. I know of more than one father who has been 'diagnosed' and started medication following his child's assessment.

Finally, how can the ADHD child be helped in the classroom?

Parents may regularly find themselves in school as a result of their child's apparent misdemeanours. It is worth remembering that for the teacher it can be difficult to accommodate a child with ADHD in the classroom, particularly if the teacher has had little experience. She might be helped if you can share with her the things which you have found helpful in managing your child. In addition, the following are all appropriate for a child who experiences ADHD in primary school, so you could suggest that:

- if he has difficulty in focusing for more than a certain length of time then it would be helpful if legitimate breaks could be given to enable him to move around and then settle down and refocus

- he gets all the equipment that he needs ready in front of him before starting so that he has no reason to get up

- attention is given to seating. He should sit near the front of the class where he can see and hear easily and where distractions are kept to a minimum. It will also enable his teacher to check that he has fully absorbed instructions and that he knows exactly what to do

- instructions should, if necessary, be repeated and should be given in short, easily absorbable chunks

- when he has to do concentrated written work, he could sit somewhere with as few distractions as possible, such as facing a blank wall away from other pupils. This type of isolated position should only be for specific types of work and should never be for long periods

- tasks should be relatively short and achievable and, where necessary, differentiated for his current levels of ability

- it is important for him to complete tasks set and to feel that he has done these successfully and that he has the capacity to do them to a level that will receive praise. In terms of work differentiation, it should not always be necessary to achieve to the level that other pupils with better skills are expected to. In other words, a small amount of good quality work should receive good feedback

- he could be given something like a squeezy ball to 'fiddle' with at certain times, for example when the whole class is having a story or other input, to help him to focus and concentrate and keep his hands to himself

- it is important to 'catch' him being good and to give him much descriptive praise, for example 'Well done, you managed to stay in your seat for ten minutes' or 'Well done, you managed to wait your turn', or whatever.

CASE STUDIES

Sally's story

This is something of a cautionary tale. Sally's difficulty with attention was identified early. She was a very engaging small girl and learnt early on how to appease those who were finding her behaviour challenging. Her parents were often worried but overall loved her spirit and were ready to laugh with her when pranks went wrong and she found herself in trouble with the school authorities.

Sally's mother talked with love and despair about her daughter's difficulties throughout her teenage years. Although Sally was a bright pupil and had no learning difficulties, she failed to thrive and attended a series of schools, each of which ended on a poor note. Incidents would lead to exclusions.

According to Sally things were never her 'fault'. This is true of many teenage pupils with ADHD; they have spent a lifetime in trouble for things left undone or for things done which should not have been done, so it becomes easier to allocate the blame somewhere else.

This ability to shrug off complaints and criticism does not mean that the ADHD pupil is not sensitive or immune to hurt or pain. It is just that she has had to find a way of managing the constant stream of complaints about her and her failures. She can become very adept at giving the 'right' answers and in giving the right response. Yes, of course she is very sorry and it will not happen again. Even though she may feel that everyone is against her she has also learnt that it is quickest and easiest to appease her critics.

Sally was an intelligent pupil and managed to pull out the stops when absolutely necessary, but much of the time she drifted and was frequently in trouble. She would be the one left holding the baby while any co-mischief makers were long since gone. Despite a chequered secondary school career she gained sufficient academic success to make her way into higher education. However, all did not go well. Away from home and with no one to check on her, she failed to turn up for many of her classes and also failed to hand in the requisite coursework. Allowances were made but eventually she was asked to leave. This is where the story ends, but what will happen next?

Sooner or later those with ADHD must start to take personal responsibility, however hard it is. The really difficult thing for parents is deciding what line to take and where to draw it. While parents may know that their beloved child would prefer not to have a problem with ADHD and all that it entails, it is her life that will be impacted if she does not find strategies for dealing with difficulties; parents will not be there forever picking up pieces and cheering her on.

There is no doubt that the day-to-day management of many children who experience ADHD can be a huge challenge for parents but it really is something which needs to be taken seriously. Very clear boundaries need to be in place from early on. Expectations must be set and there just have to be consequences which will help to shape the child's behaviour in the areas where he has difficulty. The suggestions for behaviour management should be implemented early and adhered to consistently right through schooling. It is important for the future. The combination of medication and good behaviour management has been found, in several studies, to get the best results.

Phoebe's story

Phoebe is one of those children who has experienced co-existing issues. She has struggled with attention and concentration, she has had to overcome difficulties in learning fluent reading and spelling, and on top of that she is unusually bright. It is not always easy to be exceptionally able. Interactions with average peers can be frustrating and teachers can find the very bright child an unwelcome challenge. Medication has proved to be a very useful aid as Phoebe has progressed through school.

Phoebe's early development was full of promise. She was talking at a very young age and her development seemed to be well in advance of that of other children of her age. Phoebe's parents had no reason to think that school would present any difficulties.

But, once she started school, problems cropped up. She was fidgety, her concentration was poor and she had difficulty in listening and absorbing information in class. There was nothing about her school performance to suggest to her teachers that she was unusually bright. Concerns mounted when it was apparent that she was also having difficulty with reading and maths.

Phoebe's parents were confused; it was very evident that she had an exceptional capacity to absorb information and to cross-reference ideas. She had a vast store of general knowledge; she picked up facts easily and retained them; she was obsessed by the world around her; she loved animals and wanted to know everything about them.

She was highly creative and loved to make things. She had an excellent vocabulary and enjoyed learning new words. Phoebe had a great amount of energy. She was strong minded and liked to do things her way or could get very annoyed. She did not relate easily to her peer group with whom she was often impatient and restless.

An assessment was arranged to get a better understanding of what was going on. Why was Phoebe, now aged six, struggling at school but so bright and engaged at home?

When her cognitive profile was considered alongside all the background information that her parents had provided it seemed clear that she was extremely bright but that she had a significant problem with attention and concentration. Not only was there evidence of ADHD but she also showed signs of dyslexia. The classroom was a very difficult place for her.

Despite a clear analysis of Phoebe's strengths and difficulties school staff were reluctant to recognise that alongside her areas of specific difficulty she was an unusually bright pupil. In many ways this was to be as much of a problem as ADHD, and over the following few years Phoebe's confidence suffered greatly. It can be frustrating for the bright child to be in a classroom where she can make the connections, see the point and solve the problem with ease but find it hard to pay attention, stay on task and to complete the work set, particularly if basic skills are poor.

After an unhappy year or so, Phoebe's parents sought advice about her difficulty with concentration and attention. A diagnosis of ADHD was made by an appropriate medical practitioner and she started on medication. For many parents the decision to medicate can be extremely hard; however, in this case, there was no agonising heart searching. Phoebe's mother explained that it really did get her over a hurdle and had a very positive impact on her attention.

She was also able to make progress with her reading, though it took years of hard work to crack the reading process, and it was not until she was nearing the end of primary school that her reading shot from basic reading scheme books to Harry Potter novels.

The impact of medication has had both good and bad effects. Initially she was very dependent on it; it made a positive difference to her ability to cope on a day-to-day basis and she would not miss it. By the time she was in her second year of senior school she would take it on some days and not on others. She was aware of which subjects were better when she had taken it and those where she felt better off without it. She found that she felt less creative when medicated; it made her feel more self-conscious and activities such as acting were less good. In contrast she was better at sports.

Phoebe is still on her educational journey and has more years to go before she comes out at the other end. She is still a bit of a square peg in a round hole but she is coping better in her secondary school, where her intellectual ability is acknowledged and challenged.

Harvey's story

Harvey is another child with ADHD for whom life at school has proved problematic. His impulsivity and inattentiveness has caused considerable difficulty for him and landed him in trouble. This unfinished story is included to emphasise the challenge and importance of managing behaviour while the child is still at an impressionable age.

When Harvey came for assessment at the age of nine there were no particular concerns regarding his educational progress or level of attainment. Concerns related to his behaviour. School staff reported that he was very argumentative with his peer group; he could be dismissive of others and would upset them by the insensitive and unkind comments that he made. He was seemingly unaware of the consequences of what he said and how he behaved.

Harvey would, for example, say something was easy when others were struggling; he might highlight another child's fear of the dark or tell someone that they were rubbish at maths. When challenged, he would say that it was a joke. He gained a reputation as a bully.

Harvey was also very impulsive at home; he talked a great deal, he would interrupt and he would rarely manage to sit through a family meal. He was prone to temper tantrums, though these happened less often during school holidays and at the weekends.

There were concerns about his poor concentration in class, which was affecting his ability to listen and to follow instructions. He did not fully engage with school work unless it was a topic he particularly enjoyed (for example, writing about football), and he was very fidgety.

Although Harvey could read accurately and fluently he did struggle to answer questions about what he had just read; this seemed to reflect his difficulty in maintaining mental engagement with content. He was impulsive and prone to answer quickly without adequate reflection. He was also quick to give up and often needed adult support and encouragement to re-engage with the task.

Harvey had difficulty on the tests which were timed and where he had to maintain vigilance over the test period. It is very usual for children with ADHD to find it hard to maintain focus over time; concentration seems to wax and wane, even if the activity is timed and speed is required.

Although Harvey was naturally very able at sports, he found it difficult to be a team player; he would hog the ball in football and could become aggressive. His short attention span was a handicap if he was fielding in cricket or rounders. When the ball finally came his way he would be standing on his hands or otherwise engaged so that he would miss an easy catch or fail to rapidly return a stray ball.

As you can imagine, Harvey and homework were a challenge. Over the following years he would resist help and rush off inadequate work in the minimum time.

From this description you will recognise many traits that are typical of ADHD, particularly his difficulty with impulse control. The real issue was how to try and support Harvey. Appropriate strategies were all reviewed. Harvey's parents were not keen to go down the medical route and wanted to see how well things would go with clear management and support from school.

A major difficulty for those who are living and working with the ADHD child is that it is particularly hard to influence and help to change their behaviours. Where your average child may need to be told something once (for example, please stay on your chair, or please get your games kit ready now), your ADHD child will be more likely to need to be told ten times. Parents can become worn down by the sheer effort of getting cooperation. If parents give up or make allowances the child simply learns that non-cooperation or simply failing to respond appropriately is a winning strategy at least 50 per cent of the time.

By the time Harvey was in his early teens the situation had deteriorated. The whole family was suffering. Harvey's younger sister was unhappy and had become rather withdrawn. Harvey's parents were exhausted by the frequent confrontations and were finding daily life a struggle.

Harvey's parents decided to seek advice about medication and made an appointment to see a medical specialist. A diagnosis of ADHD was confirmed but by now Harvey himself had become angry and defiant and was not cooperative. It seemed that the decision to try medication had been left too late. But all was not lost. A few months later Harvey asked if he could have a trial period of medication. The results so far have been good. He is finding it easier to manage his impulsive and angry behaviour. With this window of opportunity and with everyone working together it is hoped that Harvey will experience success in his remaining years in education.

Eva's story

Eva experiences ADHD (impulsive, inattentive). It was evident from an early age that she was very impulsive and inattentive but ADHD was not picked up as being a key cause of her distress and difficulty in school until she was well into her teens. Eva's story shows how easily ADHD can go undiagnosed and treated even though the behaviours are evident and the pupil is suffering. It also shows that it is never too late to start to understand the condition and to find ways to manage it.

Eva came for assessment at around the age of seven. She was a bubbling, energetic and engaging girl and it was fun to work with her. There was no specific concern about her academic progress and the assessment was arranged to provide information that might help her parents think about future schools. She excelled on all the tests. Her reading and spelling were both well in advance of her chronological age and the content of her written work was charming and descriptive. Eva was making good progress with maths. Her short-term auditory memory and working memory for verbal and visual/spatial information were also strong.

Although ostensibly Eva appeared to be all set to be a fast and high flyer, all was not well. In school she was well known for her careless mistakes and lack of reflection. She had difficulty in waiting her turn in conversations and would interrupt frequently. She would call out in class and found it almost impossible to remember to put her hand up. She had already gained a reputation with her peers and some of their parents as a bully. She was always eager to win; she had a strong personality and often upset other children in the way that she talked to them. At home, too, she was impetuous and talkative.

It seemed to be too early to conclude that she experienced ADHD. There were other possible explanations. Then, too, it was easy to surmise that aspects of her impatience and frustration might simply be a reflection of her high ability and general high energy levels.

Perhaps more account should have been taken of the fact that she could not sit still for long; she would get up from her chair in class under the smallest pretext. She was easily distracted and lost interest before completing work, which was, as a result, of poor quality. The possibility of ADHD was not investigated further.

Eva bumped and struggled along through the following nine years. Her performance never seemed to live up to expectations. She often lost her things and became stressed looking for them. She had a very poor sense of time. She was forgetful and needed constant reminders to help to keep her on track. Getting her thoughts onto the page was a struggle. She was frequently in trouble and was often called lazy or told that she was not trying hard enough. However, her high ability did enable her to scrape by and to deal with academic demands.

Eva's relationships with other pupils were poor. She continued to find it hard to fit in and was often perceived as rude or verbally aggressive. Over the years she was often ignored or left out and felt that others were ganging up on her. Eva also had some difficulty in getting off to sleep.

It was at this point that a diagnosis of ADHD (restless, inattentive and impulsive) was made; her key 'deficits' in relation to mental regulation, maintenance of focus, self-organisation and forward planning as well as her difficulty in controlling her temper were noted. It was clear that her experience of ADHD had also resulted in a loss of confidence and in the onset of anxiety.

The support and help she needed had to be equally wide ranging and comprehensive. Recommendations covered medical, social, dietary and educational aspects of her life. Medication was prescribed. This provided the opportunity for her to find strategies to change some of the behaviours that were causing a problem. Eva was able to benefit from learning a range of study skills, from counselling and from applying strategies to support time management.

Medication alone is not a magic answer but it does provide a window of opportunity for the ADHD student to find ways of managing difficulties and of experiencing greater success. This was true for Eva, and after a short while she was able to report general all-round improvements.

KEY POINTS

⇨ ADHD is a difficulty with attention control.

⇨ It can encompass difficulty with attention, hyperactivity and impulsivity.

⇨ It can take more than one form.

⇨ It often co-exists with other areas of specific learning difficulty or disorder.

⇨ It can be 'identified' by a psychologist but a 'diagnosis' can only be given by a medical practitioner.

⇨ Medication must be administered by a doctor.

⇨ ADHD can lead to difficulties with academic school work and social relationships. There are often behavioural issues too.

⇨ The child with ADHD can be difficult to manage at home.

⇨ There are no quick fixes or miracle cures.

⇨ Medication coupled with behaviour management has been found to be the most effective solution.

⇨ Attention to diet can, in some cases, be a help.

⇨ Routine, consistency and clear expectations should be the order of the day.

⇨ Parents (and extended family) must work together and respond consistently.

Chapter 7

AUTISM SPECTRUM DISORDER

'I am standing in a corner of the playground as usual, as far away as possible from people who might bump into me or shout, gazing into the sky and absorbed in my own thoughts. I am eight or nine years old and have begun to realise that I am different in some nameless but all-pervasive way... I think I might be an alien who has been put on this planet by mistake... I dream that one day a spaceship will fall from the sky onto the tarmac in front of me... The people who step out of the spaceship will tell me, "It's all been a dreadful mistake. You were never meant to be here. We are your people and now we've come to take you home."' (From Martian in the Playground by Clare Sainsbury)

In this extract Clare gives a vivid description of how different she felt from other pupils. Although Clare and her family were unaware of it at the time, Clare was indeed different; it was not, however, until she was 20 that she was diagnosed as having Asperger's syndrome, which is a mild form of autism.

Clare was often frightened and confused in class, in the corridors and in the playground. When she looks back on her school days she feels a combination of regret and anger for the pain she experienced. Clare's experiences are not unique – they are shared by many other children who are on the autism spectrum.

Autism is a developmental disorder which is neurological in origin and may affect as many as one in a hundred children. The difficulties and challenges associated with autism are recognised as being on a continuum. Although many autistic people do have mild, moderate or severe learning difficulties, there are also those who are of high intellectual ability.

It is important to point out that autism spectrum disorder (ASD) is a pervasive difficulty and that it has an impact on all areas of an individual's life – not just, or mainly, within the classroom. Although it is not classified as an educational difficulty (like dyslexia or dyscalculia), it does lead to difficulties within school and the classroom and it is for that reason that it is included in this book.

The focus in this chapter is on pupils, like Clare, who are intellectually capable and whose symptoms of autism are at the milder end of the full spectrum. This group of individuals has, until recently, been classified as having Asperger's syndrome or high functioning autism.

However, the DSM-5, which is the latest edition of the *Diagnostic and Statistical Manual of Mental Disorders*, produced by the American Psychiatric Association, has dropped the term Asperger's syndrome as a distinct classification and now represents all the subtypes of ASD as a single category distinguished by the severity of the symptoms. I shall therefore use the term ASD throughout this chapter but want to emphasise to the reader that I am specifically referring to those children who are intellectually able and whose language and communication difficulties are at the milder end of the spectrum.

Even within this group of children difficulties are on a continuum; while some children's difficulties are easy to spot, there are many others whose very mild symptoms are never officially diagnosed at all. These may be the children or adults who are thought to be a little quirky or perhaps a little eccentric. Their literal take on the world may mean that communication is sometimes at cross-purposes and can lead to misunderstanding.

The aim of this chapter is to consider the identifying features of these bright ASD pupils, to look at the impact that their condition has on their experience of school and to explore the ways in which they can be supported in school and at home.

What do we mean by autism?

There are three main aspects to ASD. The first is difficulty with communication. While the child with ASD may speak fluently, he may have difficulty in judging or understanding the reactions of those he is speaking to. He is likely to take things at face value.

Then there is difficulty with social relationships. Children with ASD often want to make friends but can find it difficult to mix in successfully and they will be likely to find it hard to be accepted and to be one of the crowd.

The third factor is a rigidity of thought, which can restrict imagination and creativity. Many children with ASD are of above intelligence and can be very quick to learn facts and figures but may have difficulty with abstract thinking. Imaginative and creative play may be affected. Although they may love to dress up and play Batman or act out a story, they are likely to do this in a stereotyped way. They may copy what they have seen but will not extend the play or adapt to a new storyline or change or adapt their repertoire. This also means that while they may be brilliant at maths or chemistry – subjects that are facts based – they may find it much harder to tackle the more ambiguous topics such as philosophy or religion which do not have clear-cut answers.

How do we recognise ASD? What behaviours might we look out for?

On the social front you may note that the child is a bit off centre, maybe a little strange or stiff or unnatural in a social situation. He may have difficulty getting on easily with others and seems to be a bit of a loner. He may have poor eye contact and it may be hard to get him to look at you when you speak. It may be that he does not seem to know when the joke is over and there is something a little inappropriate in the way he talks too much or too loud or fails to adjust to the situation or the people around. He may speak in a monotone manner with little intonation. He may take what you say very literally and will not read between the lines. If, for example, you call out that dinner is nearly ready you may expect your children to know that you are also implying that you wish them to wash their hands and help lay the table. This kind of implied message is likely to go right over the head of the ASD child and he will most probably just go straight to his seat and wait for his food.

In relation to his knowledge and interests you may notice that he has a great memory for small details. He may be obsessive on some topic or other. It could be a film star or ponies or flying saucers. He may talk about his interest in minute detail and be unaware when his listener is keeling over with boredom. He may sound like a little professor when he gives chapter and verse in relation to his passion for astronomy or for wildlife. What he says may be repetitive rather than adaptive.

He may show some physical differences. He may have a heightened sense of smell or taste. He may be sensitive to rough textures and may complain about labels or seams in clothes. He may be poorly coordinated and awkward or clumsy. He may really dislike loud bangs or noises. Fireworks may frighten him.

He may have some behavioural traits that are unusual. He may like to stick to routine and become upset if things are changed. It could be having his teddy bears lined up in a special way or having the bedroom door at exactly the same angle every night when he goes to bed. He may be distressed if unusual events take place and he may respond best if he is given warning of any changes in routine. He may become extremely anxious in the face of uncertainty or if he is unable to understand the situation. Anxiety is a visceral experience and can take over; it can lead to anger and to striking out or to a mini- or full-blown meltdown from which he may have considerable difficulty in recovering.

What is going on?

Our understanding of autism has increased dramatically in the past three decades. It is only 40 years ago that there was a belief that autism was caused by cold, unloving parenting. Fortunately this pejorative view is a thing of the past. In this country the scientific work of Michael Rutter, Lorna Wing, Uta Frith and Simon Baron-Cohen has contributed to our knowledge. Many people will now be familiar with the idea that children on the autism spectrum do not have the capacity to understand what is going on in the minds of others; they cannot see the world from the point of view or perspective of other people.

This ability to empathise or to infer what others are thinking is central to successful communication. It is the lack of ability to do just this which we now consider to be a key deficit for those experiencing ASD. They are slow to develop a 'theory of mind'.

We know that this crucial ability to comprehend another person's mind develops naturally during the preschool years, and by the age of four most children have become adept. They are quick to recognise if they are being tricked and they can tease and be teased. The autistic child lacks this ability and will make wrong assumptions about what other people know and think.

Clare Sainsbury illustrates this point in her book *Martian in the Playground* when she describes how, when her mother dropped her off at primary school, she would frequently ask 'Where's the frying pan?' This would be the first her mother had heard of the fact Clare had been told to bring it in for a cooking class. Clare had assumed that her mother would know what she knew and had not understood that she needed to tell her.

This lack of ability to put oneself into the mind of someone else really can help us to start to understand the ASD mind but it does not, however, explain everything. It does not explain superior skills.

What about superior skills?

You may have read about the child who can draw brilliant and detailed pictures, the child who can reproduce any tune by ear after hearing it once or the adult who, if given any date past or future, can instantly tell you on which day of the week it will fall. These individuals are the more unusual ones, but many of those on the autism spectrum have been found to have certain strengths that are out of kilter with the rest of their development. These strengths are most generally seen in relation to maths and to tasks requiring good visual/spatial skills. Why should this be?

One possible explanation for this might be due to their weak central coherence. Most of us like to get the overview, to get the gist, to see the big picture. We tend to process the parts to create a whole. In contrast, those with ASD are more likely to focus on the detail. In place of seeing the whole they will see the component parts. Thus they are not processing for overall meaning but focus in on detail. They have difficulty in seeing the wood for the trees.

There are advantages and disadvantages to this tendency. On the negative side, the ASD child may see faces, for example, as a collection of parts rather than a whole, and this could certainly interfere with his ability to 'read' facial expressions correctly. On the other side of the coin, in certain circumstances this weak central coherence can lead to superior skills of analysis in certain very specific tasks when it is necessary to deconstruct the whole into component parts. ASD children are often excellent at puzzles and shape analysis or indeed in completing any task which requires them to see the design in terms of its constituent parts rather than as a whole. They often excel on the Block Design test that I use for assessment purposes.

What is the impact of ASD on a pupil's experience of school?

Schools are places which revolve around social interaction. From the tutor group to the classroom, and from assembly to the games field, social conventions and group norms are taken for granted. Schools are social environments, and a great deal of what goes on involves social interaction and person-to-person communication. The classroom can be a difficult place for a child who lacks insight into what others are thinking and who likes routine and familiarity.

Primary school
Communication and language issues
Children with ASD can have difficulty in understanding and following instructions. They may also have difficulty in explaining their needs or answering verbal questions despite knowing the answer.

Their tendency to take things literally may also lead to misunderstandings, particularly if their teacher uses metaphor. Phrases such as 'pull your socks up', 'you're a star' and 'jump in feet first' can be confusing to the child who is literal.

Poor social skills and lack of flexible thinking
Many children with ASD find it hard to follow classroom rules and conventions. The lack of sensitivity to social conventions may lead to their blurting answers out in class and talking in a way that might be seen as rude or inappropriate. They may be unaware of the impact of their behaviour but this does not mean they cannot be hurt by others.

Cross-referencing
The ASD child can have difficulty in transferring skills or information learnt in one setting or in relation to one set of circumstances to another. For example, it might be necessary to show how adding up can be done – on the fingers, on the page across or in columns, in the head or using other materials such as counters.

Routines
The ASD child can dislike sudden changes to routine. These can lead to great anxiety and distress. When the child is distressed he is likely to panic and may then behave inappropriately without meaning to be naughty or out of line. Calming down can take a while.

Sensory overload
Too much stimulation can be a strain. If the environment is too hot or too loud or in other ways overwhelming it can cause stress. If others stand too close or he feels hemmed in he may hit out. This is due to feeling overwhelmed and is not deliberate bad behavior, though it may often be seen as such.

Reading comprehension
While the ASD child may be good at reading from a technical point of view he may find it harder to fully understand what he has read. The ASD child is likely to have a preference for fact rather than fiction.

Subject preferences
He is likely to prefer maths and science to history or English literature. The former are cut and dried while the latter are more ambiguous.

Coordination and fine motor skills
These skills are often weak and can lead to poor handwriting and work presentation. It will also impact activities requiring manipulation and precision.

Attention and concentration
These may be weak.

Auditory processing
This may be slow and he may need time to fully process what he hears.

Learning style
The ASD child can find it very helpful to have a visual aid to help keep him grounded, for example a timetable which enables him to see at a glance what the day holds. He likes routine and dislikes changes.

Issues in the playground
He may have difficulty in dealing with playground activities that involve rules and conventions. He may interpret these too rigidly or they may just not make sense to him. His poor social awareness may also make the playground a hostile place for him.

Secondary school
From the point of view of social interactions the secondary school presents many greater challenges. The child has to deal with more and different group settings. The social interactions of the peer group are becoming more complex and often more excluding. Teenagers start to care what their peers think of them rather more than what their teachers or parents

think. The ASD pupil may find himself excluded from particular groups. He is likely to be naive and unsophisticated. Unfortunately, bullying often occurs.

Poor social and communication skills in class may be perceived as rude, attention seeking or disruptive by an inexperienced teacher (or if a diagnosis has not already been made). The child in question may find it hard to work as part of a team or to take account of the point of view of others.

Poor writing skills are also likely to be evident. He may have difficulty with the physical aspects as well as in planning and organising content. There is likely to be continued difficulty in cross-referencing skills and knowledge.

The ASD pupil will often fixate on a small detail rather than see the whole. This means that when a topic is being taught in class he may get hooked on a detail and not get the big picture or understand the main teaching point.

Organisational skills are often poor and result in difficulty managing books, files, games kit and instruments. Just getting around school can be a challenge.

How can the ASD child be helped?

The ASD child needs to be understood and to be supported, accepted and helped. While it is vital that we give ASD children the tools they need to cope and to do their best it is also important that we try and see the world through their eyes and as far as possible accommodate or modify expectations to encompass their needs. If, for example, he is distressed by the feel of his socks, is there any reason why he cannot take his shoes and socks off in the classroom? The important thing is to remember that the ASD child will perceive and experience the world in a way which is different from the rest of us who are often described as 'neurotypical'.

If ASD has been identified then it is possible for teachers to create a classroom atmosphere and environment which helps to ameliorate the difficulties. For example, clear classroom rules, the teaching of social skills and play skills and clear communication can all go a long way to helping the child. Also attention to support in the playground can make life happier and easier. Support might include starting a buddy system so that the ASD child has someone to support and help him. He would also benefit from being taught about some of the unspoken playground conventions.

For parents it can be an extremely lonely path which they climb as they steer their ASD child through school. It is evident that when school staff are knowledgeable, supportive and ensure that the school environment is adapted for the socially different child then a large burden is lifted for parents.

The aim of the following list of topics and suggestions is to show the wide range of ways in which the ASD child can be helped to gain the skills needed to fit in with life in a 'neurotypical' environment. The ideas and suggestions are for all of us and not just for parents.

It is also important to stress that any one of us who lives or works alongside a child or young adult who experiences social confusion and difficulties can make an effort to adapt our world to meet with theirs while helping them to hone their skills.

Social skills training

Children with ASD have to deliberately learn the skills which come naturally to others. They need, as and when this is age appropriate, to understand that what is hard for them is getting into the minds of other people. They will have to learn how to stop and think about how someone else might act or speak. The areas in which children need ongoing help as they grow up are:

- understanding sarcasm and irony in conversation
- understanding the give-and-take nature of conversation
- understanding facial expressions
- grasping another person's emotions in a conversation
- reading body language
- employing intonation and changes in speech to communicate emotion
- making eye contact in conversation to train themselves deliberately to copy other people
- learning to listen.

Professor Rita Jordan (Emeritus Professor in Autism Studies at Birmingham University) makes the important point that teaching communication to those on the spectrum needs to include teaching about communication itself – not just teaching the means for communication.

Use of language

The ASD child will need to learn the 'pragmatics' of language, such as:

- appropriate opening sentences
- to seek clarification when confused
- to have the confidence to say 'I don't know'
- to have a few 'sympathetic' comments up his sleeve
- to learn when to reply or interrupt or change the topic.

In order to help him achieve these skills parents and teachers can:

- model good and appropriate language behaviour
- whisper what to say in his ear
- use speech and drama activities
- use social stories or comic strip conversations as a verbal or pictorial representation of different kinds of communication
- avoid using figures of speech so that speech to him is as clear as possible
- make use of videos.

Strategies to avoid sensory overload whether it may be auditory, tactile, taste or visual

It is helpful to avoid or otherwise minimise the effect of sounds, tastes and tactile or visual distress. Parents can:

- play music to camouflage sounds
- minimise background noise
- encourage the use of ear plugs
- buy duplicates of comfortable garments
- try massage
- remember only to try new foods when the child is relaxed
- enourage the child to lick or taste new foods rather than chew and swallow
- suggest using dark glasses or a visor and avoiding intense light.

Parents will also have to deal with anger, frustration and meltdown

It is important to help him to learn about and gain appropriate vocabulary to discuss emotions. Parents can:

- explore one emotion at a time
- focus on how to 'read' emotional states in other people
- help him to express his emotions.

Reporting pain

It may be necessary to ensure that the ASD child learns to report pain. He may assume that you know what he is feeling. Explain to him why this is important.

Using and developing cognitive strengths

- He is likely to have good recall of factual and trivial information. Let him enjoy this by playing quiz games.
- He is likely to have good visual abilities. Use diagrams and visual analogies and represent information in pictorial form.
- Give him a visual/pictorial timetable to help him deal with concepts of time, sequence and the order in which things are going to happen.
- Encourage his creative use of words.

Provide opportunities to improve physical skills

Many children with ASD also experience some gross and fine motor skill weaknesses. Enlist the help of an occupational therapist to work on:

- ball skills
- balance
- hand–eye coordination
- dexterity
- handwriting.

These suggestions are very general and will need to be applied appropriately for age and stage.

The teenage ASD child will face his own very particular challenges and so too will his parents. He may become particularly frustrated or angry that social interaction has developed yet more layers of complexity. The opposite sex will loom on the horizon and he may need to learn a new and specific set of strategies for managing this. He may be distressed by his difficulty in understanding boy–girl relationships.

As he heads towards the time that he will live away from home he will need to have learnt skills of independence and self-reliance. It would help if these are taught early and he is well versed in cooking, laundry, money and so on well before he sets off on his own.

CASE STUDIES

The following case studies each tell us something about the educational experiences of the individuals concerned. They also highlight the challenges which parents can face as they guide their child through school.

Nathan's story

This illustrates the kind of difficulties the ASD child faces in primary school. It is a story that also shows how, with the right help, the school experience can be positive. Nathan's story shows the benefits of early identification and intervention. In addition to receiving specialist help, Nathan also has fantastic parents whose constant involvement has been an important factor in his success. Following on from his university degree in mathematics he is employed in the security software industry as a graduate programmer.

Nathan was seven when I first met him. His parents wanted an independent assessment of his needs, which they felt had not been taken seriously by his school. His speech and communication difficulties had been recognised by their local authority (LA) but, his parents explained, his reading was 'painfully slow'. They were concerned because he was getting no extra help for literacy at school.

Nathan had been late to learn to talk. Socially he was inflexible and followed his own interests rather than other people's. He was described as a bit robotic. His understanding of language was literal and he did not get humour. He found it hard to cope with teasing. He had few friends and tended to play on his own.

During the assessment Nathan showed many behaviours (both strengths and difficulties) that are indicative of ASD. He was friendly and cooperative but made little eye contact. He excelled on the tests where he had to recall designs and on the test of pattern construction. He was good at maths. He struggled on tests where he had to deal in wider concepts and he found it hard to give word definitions. Most ASD pupils have no difficulty with reading accuracy but Nathan's reading was very weak and he showed many of the signs of dyslexia described in the chapter on that topic.

In school Nathan's difficulties with communication, social skills and adapting to rapid change caused him considerable stress and anxiety. He found it hard to understand the rules of games. He found it hard to be a loser. If he lost games he became distressed. He was frustrated by misunderstandings or when things did not work out the way that he thought that they should. Nathan had difficulty in appreciating that if others were to understand him he needed to give complete information. Unusual events distressed him. He had recently panicked when the family was stuck in a bad motorway hold-up and he became loud and repetitive when the family was late to catch a train.

Nathan was comforted and calmed when things were explained to him; he liked structure and predictability. He needed advanced warning about changes. Within the classroom things that helped Nathan were:

» a regular routine

» a warning when unusual events or changes were going to occur

» an explanation from his teachers if his behaviour appeared rude or inappropriate

» a key member of staff to relate to and a safe place to go to if he felt stressed

» a visual/pictorial/diagrammatic timetable.

Nathan received a statement of special educational needs (now referred to as an education, health and care (EHC) plan) which covered his ASD, and over the next few years he was given regular support from the local team who worked with ASD pupils and their teachers.

By the end of primary school Nathan had matured and he was considerably better able to understand classroom and playground activities and to take a full part in everyday school life. He had been receiving small-group help with social skills. He had become better at making and retaining friendships and interacting appropriately. He still liked and needed full explanations so that he could understand what was going on.

Through his secondary school years Nathan became more adept at dealing with social relationships but it was not all plain sailing; Nathan continued to have the occasional temper tantrum, which would get him into trouble and he would feel angry and bad about it. Once he became angry it would take a long time for him to calm down again.

Nathan's mother played an important role in coaching him in social skills and she pushed hard to get him involved with others outside home and school. She had encouraged him to learn an instrument and to join a band and take up swimming. By the time he went to sixth-form college he had learnt how to make friends.

Nathan achieved extremely well academically and he shone in maths and sciences. A final cause for celebration was his discovery of books and the pleasure that they can bring; despite his rocky start and the need for considerable additional support, Nathan had started to read widely and enthusiastically. This was especially pleasing for his parents who had had to fight with their LA for the additional specialist teaching support for literacy and had also employed a tutor at home.

Nathan made a group of friends at university and shared accommodation successfully. He coped well with the demands of summer vacation work in a busy environment, though he found it hard to keep on top of irregular shifts as well as having to work in different locations.

While this is all great news and very encouraging, Nathan's mother explained that social interactions and self-organisation remain a challenge. Social interaction comes at a cost. Nathan still has little empathy for others and his behaviour can be difficult. He has to work hard at social relationships and has to make a conscious effort to relate appropriately. This, his mother explained, can be a big strain and he finds it almost impossible to relax. He can be hard to live with at home where he is often rude and uncommunicative. Things are, she said, a mixed bag, but Nathan is surviving and is coping.

So, it would seem that on balance this phase of Nathan's life is going well and Nathan's mother felt that she was able to relax while Nathan was at university. It certainly seems that Nathan has benefited from an early diagnosis and from skilled input and support from the local team who gave social skills training.

From a parental perspective Nathan's parents felt that they had had to fight all the way to ensure that he had appropriate and adequate extra help. They were very aware of feeling poorly equipped to tackle teachers, headteachers and local authority personnel. Nevertheless, they did their research. They enlisted outside and independent advice and kept meticulous records of all meetings, phone calls and reports. They found the Independent Parental Special Education Advice (IPSEA) service very helpful. Advice ranged from how to write an appropriate letter to details of the law. Nathan's mother says that her advice to parents is not to accept things the way they are. Find out what you can do. The information is out there. If you know your child is struggling do not accept it even if the teacher says there is no problem. No one else will do it for you. You must do what you need to do.

Nathan's parents are tenacious and his mother is very organised. She has kept good records and was able to prepare a comprehensive and well-ordered file of relevant documentation for an important Tribunal meeting with the local authority. But, as she said, 'You can't give up, can you? If you don't do it no one else will.'

So what will happen next? For many young people who experience ASD, life will have continued challenges. The condition does not change and there will always be new hurdles and situations to navigate. For some, the transition from university to work can be helped with a little more training in life skills such as dealing with job interviews.

Nathan's story ends on a great note. He has now graduated from university and was offered a job following his first interview. This really boosted his confidence. He's now living independently and happily away from home.

Daniel's story

We will now meet Daniel and follow him during his teenage years. This glimpse into Daniel's life illustrates his difficulty in interacting socially with his peer group and the high level of stress which he feels when he misinterprets situations and comments from others. It shows his strengths in relation to fact-based school subjects and his confusion with the less clear-cut ones. We also see how much parental involvement it can take to help him keep calm and on track.

Around the age of 13 Daniel became extremely anxious and appeared to be depressed. He was unhappy at school where, he said, he had 'no friends' and where he was feeling lonely and isolated. Members of the school staff were concerned about his difficulty in fitting in. Daniel was also finding some aspects of work rather a struggle. He came for an assessment and we took a closer look at his strengths and difficulties.

On the social front, Daniel's ability to communicate with others was weak. He could not go with the flow of conversation and he would interrupt or introduce irrelevant topics. This affected his ability to get on with his peers. He would have loved to be included but did not know how to get accepted into a group. He was never invited to other people's houses, and if anyone befriended him he would blow hot and cold. He could be rigid and literal; he would misinterpret situations because he had difficulty in reading between the lines. Daniel could get on well with younger children and loved to spend time with his grandmother.

Daniel was obsessed with old movies and musicals. This was his passion. He could talk for hours on the minute details of a small aspect of the life of Audrey Hepburn or about one of her films without the slightest idea that his audience was no longer interested.

Daniel's literacy skills were a bit of a mixed bag. He could read well and accurately, but understanding what he had read was not so clear-cut. Higher-order comprehension was a challenge. Daniel enjoyed reading if the content was factual and specific, but more complex analysis was hard for him. In school where he had been reading *King Lear*, he could tell you quite literally on which page a character makes an entrance or how many lines they speak, but he could not begin to discuss how the audience might feel about the final encounter of Lear with his youngest daughter Cordelia.

Daniel was good at maths and also enjoyed the sciences but had some difficulty with his written work. He disliked writing and found it hard to structure the content unless it was free writing or did not need organising or structuring. His handwriting and work presentation were untidy and his spelling was weak. His fine motor skills as well as his hand–eye coordination were poor, which impacted the physical process of writing.

Daniel was sensitive and uncomfortable with the feel of certain fabrics. He disliked wearing some clothes; the labels in shirts could irritate and distract him.

Overall, Daniel was showing areas of difficulty typical of both dyspraxia and ASD. It was possible that he experienced an element of both. While it was not entirely clear which 'label' might be most appropriate (maybe both were needed), he could be helped in relation to both areas of difficulty. A specialist paediatrician could give a view on whether he was a child for whom a diagnosis of ASD would be appropriate. In any event he did need help to improve his social skills and to learn how to get on with others.

The years between Daniel's 13th and 18th birthdays have been challenging. Daniel's mother explained that she has had to be very much involved with all aspects of his life; she has had to help Daniel to keep calm and to keep his life organised. There have been times when she has wondered if she would ever cope. She would have loved a road map to tell her how it would happen. Parents, she thinks, need to be prepared; living with and supporting an ASD teenager takes time, energy, commitment and resources, as well as resourcefulness.

On the positive side, Daniel has coped well with certain school subjects; he is a gifted mathematician and loves sciences, which are logical and factual. He is hoping, and expecting, to get into a leading university to study engineering. The choice was simple. It is the subject that is most predictable. The timetable is set for weeks and terms at a time. He can look up and see exactly what he will be doing and when. Daniel is nervous at the prospect of living away from home but nevertheless is determined to do so.

Social skills remain a big issue and he just doesn't read people or situations. Daniel's literal take on the world and his lack of flexibility can find him in conflict with his peers who are frequently less than kind. He can find this distressing, particularly as he cannot understand what he may have done or said to incur their disapproval, and negotiating the changes which come with adolescence has also been hard.

Anxiety and stress loom large. Stress can be quite contagious and Daniel's mother gets swept up into sorting out the situations that cause Daniel huge anxiety. She has found herself up in the middle of the night to sort out an essay problem. She has spent hours on the phone to a specialist trying to find Daniel a cricket bat which met very specific specifications; Daniel was concerned that the head might be a fraction off the dimensions he thought that he needed. She might drop everything when she receives a phone call from a distraught Daniel who wants her to bring something into school.

Daniel's high levels of anxiety are often in response to misunderstandings that can arise because something has been implied rather than stated clearly or because he has taken the teacher's comments literally.

Here's an example. Daniel's biology teacher handed back a piece of work. At the end she had written: 'A wonderful bit of work – I shall expect nothing less than perfection in future.' Daniel, of course, took this literally. When it came to his next homework assignment for this teacher he became overwrought with anxiety because he couldn't get one of his diagrams to work out exactly. Daniel's mother took the brunt of this at 2am in the night.

Distress, meltdown and angst are never far away. The really hard thing is that when we understand what is happening in the mind of the pupil it falls into place. But so often this behaviour is misinterpreted and the pupil ends up in trouble.

Alexandra's story

This is not an entirely happy story but I am glad to say that we leave Alexandra engaged and successful in her college of further education. The story illustrates several points:

- *ASD does not protect children from also experiencing other areas of specific learning difficulty. Alexandra has a full house of these.*

- *Any additional areas of need must not be overlooked when it comes to provision. They need to be given equal consideration.*

- *Alexandra's story raises the issue of inclusion versus special school. It is important to keep an open mind and to decide which is best on the basis of the child's individual needs.*

- *Alexandra's story shows what a difference can be made if teaching staff have an understanding of the needs of the ASD pupil.*

Alexandra, aged ten years old, already had a statement of special educational needs when she came for an independent assessment to review her educational needs and provision. Alexandra's mother had sent me her reports from Great Ormond Street Hospital, the Wolfson Neurodisability Service, her local authority educational psychologist and the local authority advisory teacher for autism.

Alexandra's statement indicated that she was experiencing Asperger's syndrome, developmental dyspraxia, ADHD, dyslexia and dyscalculia. My assessment showed that she was essentially very bright (by that I mean that she did extremely well on tests of verbal and non-verbal reasoning). Her ability to deal with the visual tasks was, like many other pupils on the autistm spectrum, outstanding. In contrast, her working memory was average and her information processing speed was below average. She was reading successfully, but spelling was well behind and her handwriting was a bit of a disaster. Like many pupils who experience dyspraxia her hand control was weak and she wrote very slowly for her age; she used no punctuation and the words tended to run into one another, so it was almost impossible for her to read back what she had written. Letters were printed separately and were irregularly formed and went up and down off the line. However, she showed no problems with written or mental maths.

Alexandra's difficulties with ASD, dyspraxia and ADHD seemed highly relevant and were significantly impacting on her ability to function well within school. Despite her high intellectual ability she was unable to demonstrate what she knew and understood in written form, which was highly frustrating for her and it certainly needed to be addressed. She was allocated additional support in class and particularly liked the one-to-one help when it was available.

Alexandra's social interactions were not good. She tended to be on the fringe of things and was unaware of how to interact appropriately with other children. She was rarely invited to anyone else's house. She was rigid and literal in her interactions. She was embarrassed by her difficulties; she knew that it was hard for her to learn things that other children found easy. She felt useless. She found it hard to maintain attention and often daydreamed. She was frequently told off and her name 'went on the whiteboard' for things which she could not help.

Our hearts go out to her when we think what she has had to contend with on a daily basis in school. Her keen self-awareness must have made her feel extremely sad. She was 'gifted' intellectually, yet very 'disabled' when it came to performing academically and socially. She had a very complex neurodevelopmental profile.

Suggestions for helping her covered six pages. These related to her dyspraxia, spelling, ADHD and ASD. Below are the suggestions relevant to ASD. Alexandra needed:

» small-group social skills training. She needed an opportunity to discuss and learn about 'appropriate behaviour' in a supportive and unthreatening environment

» a regular routine to follow

» a warning when unusual events or changes were going to occur

» an explanation if her behaviour appeared rude or inappropriate

» a safe place to go and key member of staff to relate to if she felt stressed

» to be allowed some time out of activities where she had particular difficulty such as sports and PE

» recognition of her high intellectual ability

» recognition and appreciation of her strengths.

Because of Alexandra's various problems it seemed important that school staff should be helped to understand the implications of ASD and to modify their behaviour in relation to her.

Six years later Alexandra had completed her GCSE year. Alexandra's mother explained that secondary school had been a disaster. Alexandra's complex needs were not met. Emotionally she was distraught and she was self-harming. She was unable to articulate her problems and unhappiness.

Alexandra's mother sounded tired and dispirited. 'There is nothing,' she said, 'that you can do; you are at the mercy of people in authority. Individual teachers have good intentions. But there is no one in the school with a proper understanding of autism. The school has no autism strategy. The LA has no countywide policy. Every school has free rein to do as they wish.'

Understandably, Alexandra's mother was more concerned about her daughter's happiness than her academic achievements, but she felt bitterly let down and disappointed that this essentially able child was not achieving.

If she could have turned the clock back she would have pushed for Alexandra to attend a specialist school, even if this had meant boarding, on the basis that staff in a specialist school would have had a better understanding of Alexandra's ASD difficulties.

Alexandra has now left her secondary school and attends a local further education college where she is studying art and design. The difference has been astounding. Alexandra's mother explained that it was like a different world. It boils down, she said, to having a lead practitioner for autism and autism-aware members of staff. For the first time ever, Alexandra is now achieving despite her disabilities.

Over the years Alexandra and her mother have attended a local support group for 'spectrum girls' aged between 3 and 25. This has been largely beneficial and has provided them both with supportive friendships.

There does appear to be a bit of a postcode lottery regarding provision. Alexandra's mother is involved in lobbying for improved provision within their local authority. There are many pupils who have had no help. Their behaviour has then led to exclusion.

This is not, as I said at the beginning, a feel-good story. If you are the parent or teacher of an ASD child with co-occurring difficulties the hard lesson is that:

» no matter how 'clever' the child is, if he does not have appropriate specialist help for the other specific difficulties he will struggle to access the curriculum and to learn well

» it is really important to look at the child's strengths and interests and to work with these

» it is important to consider whether special day or boarding school might be better for the ASD child. Inclusion has been promoted like the Holy Grail. At times this can seem to have been held up as the politically and socially best way forward at the expense of good specialist education, and over time we have lost some excellent specialist provision. However, there are good specialist schools out there, and the 2015 Special Educational Needs and Disability Code of Practice emphasises the need to take account of parents' and pupils' wishes in relation to provision.

Simon's story

Quirky or on the spectrum? This short study of Simon is to show that identifying ASD can be difficult and also that those pupils who may show symptoms that might accurately place them on the very

mild end of the spectrum may never need a 'diagnosis' and they may cope well, if a little eccentrically, with life.

Simon came for assessment when he was approaching seven. His parents were aware that he was advanced in terms of his mathematical ability and in other areas such as chess, music and science. However, they did have a number of concerns: he was having difficulty in socialising with his peer group, he seemed unhappy and he expressed boredom with school. They hoped that an assessment might look at his educational needs and indicate the best way to extend him.

Simon turned out to be quite a complex character. He was bright and there were no evident learning difficulties; however, there was clearly a gulf between his poor social skills compared with his strengths in maths, chess and science.

Simon made poor eye contact but loved chatting to adults – this is quite a usual trait for a child with social communication difficulties. The adult will follow the child's interests and the child does not have to adapt as he would if conversing with his peer group. Also, he liked to talk about complex things.

Simon could become fussed and anxious if the environment he was in felt too noisy or too busy – again a trait associated with ASD. He was also sensitive to clothes, particularly if he felt that they rubbed or itched.

At home Simon could be moody and stubborn; he was fearful of new situations that impacted on his behaviour, making him uncooperative and often unhappy.

By the end of Simon's assessment there seemed to be sufficient information to broach the topic of whether Simon's difficulties and behaviours might possibly be indicative of ASD. This was not something his parents had considered and they did not think it likely. The subject was left, but they were advised where they could go should they wish to follow it up. We also discussed ways of extending him and providing him with challenges in the areas where he was doing particularly well.

Simon's parents did not follow up on the social communication issues but focused on supporting his academic progress. By the age of 13 Simon was flying academically. He was also a more settled and happy pupil. But, his mother said, Simon was very much 'his own man', single minded, determined and eccentric – certainly it was unlikely he would do things just to please others, and it was this aspect of his personal development that she continued to keep an eye on. She went on to explain that on one side of the family there are a number of unusually high-achieving but socially challenged individuals and that this is very much accepted as the norm as far as they are concerned. So, Simon may be one of those quirky and unusual characters who are functioning well but who appear to share some characteristics and behavioural traits associated with ASD.

Sarah's story

I shall end with Sarah. She is 40 years old and has just had a diagnosis of ASD. She feels delighted and liberated. Although Sarah is neither a pupil nor student I am including her because she so clearly shows us the power and importance of the self-understanding which a diagnosis can bring. For Sarah it has meant that many things now fall into place. She understands why she had so often felt that she was different, why she didn't fit in and why she had low self-esteem.

Those who know Sarah will have noticed that her communication style is a little brisk. No frills or redundancies. They may also have noticed that changes in routine stressed her. Her work colleagues had often joked about the way she took things literally. Although she had worked for several years as a carer helping young men with ASD and knew a fair bit about the condition, it had evidently never crossed her mind that she too might fit the diagnosis. She knew she did the job well; she could tune in to their needs and had an almost intuitive understanding of how they felt and thought. But it was not until one day as she was reading a particular book on ASD that things suddenly clicked and she realised 'that's me'.

Sarah feels that a 'diagnosis' is paramount. She says that now she knows she is on the spectrum she can accept herself and be more forgiving to herself for her difficulties and foibles. She has also enjoyed the contact she has made with other ASD women. She likes to chat to them and has found that they are artistic and intuitive.

She understands now why there were days when she would open her front door, step outside and feel so overwhelmed by the brightness of the sky or the loudness of the noises that she would have to retreat back into the house. She understands now why her heart rate was permanently high. Stress caused her to feel anxious and panicky. She is having help to deal with this.

Sarah's spatial skills are weak and she has really berated herself over her panic and misery if she has to drive an unfamiliar route without studying the map first. She now accepts this aspect of herself.

Looking back to her school days she said that things were okay until she got to puberty. Her literalness caused problems; she was bullied and used to believe what people said. She couldn't understand why people would lie.

Shortly after Sarah had her diagnosis confirmed she sat down and over the next two weeks she wrote her story. It is now in print and is called *OMG! I've got Asperger's*. It is a quick and very immediate read. There is a message for the rest of us. While the book is very much a celebration of who she is and the joy of gathering knowledge and understanding of why she is as she is, there is an underlying anger with the rest of us who have been so slow and unimaginative in understanding her world. Much of her pain has been caused by misunderstandings and miscommunications.

The message is clear. We need to step into the shoes of those pupils with ASD and really try to understand the world as they see it.

KEY POINTS

⇨ Autism (ASD) is a serious and lifelong developmental disability affecting up to one in a hundred pupils. Difficulties are on a continuum ranging from mild to serious.

⇨ The defining feature of autism is that those on the spectrum lack instinctive social understanding. They must learn and be taught explicitly all the things that others have acquired naturally. ASD may be accompanied by mild, moderate or severe learning difficulties.

⇨ Intellectually able pupils whose signs of autism are mild have, until recently, been classified as having Asperger's syndrome or high functioning autism.

⇨ On its own ASD is not a specific learning difficulty but it can co-occur with dyslexia, dyspraxia and ADHD.

⇨ Although what has been generally referred to as Asperger's syndrome is not a specific learning difficulty, it impacts on many aspects of social and academic life in school.

⇨ The ASD child can be supported to develop appropriate skills in relation to social communication, self-regulation and self-help.

⇨ Above all, ASD pupils can best be supported if their particular difficulties and their needs are understood by teachers and peers.

Chapter 8

AUDITORY PROCESSING DISORDER

At the age of 13 Stella was being badly bullied in her senior school. Throughout her schooling she had experienced difficulty with her school work and in dealing with social relationships. Her parents were struggling to find out what was wrong. A previous assessment had suggested that she was none too bright and that there might be emotional issues. Stella's mother can still feel her despair and distress when she remembers back to that time. The underlying cause of Stella's difficulties was eventually identified. She experienced auditory processing disorder (APD). Once it was identified she could begin to have appropriate help.

The aim of this chapter is to provide a description of APD and the impact that this can have on a child's ability to learn and to cope within the classroom. APD can be difficult to identify. The reasons for this are considered. The role of the audiologist as part of the assessment process is described and suggestions are given for supporting children who experience APD.

What is auditory processing disorder?

Auditory processing refers to the way in which the brain recognises and interprets the sounds around us. Children with auditory processing disorder have difficulty in 'interpreting' what they hear. While their hearing acuity is good and they have no difficulty in passing hearing tests they will often be unable to distinguish between the sounds in words, even though the sounds may be loud and clear. The comment 'she went to feed the dog' might be misheard as 'she won't feel too good'.

The part of the brain that should be turning sounds into language and hearing into listening is not doing its job properly. Children who experience APD have particular difficulty in filtering speech sounds from general environmental noise. This difficulty is magnified when the child is in an environment which is noisy. The average classroom situation is just such a challenging environment.

The classroom environment

Classrooms can be noisy places; they are rarely designed and constructed to create good acoustic conditions. Bare floors and large glass windows do not absorb sound and noise echoes off these hard surfaces. There is generally a lack of any fabric or soft furnishings to absorb the sound of scraping chairs and the clamour of voices.

The environmental noise in a class of young children runs to 60–64 decibels. The teacher's voice reaches a level of 65 decibels. This means that the teacher's voice is sometimes below and sometimes just above the background noise. The problem for children with APD is that they find it almost impossible to interpret what their teacher is saying unless speech sounds are up to 20 decibels louder than the environmental noise.

If we keep in mind that between 50 and 70 per cent of the school day is taken up with listening – to the teacher, to peers, to audio media – we can appreciate that there will be serious consequences for children with APD.

What is the impact of APD?

Within the classroom the child with APD is likely to:

- mishear and therefore misunderstand much of what is said
- have difficulty distinguishing words which sound the same
- find it difficult to interpret and follow instructions
- be unsure or confused about what he or she is meant to be doing
- require additional time to process information.

Secondary difficulties

The child with APD who is constantly struggling to make sense of what he hears will be very likely to experience additional difficulties as a result of his disability. It is highly possible that it will lead to:

- mispronunciation of words
- limited vocabulary
- difficulty with all aspects of literacy
- poor academic performance
- problems with social interaction and relationships
- lack of self-confidence.

It's easy to imagine just how much effort must be used on a daily basis as the APD child tries to process and make sense of what has been said. The child with APD, if he is brave, may ask for frequent repeats. The shy child will most likely do his best to copy others or just appear to be slow and unresponsive. This is likely to be exhausting. Who can blame the child who gives up and decides to opt out or to behave badly?

How can we identify APD?

There seems to be increasing awareness of APD, but it remains particularly difficult to identify because it can so easily be confused with other areas of specific difficulty. The behaviours below which might suggest that a child experiences APD are much the same as the ones that can indicate ADHD, dyslexia, a poor working memory or a specific language difficulty.

The child with APD may well:

- have a short attention span
- be easily distracted
- be restless or bored in classrooms and group discussions
- have difficulty following instructions
- have experienced a delay or problem in language development
- ask for things to be repeated
- misunderstand what is said
- find that difficulties are exacerbated in the presence of background noise
- seem to have a poor auditory memory
- respond slowly in conversation
- have difficulty with phonics
- mispronounce words
- have difficulty with reading accuracy and comprehension
- use completely wrong words sometimes
- tire easily.

The similarity between the behaviours of those with APD and those with other areas of specific learning difficulty means that it is all too easy for children to be wrongly diagnosed as experiencing dyslexia or ADHD while their APD may go unnoticed. It is also possible that they are simply regarded as slow and unintelligent.

How can a clear identification of APD be made?

Identification can only be made by an audiologist. However, in order to fully understand the nature and magnitude of the secondary problems which are likely to have arisen, it can be very helpful to have a multidisciplinary assessment. Thus, a teacher or educational psychologist may shed light on academic difficulties. The psychologist may evaluate cognitive functioning in a variety of different areas and a speech and language therapist can investigate oral language, speech and related capabilities.

Some of these professionals may actually use tests that incorporate the term 'auditory processing' in their assessment and they may even suggest that a child exhibits an auditory processing difficulty. But it is essential to know that however valuable the information from the multidisciplinary team is in understanding the child's overall areas of strength and weakness, none of the test tools used by these professionals are diagnostic tools for APD, and the actual identification of APD must be made by an audiologist. The audiologist is the only professional who can do this.

The audiologist will give a series of tests in a soundproofed room. These tests require the listener to attend to a variety of signals and to respond to them via repetition, pushing a button, or in some other way. Other tests that measure the auditory system's physiological responses to sound may also be administered. Most of the tests for APD require that a child be at least seven or eight years old because the variability in brain function is so marked in younger children that test interpretation may not be possible.

What can parents and schools do to support children with APD?

There are six key ways in which parents and teachers can together support the child:

1. Modify the learning environment – including the use of technology to aid auditory processing.

2. Adapt teaching styles and methods.

3. Address any delays and weaknesses in learning which have resulted from APD, such as delayed reading.

4. Teach strategies to cope with the difficulty.

5. Teach strategies to become an active listener.

6. Treat the APD.

These points are discussed in detail below.

Modify the learning environment

The best way to support pupils with these difficulties is to adapt their learning environment. Consideration should be given to improving the acoustics in the room and to seating.

- Try to diminish any background noise. The pupil should not sit by a window where outside noises will be intrusive. Shutting doors and windows in the classroom can help the child to 'hear' the teacher.

- Incorporate soft furnishings into the room, such as rugs or cushions. This should absorb some noise and make the room seem quieter.

- Seat the pupil at the front of the class so that he can see and hear easily, and keep him away from pupils who might be disruptive.

- Allow the pupil to see the speaker, as many pupils with APD rely on some lip reading.

- Find periods when the pupil can work in a quiet environment.

Technological help

It is possible to give very effective support through the use of a wireless FM (frequency modulation) system. This direct audio link between teacher and child enables the child to listen to the teacher's voice directly through a small receiver (rather like a hearing aid) which is hooked onto and inserted in the child's ear. The teacher's voice is thus transmitted direct to the child and it is no longer necessary to have to filter out the background noise. The teacher's voice can be adjusted up to 20 decibels louder than the environmental noise, which enables the child to hear and process the teacher's voice at any time without difficulty. The child can switch the device on and off at will. One such system is called EduLink and is produced by Phonak.

It is an exciting development, and although not a miracle cure those pupils I have known who have used it have found it exceptionally helpful. Rather than struggling to process what is being said the other side of the classroom against the background noise of other things going on, the pupil has the benefit of a clear and easily audible voice directly in their ear.

Adapt teaching style and mode of interacting

Some modification to the teaching style is immensely helpful:

- Instructions should be given at a reasonable measured pace giving the pupil sufficient time to 'process' what he hears.

- Information should be 'chunked' into small amounts and sentence structures should be simple (this approach is helpful to all pupils).

- The pupil should be encouraged to ask for a repetition if he has not understood. Repetitions of information should be given clearly and slowly, not faster and louder (the problem is not auditory acuity – the pupil can hear okay!).

- It can help to accompany verbal instructions with a picture or other visual aid or with written notes to which he can then refer.

- Instructions could be written on the board.

- Memory aids (such as wall charts, posters, useful spellings) may help.

- When the pupil starts a new task after listening, the teacher should check that it is fully understood.

- The pupil should be given 'thinking' time to process what he has heard before being pressed into a response.

- If the pupil is having difficulty in sustaining attention and staying on task, perhaps some breaks could be given to enable him to move around or simply have 'time out' before he settles down again and refocuses. It can be particularly tiring for a pupil with 'listening' difficulties to cope with all the demands of the classroom and he can get overwhelmed and exhausted.

- There should be close liaison with home if there are new topics which might be reinforced at home. A notebook for two-way comments might be helpful.

Interaction at home

Several of the suggestions above are also relevant in the home environment but parents can also remember that they can help to increase their child's listening ability:

- Do not try and have an important or significant conversation when your child is in another room, watching television or listening to music, or when appliances are on. Even a running tap can be an interference.

- Get your child's attention and ensure he is ready to listen before you start to talk. Also face him directly and make sure he is looking at you.

- Use short, simple sentences with a pause between key information or ideas.

- Encourage him to ask you to repeat anything he doesn't understand.

Address any delays in learning which may have resulted from APD

An educational assessment would be useful because it should provide a good analysis of any secondary difficulties which have arisen due to APD and point parents and teachers in the right direction. Literacy skills are almost certain to have been affected.

Suggestions for helping with any areas of difficulty or delay can be found elsewhere in this book; for example, the ideas set out in the chapters on dyslexia, reading, ADHD and language may all have some relevance.

Teach strategies to cope with the difficulty

Children with APD need to learn to make the most of their existing cognitive strengths and work on any weaker areas. An educational psychologist's assessment can highlight a pupil's cognitive profile and identify areas to develop and to work on. The key areas to develop are language, thinking, memory and attention (see the relevant chapters).

Teach strategies to become an active listener

Children with APD need help to take responsibility for their own listening success and to be active participants in daily listening activities through a variety of active listening and problem-solving techniques. Resources for encouraging good listening can be found at the end of the book. There are also suggestions for listening activities in Appendix 2.

Treat the APD

There is no one miracle approach to treating APD and it will need to be individualised and deficit-specific, which is why it is so important to have an accurate and careful diagnosis by an audiologist. Your audiologist will be able to give guidance on listening therapies and programmes. The aim of such programmes is to remediate the disorder itself.

Treatment includes a wide variety of exercises that target specific auditory deficits. Therapy can range from computer-assisted software programs like Fast ForWord to one-on-one training with a speech and language therapist. Here are some common approaches:

- To overcome sound discrimination problems, a professional trains the child's brain to differentiate sounds, first in a quiet environment, then with increasingly louder background noise.

- To sharpen auditory memory, an audiologist uses sequencing routines – having the child repeat a series of numbers and directions – to exercise the listening skills.

- To manage language-processing problems, a therapist will train and encourage a child to ask a teacher, adult or peer to repeat or rephrase an instruction or comment. The therapist and child might also work on developing a customised note-taking system that enables him to capture the information being taught in the classroom.

The degree to which an individual child's auditory deficits will improve with therapy cannot be determined in advance. Whereas some children with APD experience complete amelioration of their difficulties or seem to 'grow out of' their disorders, others may exhibit some residual degree of deficit for ever.

However, with appropriate intervention, all children with APD can learn to become active participants in their own listening, learning and communication success rather than victims of an insidious impairment. Thus, when the journey is navigated carefully, accurately and appropriately, there can be light at the end of the tunnel for the child afflicted with APD.

CASE STUDIES

Stella's story

This story provides a vivid example of the cognitive, social and emotional difficulties which children with APD can experience before a diagnosis is made. It is an encouraging story because it shows how the right support can make all the difference and allow the failing child to become a successful and confident student. It does highlight the potential difficulty in identifying APD and the importance of getting an audiologist's involvement.

When Stella came for assessment she peered out through a screen of beautiful, thick hair and I remember thinking how she quite literally seemed to use it as a curtain behind which she could retreat. She was already 13 years old and her parents were deeply concerned.

Throughout her schooling she had experienced difficulty with her school work and in dealing with social relationships. In primary school she struggled, but because she was quiet and well behaved her difficulties were easy to overlook. All the while Stella's parents were certain that all was not well. They had her hearing checked but this did not pick up any problem. They had an EP assessment but unfortunately this was not helpful. The report suggested that she was none too bright and that there might be family issues. (Stella's mother can feel the anger rise when she remembers back to that time.)

Stella duly moved on to secondary school and it was there that that things came to a head. She was still quiet, withdrawn and non-communicative. Her attention was also poor. But more worrying was the fact that she was being badly bullied and appeared to be self-harming.

Stella's parents were desperate to find out what was wrong. They knew she was an able child and that there must be an explanation for her academic and social difficulties. In desperation they arranged an appointment with an experienced child and adolescent psychiatrist.

Here finally they found the support and expertise they needed. The psychiatrist agreed that she was indeed of good ability but experiencing an area of specific difficulty. He was able to let them know that the self-harming was not serious and that it was a cry for help rather than anything more sinister. He suggested that she have a multidisciplinary assessment to get a good 360-degree view of her strengths and difficulties.

A series of assessments were arranged. These were with a speech and language therapist, a consultant audio physician and myself.

Stella's educational psychology assessment revealed that (as her parents had always suspected) she was of good general ability but that she had significant difficulties with her 'expressive' language and her literacy skills were delayed. It was, however, the audio physician's assessment that proved to be most important and it was the audio physician who identified APD. Suddenly everything fell into place.

Stella's parents felt the utmost relief and at last were able to work on the areas where she needed help. Even now, a good number of years on, Stella's mother talks with the utmost gratitude about the relief of getting a good and accurate 'diagnosis' and of the value of such a multidisciplinary assessment with input from a range of 'specialists'.

Stella had difficulty with the differentiation of sound. This was made worse in situations where there was background noise to contend with. Let's imagine for a moment that when Stella was in primary school her class teacher had asked the children to 'tidy away the blue books, then come and sit on the carpet ready for a story'. Stella might have heard 'tid way the voodoo then cow and see on the carp ready for tory'. If this was a familiar request and the class were used to doing the same thing on a daily basis she would probably have been able to work out what she had been asked to do. However, if this was a totally new set of instructions she would have had little to go on as she tried to make sense of what she had heard.

Primary schools are often cosy places, with carpets and beanbags to reduce sound. Despite this, many factors within Stella's primary school mitigated against her. The pupils sat at tables. There was a background hum of chat. Her mother recalls the joy of her last year when she had a rather old-fashioned teacher. He sat all children facing the front and demanded a silent classroom and no bullying. Facing the front was good for Stella. We all aid our listening and comprehension through lip reading, though we do this unconsciously. So for Stella, facing her teacher so that she could watch him talk was a definite bonus, as was the silence and the lack of bullying.

After Stella's diagnosis she had speech and language therapy and followed the intensive 'listening' program Fast ForWord. It all made a difference. It increased her vocabulary and her confidence. Therapy was given in conjunction with a move to a much more supportive school which really concentrated on the individual child. Stella also used the FM wireless system EduLink in the classroom. This made it easier for her to 'hear' what her teachers were saying in class. Stella blossomed. Although she struggled with academic work she was a creative pupil, and with the help of a wonderful art teacher she was able to move on to college to take an art degree.

The college supported her well. She had a note taker to help her in lectures because she was unable to process speech sufficiently quickly to note take for herself. She was reading 'okay', but comprehension presented some challenges. The text in many of the academic books that she was required to read often seemed complex and impenetrable, so she needed ongoing help with that.

Although it was still hard for Stella to follow very fast conversations, she made a small group of good friends. She put herself forward to be a student rep and to show prospective students around on open day. She also got herself a part-time job to augment her living costs. These things represented a big step forward from the previously anxious and withdrawn teenager.

The best news of all comes next. Stella won a prestigious scholarship to study for a master's degree in a well-known academy in the USA. She is there now, at the time of writing, and her parents are in awe of her bravery and determination.

One last word from her mother. Never give up. Never stop believing. If things do not seem right, turn every stone to find a way forward.

KEY POINTS

⇨ APD is an auditory processing disorder which affects a child's ability to recognise and interpret speech sounds.

⇨ Not all learning, language and communication deficits are due to APD.

⇨ No matter how many symptoms of APD a child has, only careful and accurate diagnosis can determine if APD is indeed present.

⇨ Although a multidisciplinary team approach is important in fully understanding the cluster of problems associated with APD, the diagnosis of APD can only be made by an audiologist.

⇨ The treatment of APD is highly individualised. There is no one treatment approach that is appropriate for all children with APD.

⇨ With good support children can make good progress and learn to cope.

Chapter 9

SPECIFIC LANGUAGE IMPAIRMENT

Ava was 15 years old when she came for an educational assessment. During her assessment she often said 'I don't understand' and needed to have things repeated. She gave quick and excellent answers to questions when just one or two words were required, but when she had to provide a longer explanation she had great difficulty in expressing herself. Although she had good intellectual ability and scored above average on most tests, her reading comprehension skills were at a ten-year-old level and her listening comprehension skills were at a nine-year-old level. Ava had a specific language impairment (SLI) but somehow she had struggled through, and her particular weaknesses had been difficult for parents and teachers to identify.

It is estimated that between 3 and 10 per cent of children experience specific language impairment. SLI has, however, been something of a Cinderella in that difficulties can easily go undiagnosed. It is all too easy for the kind of problems that arise if a young child has difficulty speaking or understanding speech or text for it to be misdiagnosed as dyslexia, ADHD or some other specific learning difficulty. In this chapter we will look at what is meant by a specific language impairment, how we might identify it and what difficulties ensue.

What exactly is an SLI?

The term specific language impairment relates to difficulty with 'expressive' and/or 'receptive' language. Expressive language means talking and using language to convey meaning; receptive language means the ability to understand spoken and written language.

The term speech and language impairment does not include problems with speech production (producing clear speech sounds), phonological awareness (hearing the sounds within words) or understanding the normal social conventions of interaction (turn taking, listening and responding appropriately).

In this chapter we will focus on the difficulties with understanding and speaking which are classified as SLI. However, because the whole topic of speech and language is complex, I would like to start by expanding a little on those elements of language and communication which are *not* regarded as being part of an SLI but which can cause difficulties of their own.

Other Language Elements
Speech production

Some children find it hard to pronounce words and to articulate specific sounds. Speech sounds may be very unclear and can sometimes sound 'slushy'. This may be caused by the muscles of the mouth not working efficiently to produce the right sounds. This is sometimes referred to as dysarthria.

Children with verbal dyspraxia also have difficulty in making and coordinating the precise movements required for the production of clear speech. They have difficulty in producing individual speech sounds and in sequencing sounds together in words. As a result their speech can be unintelligible, even to family members.

Poor speech articulation may also be due to an inability to 'hear' speech sounds either because of a hearing loss or because of phonological weakness. These children need support to overcome difficulties but their speech production difficulties are not, of themselves, a language and communication issue.

Phonological awareness

As you may remember from earlier chapters, in order to learn to talk (and then to read and spell) a child needs to be able to hear and distinguish the small speech sounds (phonemes) used in his native language. An inability to do this with ease is referred to as poor phonological awareness. This may be due to a hearing loss – permanent or intermittent – or may relate to an auditory processing difficulty. These issues have been taken up in other chapters. They are not, of themselves, a language and communication disability but will impact on language.

Social communication skills

Social communication skills refer to our use of language in a social context. For example, our ability to use language appropriately depending on who is listening, to read between the lines, to understand jokes and innuendo, and to understand what it is socially acceptable to say to whom and under what conditions. It also includes our ability to read the body language and facial expressions of the person we are talking to and thus to adjust to whether they are looking engaged, bored or desperate to go.

These skills develop with age. Learning starts from the moment that a baby gurgles and laughs in response to an attentive parent, and continues through childhood. The majority of children develop these skills naturally through their everyday social interactions. There are, however, a few children for whom social communication skills are not acquired automatically or who are simply awkward and inept. Around one in a hundred children may be identified as being on the autistm spectrum, but there will be others whose difficulties do not fulfil the criteria for such a diagnosis but who may seem awkward or inappropriate in the way they relate to others.

So now let's return to SLI

So, we see that SLI is as prevalent as the other specific difficulties described in this book, and like the other areas of specific learning difficulties it is an invisible disability, it tends to run in families, it can have a big impact on educational progress and it can co-exist with any one (or more) of the other specific learning difficulties. Children with an SLI are just as intelligent as other children but they will need the support and expertise of a speech and language therapist. The role of the therapist is to help them to learn and to develop language skills. As with other specific learning difficulties, problems can be mild or severe and can come in varying combinations.

Understanding language

The child with receptive language impairment might:

- have difficulty understanding what other people have said
- find it hard to follow spoken directions or instructions
- find it hard to relate to his peer group
- find it hard to organise his thoughts.

Inevitably there will be repercussions within the classroom. If a child has difficulty in understanding what his teacher has said he may react in a number of ways. He may keep his head down and try to copy what others are doing. He may opt out, appear inattentive and be slow to get going with his work; he may interrupt others and seem to be a bit of a trouble maker. His work may not relate to the instructions given. Reading comprehension will be impacted even if he can read easily and accurately. This is true whether he is six or 16.

Expressive language

The child with an expressive language disorder might:

- have difficulty in speaking in a grammatically correct way
- have difficulty forming sentences
- speak in a way which muddles correct word order
- have a limited vocabulary
- leave words out of sentences when he talks
- muddle up tenses
- mix up words
- use some phrases over and over and/or repeat parts of questions
- omit word endings such as plural 's' or comparatives (bigg*er*).

Within school he is going to find it hard to contribute verbally in class unless given support and adequate time, and he is likely to have some difficulty in keeping up with the cut and thrust of conversation with his peers. He may consequently be quiet and reluctant to contribute. His written work may include words in the wrong order, words in the wrong tense or words which have been truncated. Many children with language impairment have difficulty in the acquisition and development of literacy skills.

It is not hard to see that if left unrecognised and untreated these language difficulties will have a snowball effect, and as the child progresses through school he is likely to struggle and to find it hard to cope educationally and socially.

Why do these difficulties go unnoticed?

It may not always be easy for parents to recognise this type of language difficulty. First of all it is not unusual for parents to equate language skills with how clearly a child pronounces words. So, if the words he says sound clear and recognisable, then there is a tendency to think all is well even if they are muddled and sometimes do not make sense. It is easy to get used to the way in which a child communicates. Parents may take his muddled or restricted responses for granted or, if he is quiet, they may just think he is lazy or allowing his siblings to talk for him. Parents of boys have been lulled into thinking that boys are slower than girls when it comes to talking and that he will get there in the end.

Where understanding is concerned, parents may adjust the way in which they speak to him almost without realising it. Also, he may well get the gist of what is said even if the details are confused, so it may feel as though communication is taking place.

The confusion of co-existing difficulties

If specific language impairment has not been picked up before a child starts school the problems that he encounters in class may well be attributed to alternative causes or to other learning difficulties.

When other learning difficulties co-exist with poor language it can be hard to know if these are separate difficulties or to what degree they influence each other. For example:

- Many children with language impairment also have difficulty with literacy. In such cases it is all too easy for the literacy difficulties to be ascribed to *dyslexia* and the language impairment to be overlooked. If language difficulties have not been identified at the time that the child starts to have difficulty with reading then parents and teachers inevitably focus on the reading difficulties.

- In other instances, poor language may appear to be the result of an *auditory processing disorder*; whichever comes first, they both impact on the child's ability to progress well in school, and both areas of difficulty need to be assessed by the appropriate specialist.

- A language impairment can also lead to behavioural traits which can easily be confused with *ADHD*; for example, if the child appears to switch off, act out, look dreamy or appear inattentive.

- Poor listening may also be confused with a *weak working memory*, if, for example, he does not seem to have fully processed what has been said or asks for a repetition.

- The poor social skills which may result from the effort of interacting when it is not clear what others have said or the frustration of not being fully understood may be confused with a *social communication difficulty*.

The earlier an SLI can be identified the better. If you, the parent, think that it is possible your child might experience a problem with language processing I would strongly suggest that you get a speech and language assessment. If there is no problem then you can rule it out, but if there is an area of difficulty then appropriate help can be organised.

What can be done to help children with language impairment?

The key task for parents and teachers, once they are aware of a problem, is to help make the child's world more understandable and navigable. In so doing they will help the child to gain the confidence to interact and make his needs known.

The child with language impairment will have to be explicitly taught the things that unimpaired children know implicitly. The professional to whom parents can turn for help is the speech and language therapist (SpLT). It is the SpLT who is able to assess a child's areas of difficulty and to provide a programme of help. An SpLT can work with the child to:

- develop strategies to cope; for example, when he cannot think of the word he needs (but can imagine it in his head), he can learn how to describe the word rather than give up. If the word was 'horse' then he could say you ride it and it is like a donkey

- find ways to indicate when he has not understood

- gain the confidence to ask for a repetition or alternative phrasing when he has heard something which he has not fully understood

- gain the confidence to ask follow-up questions when things are not entirely clear.

The SpLT can work with parents so that they can continue to support at home and gain a greater understanding of the issues. Together they can work with the child to improve his:

- understanding of the meaning of words

- understanding of different types of sentences

- use of words in a sentence

- use of joining words such as but or because

- use of question words such as why, when or what

- vocabulary

- use of phrases
- conversational skills.

Parents can make use of word games and activities such as sentence completion. Any activity that requires precise verbal instructions or interactions will be helpful. Many basic stimuli can be used to make up and tell a story. Postcards or pictures from magazines can be studied and then described. Newspaper articles can be retold, and short stories recapped. Parents can provide a language-rich environment and support their child's progress.

Acquiring language skills can be a huge task for many SLI children.

Help in the classroom

It is important that all who teach a child with an SLI are made aware of the difficulty. It is likely that they may not be familiar with the problem or with the implications for the child in the classroom. Parents should not be afraid to provide useful information.

At a minimum the teacher will need to check that the child has understood verbal instructions; if necessary, these will need to be broken down into smaller steps with visual cues and prompts to support her understanding.

If the child is looking a little blank, it is important to simplify or rephrase instructions perhaps more slowly and check to see that she has understood. The child should also sit near the front of the class where the teacher can check that she is attending before instructions are given.

Visual aids can be a good support for children who have difficulty in understanding. A visual timetable will enable her to understand what she is doing over a period of time such as the school day. It will give structure to the day and can reduce anxiety levels. Symbols can be used to represent the tasks, activities or lessons, and these can be taught to the pupil.

A home–school book would be useful so that both parent and teacher are aware of what she has been doing and learning. That way parents can discuss and ask about school activities. The teacher can pick up on and chat about home activities (birthday parties, trips out and so forth).

The kind of strategies outlined in the chapter on working memory and some of those suggested in the chapter on dyslexia would also be appropriate.

Support for reading comprehension can be found in the chapter on reading.

Support at home

- Enlist support from the extended family and make them aware of any specific difficulties. They also need to be reminded to talk in language that is not too complex or too fast.

- You and they should use simple sentences with a pause between key information and ideas.

- Siblings will also need to be encouraged to make sure that their language-impaired brother or sister is given ample talking space and time and that they are allowed to talk uninterrupted.

- Do not try and have an important conversation with your child when she is in another room or engaged in an interesting activity.

- Make sure that you get her attention before you start to talk.

Address any delays in learning which may have resulted from the SLI

An educational assessment would be useful because it should provide a good analysis of any secondary difficulties that have arisen due to SLI and point parents and teachers in the right direction. Literacy skills are almost certain to have been affected, and reading comprehension is often impacted.

Suggestions for helping with any areas of difficulty or delay can be found elsewhere in this book; for example, the ideas set out in the chapters on dyslexia, reading, ADHD and language may all have some relevance.

CASE STUDY

Ava's story

This story shows us how difficult, but how important, it can be to identify a mild language impairment. It illustrates the importance of addressing these language difficulties and of addressing the academic difficulties that can arise as a result of the language impairment.

Ava was well into secondary school when she came for assessment. She was struggling to keep up with her peer group in school and did not seem to be achieving at the level that her parents had anticipated. At home she was always so bright, alert and interested in things. She was passionate about fairness and justice, she was interested in all that was going on in the world. Her parents could not understand what the problem might be.

Ava's confidence was suffering. To make things worse she had three very academic siblings who were all doing well in school; Ava was particularly sensitive to any inadvertent comparisons made between her and her siblings. Ava's teachers were evidently not unduly worried and tended to dismiss any concerns with a response to the effect that she was a lovely girl – bless her – but that if only she would concentrate she might do better.

Assessment showed that Ava was a child of good ability but she had very evident problems with language and with reading comprehension. This was most certainly enough to account for her disappointing academic performance and the fact that she appeared, at times, to lack concentration. There were no underlying problems with either her working memory or indeed her ability to maintain attention.

What about her difficulties? Ava found it hard to express herself and to convey what was on her mind. She often seemed to know the answer to questions but simply could not articulate it fluently and freely. She was also having some difficulty with understanding. She often said 'I don't understand' and needed to have things repeated. A test of her listening comprehension produced a score that was on a par with an average nine-year-old – no wonder that she often appeared inattentive in class. She must surely have found herself frequently confused and unsure of an instruction or explanation.

The second area in which Ava was experiencing difficulty was with reading comprehension. She could read accurately but she was not taking in, understanding and absorbing the content. While her reading accuracy (her ability to look at and read individual words) was excellent, her comprehension of the texts that she read was well below average and her speed of reading was also slow. Complex sentence structure and unusual vocabulary exacerbated the situation.

Discussion with Ava's parents revealed that this difficulty with reading comprehension had been evident throughout her schooling. They also explained that when Ava was younger she had had difficulty with speaking in a grammatically correct manner. They had noticed that sometimes she struggled to find the words she needed and that sometimes she would listen but not seem to follow what had been said to her.

It seemed highly likely that Ava was experiencing a specific language impairment. This may not have been very extreme but it was certainly enough to make aspects of classroom learning a real struggle. What Ava needed now was a speech and language assessment to ascertain the extent of her difficulties. This was put in place and it was confirmed that Ava did experience a specific language difficulty affecting both her listening and speaking. Over the following year or so Ava's language weaknesses were addressed through language therapy and a listening programme.

Meanwhile back in school, Ava needed specialist input to ensure that she could make up lost ground on the learning front. She needed support with her spelling (see Chapter 15, Tips for Spelling). She needed very specific help with her reading comprehension (see Chapter 14, Tips for Reading) and she needed to develop good study skills and habits (see Chapter 24, Habits, Strategies and Study Skills).

Now that they were aware of the underlying causes of Ava's slow progress, her parents were also able to adapt the way they interacted with her and found ways to support her language development (Chapter 21, Tips to Enhance Language and Communication Skills, has ideas for helping to enhance listening and speaking).

It was also going to be important that all who taught her were made aware of her specific language difficulties and given advice about how they could help to minimise the impact of poor comprehension as well as asked to make allowances for her difficulty in expressing herself fluently and freely. Many of the suggestions made in Chapter 2, Working Memory, are pertinent.

Key points for teachers to remember include the following:

» Wait until you know she is listening before giving an instruction or starting to talk.

» Give instructions clearly in short bites.

» Allow time for her to process what you say before you continue.

» Do not talk too fast.

» Use language which can be easily processed, i.e. simple sentence structure.

» Repeat instructions calmly, slowly and without irritation.

» When she starts a new task after listening to instructions, check that she has processed what she has to do and can carry it out.

» If necessary, give a written list of what needs to be remembered (use pictures for a pre-reader).

Clear communication can also be enhanced by using visual aids:

» Use memory aids, i.e. wall charts, posters, useful spellings, dictionaries, cubes, counters, number lines. These may all help with homework and are not just useful for the classroom.

>> Accompany verbal instructions with a picture or some other form of visual aid.

So, what happened? Ava and her parents were all relieved to find that there was a reason for Ava's struggles. Over the following few years she worked hard on the areas where she needed help. School staff were empathetic and responded well to her needs.

She gained confidence in herself and in her abilities. She learnt to ask for explanations if she was confused. Her work improved and her marks went up. Ava coped well with her public exams and gained good grades.

Ava decided, however, that although she felt she could most probably manage, she would not pursue an academic degree. It would have been hard work and there were no subjects that she felt sufficiently passionate about to want to give it a go. She has gone instead to college where she has chosen to complete a range of practical courses to give her good skills for entry to work.

KEY POINTS

⇨ A specific language impairment (SLI) is an impairment of receptive (understanding) and/or expressive (spoken) language which affects between 3 and 10 per cent of children.

⇨ It is an invisible, heritable difficulty, which can impact on educational progress. It can affect any child, regardless of intellectual ability.

⇨ It is not always easy to identify. It can easily be confused with other areas of specific difficulty, such as dyslexia, APD, ADHD and poor working memory.

⇨ It may co-occur with other areas of specific language difficulties.

⇨ Identification and support can be sought from a speech and language therapist.

⇨ It will help the child's teacher if he or she is given as much information as possible about the child's condition and, where necessary, tips for classroom support.

⇨ Delays or difficulties in learning that may have occurred because of the SLI should also be addressed alongside the language support.

Chapter 10

VISUAL PROCESSING DIFFICULTY

Shira seemed to have no difficulty in learning to read, although the process was slow and as she got older she was rarely to be seen with a book in her hands. It was assumed that she might be a bit dyslexic, but she was getting on okay in school so no one worried unduly. Reluctance to read was not, however, the only hint that Shira might be having visual processing difficulties. She was having difficulty in copying from the board and she had terrible difficulty in remembering and reproducing shapes. Aspects of maths were difficult for her. She would misread symbols, and geometry was a struggle.

Vision, like hearing, is involved in almost all forms of learning; if any aspect of vision is faulty it will be likely to impact on a child's classroom experience and interfere with his learning. There are two important aspects of vision. The first is visual acuity; this is the eye's response to the light shining into it. This determines whether we have perfect vision or whether we are long or short sighted. The second is visual processing; this is our ability to interpret and understand the information that comes through the eye.

Parents are generally vigilant about ensuring that their children visit the optician and have their sight tested and that, if necessary, glasses are prescribed for long or short sight. What is more likely to go undetected is any form of problem with visual processing and this is what we will be looking at in this chapter.

Visual processing is a complex business and there is plenty of scope for inefficient or faulty procedures. Many aspects of a child's learning and performance can be affected if visual processing is less than optimal. Reading, spelling, writing, maths, copying and even tying up shoelaces can, for example, all be affected. The problem is that difficulty in any of these areas can all too often be attributed to other causes (dyslexia, dyspraxia, ADHD), and the contribution made by visual processing weaknesses may well be overlooked.

The aim of this chapter is to:

• describe a range of visual processing difficulties

- flag up the ways in which they can affect performance
- consider the symptoms which parents should be able to recognise as possible visual difficulties
- look at the relationship between visual processing difficulties and different areas of specific learning difficulties
- make suggestions for formal identification and for remediation.

What do we mean by visual processing?

When we think of eyesight we generally think in terms of accuracy as in 20/20 vision. Our first concern for children is to make sure that they can see clearly. We know that it is important for children to have good visual acuity so that they can see all that is happening both near and far and in the classroom. If a child has had his eyes tested by the high street optician and has demonstrated good vision by looking across the room and reading the letters on the reading chart then most parents would relax and tick the sight box.

This does not, however, tell us the whole story and there are other important aspects of vision that can have a dramatic impact on a child's experience and progress with learning. Vision involves the ability to take incoming visual information, process that information and obtain meaning from it. We need to be able to understand what we have seen, from squiggles on the page to geometric shapes.

Visual processing is what happens between the eye and the brain. There are many steps in this process, but let's keep it simple. The eye picks up information from the world around in the form of light waves, which fall on the retina; the light is then converted into electrochemical signals. The optic nerve routes these signals to the different parts of the brain that specialise in 'seeing' such things as shapes, contrasts, movement, colour, orientation and depth.

Most of these higher-order brain activities are influenced by expectations based on past experience. In other words, they are learnt. From the moment babies are born their brains start to learn how to interpret the signals coming in via the optic nerve. If all goes well the eye and brain will work efficiently together.

However, before the brain gets involved in interpreting incoming signals, the eyes need to be in good physical shape. Even if a child has been given the all clear on visual acuity it is still possible that he may be having some difficulty with eye movement and control. He may have difficulty with:

- eye tracking (eye movement control). When we are reading our eyes should move smoothly along the line stopping once or twice to enable us to 'see' the print. Poor readers may have difficulty with tracking and their eyes may flick back and forth along the line fixating at numerous points

- focusing near to far. This is the ability to keep the eyes focused as an object moves from far vision into near vision. To test this you can stretch your arm out in front of your face with the index finger raised. Slowly bring the finger in towards your nose

- sustaining clear focus up close

- eye teaming (binocular coordination).

Once the brain gets involved we are onto the aspects of visual processing which are learnt and which develop with experience. Visual processing involves:

- depth perception – seeing the world in 3D and judging the distance of an object

- visual motor integration – coordinating visual input with physical actions

- visual form perception – understanding the relationship of objects within the environment

- visual memory – recalling the traits of objects or forms

- visual attention – focusing on what's important and filtering out the irrelevant

- visual discrimination – noting similarities and differences based on shape, colour and size

- visual sequential memory – remembering a sequence of objects in the right order

- visual figure ground – picking out one object from a busy background

- visual form constancy – recognising an object whichever way around it may be presented or however large or small it may become

- visual closure – recognising an object even if a part of it is missing.

How can we tell if a child experiences visual processing difficulties?

Poor visual processing can have an impact on a wide range of activities that involve vision. The child with weak or slow processing may:

- experience difficulties with reading and interpreting symbols. He may, for example, lose his place when he is reading, miss out words or reread the same word, like to use a finger or marker to keep his place, struggle to find information on a page, and find it hard to change focus as he looks up at the board and then back to work on his desk

- show physical symptoms of strain. With close work he may complain about headaches (around the temple or eyes), find it hard to maintain concentration, experience blurred or double vision, often rub his eyes, become tired when he is reading, and put his head very near to his work or look at it from an angle

- appear inattentive or lacking in focus. He may manage to read individual words but have difficulty with sentences, read a whole page of text, turn the page and forget what he has just read, and lack interest in or be inattentive during films, videos or watching television

- have difficulty with activities that involve interpretation of visual/spatial information. He may dislike completing jigsaws, have untidy handwriting, have difficulty in keeping his writing within lines or margins, misread maths function signs, omit steps and confuse visually similar formulas, and have difficulty with spatial concepts in maths. He may be slow to scan for matching shapes and find it hard to recognise and match shapes

- have difficulty with visual/spatial motor skills. We use vision to direct our actions and movements in relation to our immediate environment. He may have poor judgement of distances (tripping or spilling), difficulty in identifying where things are in space, poor map reading, and difficulty with graphs, tables and other forms of graphic representation

- experience problems with visual memory. He may have difficulty remembering sight words, and write letters and numbers incorrectly. He may get letters and numbers in the wrong order

- lack the ability to visualise with ease. When we talk about visualisation we refer to the ability to 'see things in the mind's eye'. The capacity to visualise is closely aligned with the ability to think. Many complex ideas are easier to cope with when they can be represented graphically. Ideas can be contained within diagrams, maps, charts, coordinates and so forth. The ability to see these in the mind's eye (when they are absent) can aid thought.

But hang on there, haven't these problems been mentioned already in earlier chapters? Isn't there something very familiar about this list? I guess you will have had little difficulty in spotting the fact that just about every one of these behaviours which are listed as possible indicators of a visual processing difficulty have already featured on the checklists for dyslexia, dyspraxia, dyscalculia and ADHD. How can we make sense of this?

Well, visual processing difficulties and other specific learning difficulties are not mutually exclusive. Visual processing difficulties are likely, in the situations described above, to be making a significant contribution to the literacy or attention difficulties which the child is experiencing. The degree to which poor visual processing is contributing to these difficulties can easily go unrecognised and untreated if they are not identified. The important thing to keep in mind is that visual difficulties are on a spectrum – they may be mild or they may be significant, so their impact will vary.

So, for one child difficulty with reading may be almost entirely due to visual weaknesses, but for another poor reading may be largely due to poor phonological awareness and weak working memory. Visual therapy may completely alleviate the first child's reading problems but will have little impact on the reading skills of the second child.

The same will apply to the clumsy child who bumps into things, who has poor handwriting and cannot keep letters within two lines, or who has non-existent ball skills. It is possible that weak visual/spatial skills (difficulty in judging distance and positions in space) may be a significant underlying cause of the problem, but it might be that very poor physical coordination is the causal factor.

It is becoming clear that children who are experiencing areas of specific learning difficulty really do need to have a proper and full assessment of their vision in order to establish to what degree vision may be contributing to their difficulties.

Which professionals can help?

There are three groups of professionals who can give you some information about your child's vision and visual processing.

The educational psychologist

The educational psychologist can test a child's visual memory, visual sequencing, the speed with which he can process visual information and his capacity to deal with visual/spatial information. These are cognitive tasks and are very much to do with what is going on in the brain.

The occupational therapist

The occupational therapist can test hand–eye coordination, visual/motor integration, visual memory, visual sequencing. The OT is able to explain such things as when, for example, a child has difficulty in copying a particular shape and whether this is due to poor hand–eye coordination or because the child is not perceiving the shape appropriately. We rely on vision a great deal when we are carrying out physical activities. If there are difficulties then the OT is able to work with the child to improve these visual processing skills.

The behavioural optometrist

The third group of professionals who are eye experts are the opticians, optometrists and orthoptists. Between them their role is to look at the health of our eyes and also to look at how efficiently our eyes are working. The titles of these professionals can be a little confusing to the layman. In this section I shall be focusing on the work of the behavioural optometrist, but before looking to see what he does let me run through the rest of them and what they can do.

We are all familiar with the high street *optician* (more properly known as an optometrist), who is qualified to measure visual acuity and to prescribe glasses and contact lenses. We would also expect her to check the health of our eyes and to refer us when necessary if she suspects any problems. We would not expect her to test all areas of visual processing.

Next on the list are the *orthoptists*, who are qualified to check binocular vision, motility (this means eye movement), lazy eyes and squints. They are normally encountered in a hospital eye clinic setting working with a paediatric ophthalmologist (who is a specialist eye doctor). They may measure squints and misalignments of the eyes, often pre-surgery, and may prescribe orthoptic eye exercises.

It is, however, the *behavioural optometrist* who is of interest to us in this chapter. These are the professionals to whom we can turn for support, help and visual therapy if it is indicated. Behavioural optometry is an expanded (but specialist) area of the work done by orthoptists.

The behavioural optometrist can test a wide range of visual processes and can decide if visual therapy would be of value to your child. The behavioural optometrist's interventions are based on the knowledge that vision (in terms of the way in which the brain interprets the electrical impulses sent in from the retina) is a learnt process. If it is learnt then it can be shaped, changed and improved.

Which visual processing difficulties can be ameliorated?

- Tracking – this is the ability to maintain visual attention on a moving object or to move the eyes smoothly along a line of print without losing place. Poor tracking can interfere with reading and learning to read.

- Accommodation – this refers to the ability of the eyes to work together to produce a clear image. Difficulty with accommodation will lead to discomfort and a preference for larger print. When print is too small it is hard for the reader to see individual letters.

- Binocular coordination – this is where the eyes should work as a coordinated team to aim simultaneously at the same target. Difficulties here may mean that text can appear distorted.

If the behavioural optometrist discovers that a child is not focusing properly when he is looking at things close to, or that his eyes are drifting apart when he is trying to focus close to, then a reading correction (glasses) can often make a positive difference straightaway and this can be followed by therapy.

Therapy generally consists of exercises, which may take ten minutes a day and last for a number of months.

It is important to keep in mind that treating visual difficulties will not directly address any educational weaknesses such as poor reading or spelling or maths. However, if the vision can be improved it will make it considerably easier for the child to work on his weaker skills and in many cases it has been found to bring about very rapid improvements.

If visual difficulties have been contributing to poor visual/spatial skills, poor hand–eye coordination or any other physical coordination, then an improvement in visual processing will also speed up and support the improvement of these visual/spatial and physical skills.

Which children can be helped?

An experienced behavioural optometrist described it as follows: visual difficulties, she explained, are on a spectrum. If we take two dyslexic pupils who are reading at a similar level, one may have clear and evident visual problems while the other may have only very slight visual processing weaknesses. If the visual processing issues are addressed for the first child, his reading scores will improve and it may well be that his reading difficulties become a thing of the past. However, visual therapy will have a limited impact on the reading of the second child.

The same will apply if we compare two dyspraxic or two ADHD children with or without visual processing difficulties. In the case of the dyspraxic children, help with visual aspects of visual/spatial difficulties may help one but not the other, although most of these coordination difficulties do have a visual component because we learn so much through the visual system.

Are tinted glasses helpful?

Tinted glasses hit the headlines from time to time, often under the heading 'Cure for dyslexia'. A miracle cure is, of course, just what we all want, so it is tempting to seek solace in a few sheets of tinted plastic. It requires less effort than visual therapy and we can feel proactive and hopeful. Of course, it really can help some children who are sensitive to bright light, glare, high contrast, pattern and colours and it can make the reading process feel more comfortable. What it does not do is improve the underlying visual processing difficulty. That said, it is worth experimenting with lighting and overlays to discover if this is helpful for your child.

Is there anything else parents and teachers can do to help?

First, there are things that you can do and discuss with your child at home:

- Develop self-knowledge. As ever, it is helpful for children to know where they have strengths and where they have weaknesses. Then they are aware of whether additional effort may be needed and when they should be vigilant and paying good attention. They should also be helped to use their strengths.

- Together list the tasks that are causing difficulty, and brainstorm strategies which the child might try.

- Help to develop his observational skills and memory. Let him look at a picture or postcard of something interesting. First, ask him to describe what he sees. Then as a next stage, let him look at the picture for a period, then turn it over and again ask him to describe what he has seen.

- Encourage him to use his voice to support visual memory. You might have him look at a shape for a moment or two, then turn it over and see if he can reproduce it. Is it accurate or has he misremembered details? Then try showing him a shape but ask him to describe its salient features. Then turn it over and ask him to reproduce it. Chances are that the second effort will be an improvement on the first.

- Give practice in observing differences. Activities such as Where's Wally? may help.

- Encourage the use of voice to give meaning to what is being observed. Help him to practise describing visual images. Present visual conundrums, puzzles, matrices or designs and get him to describe and talk through the issues.

- Help him to develop appropriate vocabulary to aid visual discrimination. *We are more readily able to recognise and distinguish that which we label.*

- Encourage him to use his own voice to keep track of what the hand and eye are doing. Talk through and describe the thought processes that are happening as he works to understand a diagram, map or chart.

These activities, which encourage observational skills accompanied by systematic analysis and the use of voice and verbal labels, are very powerful techniques. As ever, try and make sure that anything you do together is fun.

Then there are things that parents and teachers can do to help:

- Consider where enlarged print might be useful. For children who are learning music it can sometimes help to have the score enlarged on a photocopier.

- Eliminate visual distractions.

- Keep work sheets plain and uncluttered.

- Let him try out a Kindle and see if it helps to adjust background lighting and size of print.

- Find ways of getting around the need to copy.

- Make sure that written instructions are broken into steps and numbered.

- Check the chapter on habits, strategies and study skills for more relevant ideas.

Things which the pupil can do to help himself:

- Use highlighters to draw attention to important information.

- Colour code things which are easily visually muddled.

- Apply spelling rules rather than rely on how a word looks.

- Practise proofreading skills.

CASE STUDIES

Carly's story

Carly's story illustrates a common difficulty that some children face around Year 3 when demands increase, illustrations reduce, text is smaller and there is more on the page, and when some initially good readers start to experience difficulties.

Carly was halfway through Year 3 when she became withdrawn and no longer chatted happily to her family about her day in school. Her parents also noticed how hard it was to get her to read with them in the evenings.

They became more seriously concerned when Carly's teacher confirmed that she had noticed that within class Carly had become quiet and seemed unhappy. She also pointed out that Carly's concentration seemed to have dipped and the quality of her work had fallen.

Shortly after this Carly's mother spotted her sitting at her desk looking miserable and with a hand over one eye. She asked why, and Carly explained it was because the print looked double and it all seemed too hard.

An appointment was made with a behavioural optometrist. It was confirmed that Carly was getting double vision and that, in addition, the letters often appeared to be moving on the page. So this certainly seemed to be the likely cause of her fatigue, her poor concentration and general unhappiness. As she thought back, Carly's mother remembered that she had also noticed how Carly had been turning her head to one side when she had close work to do and that this had been going on for several months. Carly was prescribed particular glasses which helped to sharpen and clarify letter images and to make sure she was seeing a single image; she was also given exercises to support her reading. Carly was almost instantly happier, more engaged and able to concentrate. Her reading improved in leaps and bounds.

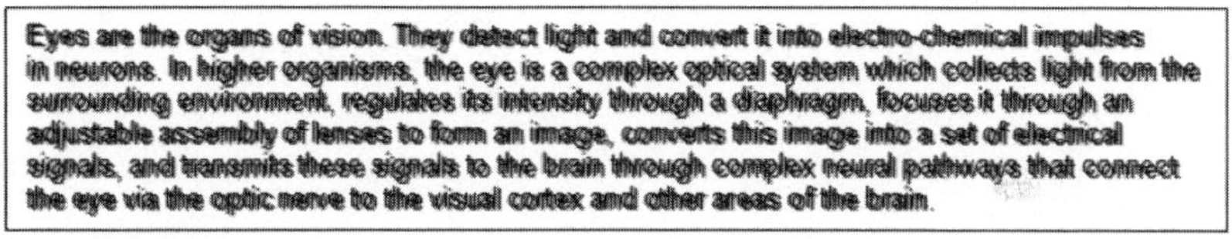

Eyes are the organs of vision. They detect light and convert it into electro-chemical impulses in neurons. In higher organisms, the eye is a complex optical system which collects light from the surrounding environment, regulates its intensity through a diaphragm, focuses it through an adjustable assembly of lenses to form an image, converts this image into a set of electrical signals, and transmits these signals to the brain through complex neural pathways that connect the eye via the optic nerve to the visual cortex and other areas of the brain.

Figure 10.1 The way that letters had been looking for Carly

Jack's story

Jack's story illustrates how difficulty with focus can impact on reading, writing and copying. It also shows how poor visual/spatial skills can result in apparent clumsiness and poor ball skills.

Nine-year-old Jack was bright, bubbly and sociable. He loved learning and would arrive enthusiastically at school each morning. But by 10am he was exhausted and would often be seen rubbing his eyes. Jack struggled to maintain concentration, and the effort required for reading, writing and copying was enormous. Jack also experienced headaches following desk work.

The classroom was not the only place where Jack had difficulties. His parents had noticed how hard it was for him to look where he was going and to walk from one place to another without bumping into things. Jack's clumsiness and poor ball skills were also evident when he played sport at school. Jack was frequently sustaining injuries and coming home with bruises.

Assessment by a behavioural optometrist showed that several aspects of Jack's vision had not developed well. He was prescribed special lenses, which helped to reduce his visual fatigue. Exercises soon improved his ability to focus both eyes together and to accurately locate and track items in space.

It was not long before Jack's teacher noticed a great improvement in his concentration, the accuracy of his copying and his improved reading and writing. To Jack's delight he even made it into the school football team – and reduced the number of bruises!

Jack's poor ability to focus both eyes together meant that print appeared blurred. The smaller the print the harder it was for him to figure out what he was looking at.

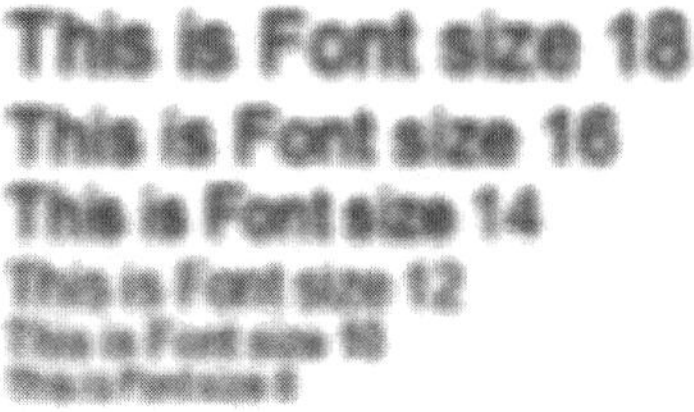

Figure 10.2 The way letters appeared to Jack

Shira's story

Shira's story illustrates how easy it is to let visual difficulties go either undetected or at least untreated. As with other areas of specific learning difficulty there are no magic bullets or quick fixes. Help from an occupational or visual/perceptual therapist along with acquiring good strategies and habits can begin to ameliorate the problem.

Shira seemed to have no difficulty in learning to read, though the process was possibly a little slow. The house was full of books and the rest of the family were avid readers, so it was something of a surprise that by the age of seven or eight Shira showed no interest in books. She was also experiencing difficulty with spelling and would make the same mistakes over and over again. She just didn't seem to recognise whether certain words looked right or not. It was assumed that she might be a bit dyslexic, but she was getting on okay in school so no one worried unduly.

Reluctance to read was not the only hint that Shira might be having visual processing difficulties. She was having difficulty in copying from the board and she had terrible difficulty in remembering and reproducing shapes. Aspects of maths were difficult for her. She would misread symbols, and geometry was a struggle.

She continued to be a slow reader and also found that as soon as she had turned the page she had forgotten what she had read. As she neared the end of Year 8 (aged 13) she was having to work hard to keep up and began to feel anxious. Anxiety began to impact on the way she was functioning. Shira needed help. This came from two directions. First, she received regular counselling to help with her anxiety, and second, it was at this stage that an educational psychologist's assessment was suggested.

The assessment took place. It was no surprise to find that she had good verbal ability (she was bright, could make connections, had a good vocabulary and could express herself well) and that her general intellectual ability was in the upper half of the average range. It was also very interesting, though not a great surprise, to find that she had significant difficulties with almost all aspects of visual processing.

Shira scored poorly on tests that looked at her visual/spatial skills. She was down in the bottom 1 per cent on the tests that sampled her memory for visual information. The speed at which she could process visual information was also 'extremely' slow. This meant that her ability to scan for a word or look for information on the whiteboard would be laborious and slow. No wonder Shira had struggled with all things dependent on good visual analysis, reasoning and memory. Shira was experiencing a specific learning difficulty relating to her visual processing.

It was recommended that she should have a behavioural optometrist's assessment. It was also suggested that a period of support from a visual/perceptual therapist or appropriate occupational therapist would help her to improve skills and find strategies to cope.

Unlike Carly and Jack, no specific issues that could be readily addressed were uncovered by the optometrist's assessment. This did not mean, however, that Shira would not benefit from working on her visual processing skills with the recommended visual/perceptual therapist.

It was also recommended that:

» Shira should be helped to understand her strengths and weaknesses as a student. She had good verbal skills and was a good communicator. She was able to learn better when she heard information. So, for example, instead of trying to memorise information from a mind map she should learn from an audio recording

» Shira should be helped to keep distracting visual information on a page to a minimum. She should try to cover up redundant information so that she can focus on what is relevant

» Shira's difficulty in copying accurately should be taken seriously and alternative methods of providing her with notes or information which others might be taking down from the board should be devised. She should not have to copy in class

» Shira should learn to touch type and to use a laptop for her work. This was suggested on the basis that she would find it easier to visually process typed work than handwritten work. She could alter the script and the size to that which she found easiest

» consideration should be given to Shira's workload. Where possible it should be reduced to take account of the additional effort she had to put into everyday learning

» Shira's visual difficulties were sufficiently marked to warrant use of a laptop and additional time for internal and public exams.

Shira has worked hard. She feels calmer and more confident. She was delighted to do very well in her GCSE exams and is now embarking on her A-level courses.

KEY POINTS

⇨ Vision involves more than visual acuity and 20/20 vision.

⇨ Visual processing includes efficient eye movements and coordination, the transfer of information via the optic nerve to different brain locations, and the brain's interpretation and understanding of that data.

⇨ Poor processing can impact on basic skills such as reading and maths. It can cause strain and fatigue; it can impact some activities requiring hand–eye coordination.

⇨ There is a significant overlap with the difficulties that are also indicative of dyslexia, dyspraxia, ADHD and dyscalculia.

⇨ Assessment by a behavioural optometrist will be able to identify areas and significance of any problems.

⇨ This can lead to visual therapy, which in many cases is of benefit.

Chapter 11

AN EDUCATIONAL PSYCHOLOGIST'S ASSESSMENT

'My son's educational assessment was fantastic! It enabled me to be proactive. It gave me an understanding of his strengths and difficulties. It gave me a clear view of how to support and help him and it gave me the power to liaise with his school and to say "this is what we need to do". School staff found his assessment report clear and helpful.' (A parent)

The assessment process will vary from educational psychologist to educational psychologist (EP) and from country to country. However, there are likely to be more similarities than differences. Across the developed world the training and experience of education psychologists and school psychologists is broadly comparable. They are experts in child development, education, educational difficulties, psychology and learning, and they will have had extensive training. Their shared aim is to support teachers, parents and pupils and to enable children to successfully access the curriculum.

In the UK there are two main routes for getting a child assessed. If your child is in private school you will need to find an independent EP. If, however, your child attends a state school he or she could be assessed by the EP attached to that school. I say 'could' because it is not always easy to arrange for this. If your child's difficulties are thought to be mild it is unlikely that he will be considered to be a sufficient priority for EP time and attention. Unfortunately, EPs are a scarce resource even though their expertise is much needed within the education system.

Whether children are in state or private school, many parents value the advice of an independent psychologist because they are outside the system. There are pros and cons to this. For some parents it can be daunting to have to deal with the powers that be within their local authority (LA), and even headteachers can at times be intimidating, so having the support and expertise of an independent advocate can be empowering and confidence giving.

The focus of this chapter is on independent assessment, but at the end of the chapter you will find information about seeking assessment and specialist provision from your LA.

When is it appropriate to have a child assessed?

Over the years many parents have phoned me, often hesitantly and anxiously, concerned about some aspect of their child's educational progress, behaviour or wellbeing. They want to know what is going wrong and they want to know how to help.

Concerns are wide ranging; they may be to do with concentration, motivation, organisation, maths, reading, handwriting, spelling or problems getting along socially. Or they might just want advice about choosing the right school.

Once they hear a friendly voice at the other end of the phone their concerns often pour out. It can be a lonely and worrying time for parents when they think that there may be a problem and they are unsure what they can do. They are generally reassured when they find out that an assessment is a practical process which is often fun for all and which can successfully:

- clarify the problem

- identify any underlying causes

- provide appropriate suggestions for parents and school staff regarding the best way to help the child.

The assessment procedure that many independent EPs follow to achieve these aims is as follows:

- Gather information. It is important to build up the 'big picture' of the child and, to do that, feedback from all relevant sources is important. Generally this is just parents and school staff, but if the child has any other relevant reports it really helps if the EP can see them.

- Meet and work with the child. This generally takes around two hours. The child will complete an IQ test and will also be asked to carry out a range of literacy and maths tests. Further diagnostic tests may be given if necessary and appropriate.

- Meet and give feedback to parents. This is generally an appointment lasting about an hour and in most cases will follow straight on from work with the child. The EP should be able to talk parents through test results, share views, outline the implications arising from any identification of difficulties and consider ways forward.

- Write a report summarising the assessment findings and setting out suggestions and recommendations.

Information gathering

It may not be immediately obvious but this is a vitally important part of the assessment. The EP should be building a big picture about the child and finding out about all those things that we know can have an impact on learning. No amount of testing will reveal that a child is not paying attention in class because he is really worried about a parent who is unwell. We cannot conclude a child is dyslexic because he cannot read unless we know how well or how much he has been taught and whether he has ever had a hearing or sight problem.

For parents, this part of the assessment means completing a family questionnaire. The EP may also ask for the parents' permission to send a questionnaire to the child's school.

Questions are likely to be in sections which cover: basic skills, developmental history, health, hearing, sight, appetite, sleep, physical development, fine motor skills, gross motor skills, speech, language and communication, school experiences, family experiences, strengths, attention and concentration, and planning and organising skills.

Is it necessary to complete a family questionnaire?

I doubt that any psychologist would refuse to carry out an assessment if parents had not completed a questionnaire, but it is in the interests of the child that the psychologist knows as much as possible about him before they sit down to work together.

How important is the information given on the questionnaire?

The questions are there for a reason. Information requested on the questionnaire might turn out to be very important in helping the EP to make a correct identification of the problem.

Some parents are very cautious about filling in the questionnaire. They worry that they may influence the psychologist and above all they want an unbiased view. I can sympathise with this. However, I would wholeheartedly advise you to be candid. Withholding information really does make the psychologist's job so much harder.

We are not clairvoyants and we do not have magic powers! Test results alone are insufficient to understand or confirm the nature of a child's difficulties.

Some parents withhold information because they do not see why it might be important, but this can be a mistake and, at worst, can mean that a difficulty goes unidentified.

Parents should also feel confident to share small niggling doubts; far from planting ideas in the psychologist's mind they may, in fact, be giving the psychologist the opening she is looking for to raise a difficult topic.

Assessment is based on evidence, but getting the right evidence and making the right judgement is a skill.

How important is the school questionnaire?

Many parents can feel a little uncomfortable about this. However, trust the psychologist! Some children are quite different at home and at school so it's good to have the wider perspective. Even if you worry that your child's headteacher or class teacher is going to give a bad report, it is still worth allowing the psychologist to go ahead and get information. It is part of the big picture. Psychologists will make their own judgement and it helps to know the way in which your child is perceived in school. If the teacher has a negative view of your child this may tell us a great deal about the way your child is being treated, and reveal more about the teacher than your child. This could be important in terms of giving feedback and advice to school.

Should I take samples of school work?

This can be really important. During an assessment there is insufficient time to get more than a small sample of writing and maths. It can be useful to see what your child is producing in school. How long are his stories? What is his spelling like when he is focusing on content? Is he having extra work or help? What does this cover? If maths is an issue, it is useful to see what he is doing in school. Is he having problems getting large untidy digits into small squares? Can he do sums of the same type but run into difficulty when they are mixed? All additional information helps with forming a hypothesis regarding the cause of his difficulties.

What will the psychologist do when working with my child?

Minimally, it is likely that the psychologist will carry out literacy tests, maths tests and an IQ test. Further diagnostic tests may follow depending on whether they are needed and appropriate.

Not all psychologists assess in exactly the same way. Indeed, within the profession there is often discussion and disagreement about what is best practice and about the use of IQ tests.

The kind of assessment procedures carried out by an EP who is working for a local authority or is employed directly by school may be different. Some EPs may only observe in class, some do not use any normative tests (i.e. tests which measure ability or level of skill compared with other children) and some use a consultative approach where they support parents and teachers but may not see the child at all.

If you are thinking of making an appointment for a private assessment you should feel confident about talking to the psychologist ahead of time to make sure that you know what to expect and are happy about it. One of the most important things is that the psychologist is able to give advice about 'what next?' and what parents and teachers need to do to support the child in question.

Below I will describe the assessment model that is used by psychologists who have worked in my practice and is most frequently used by psychologists in private practice. Although it may not be universal it does provide something against which to compare what others might provide for you if you are seeking assessment.

The tests

The IQ test

Your child will complete an IQ test. It could be the British Ability Scales (BAS) or it could be the Wechsler Intelligence Scales for Children, fourth edition (WISC-IV). Incidentally, the Wechsler IQ test originated in the USA and is used in many countries. Here in the UK it has been standardised (adapted) to ensure that it is a fair test for our particular population of children. Over time the test has been updated. The fourth edition is in use at the time of writing, but there is a fifth edition in the pipeline which will be available in the next year or so.

The WISC-IV UK is made up of ten subtests which sample ability in relation to:

- verbal ability
- non-verbal ability
- working memory
- processing speed.

The first two sample intellectual ability, while the second two pick up on information processing ability. The key reason for doing this test is to see where there may be strengths or weaknesses. Many children who are struggling or having some difficulty do not produce scores which are even across the four domains. Discrepancies may point to a specific learning difficulty. This can only be determined in conjunction with all the other information collected. It is useful to get an idea of overall ability to deal with these tests, particularly as there is a strong correlation between verbal ability and academic attainment. It gives us an idea if the child is underperforming.

Most children seem to actively enjoy completing the tests. They are quite rapid – there is no time to get bored and they are administered so that a verbal test is followed by a hands-on 'doing' test. My aim has always been to make sure that the child leaves with a grin on his face, feeling that he has done well. This part of the assessment can take between one and one-and-a-half hours.

Literacy tests

There are many reading tests on the market. The Wechsler Individual Achievement Test (WIAT) is the one that is most often used in conjunction with the WISC. This is helpful because they have been developed together and the IQ scores can be used to 'predict' how well the child should be reading. It is also well constructed and consists of four main parts.

- Word reading – for the younger or very inexperienced child the test begins by sampling his knowledge of letter names and sounds. It then progresses to a list of words which are initially simple but become longer and more difficult. The words are presented on their own and therefore have no helpful context.

- Nonsense word reading – this test is the reading of 'nonsense' words. The child is presented with a list of increasingly difficult words, none of which are real words. They are words such as 'pon', 'fum' and 'sluck', and progress to 'tellitry' and 'imational'. To be successful the child must know about the odd conventions of the English language and be able to apply spelling rules.

After the child has read through the first simple consonant-vowel-consonant (CVC) words he will find that sounding out letter by letter will not help. Furthermore, there are no clues to help the bright child guess. This test is particularly good at picking out children who are 'dyslexic'. Even the teenager who has compensated well and who gets a good score on both the individual word reading test and on the comprehension test can find this challenging and is likely to make numerous small errors. He is likely to transpose letters or to leave them out all together.

- Comprehension – in this test the child reads a number of texts. He is timed on those which he is allowed to read 'in his head'. Each text is followed by a number of questions. This picks up both his speed of reading and the degree to which he is able to process the meaning as he reads. This can be revealing. Some children with poor ability to decode can be brilliant at making sense of what they read, even if it is incomplete or inaccurate. Others struggle so hard to 'decode' unknown words that by the time they have finished the sentence they have lost all idea of what it was about.

- Spelling – the spelling section of the WIAT is a straightforward spelling test. Words are read out and the child has to write them down. They start simple with easy CVC words and progress so that the child has to demonstrate if he knows the vagaries of our spelling system.

Free writing tests

I have always found it very revealing to ask the child to spend five minutes completing a piece of free writing. There are, however, commercial tests that can be used to assess aspects of a child's written language.

Free writing provides useful evidence of many things, including:

- spelling under normal conditions (while thinking of content)
- punctuation
- handwriting
- speed of writing
- willingness and ability to write on demand.

Observations as the child writes show other useful things such as whether he:

- writes continuously or stops and stares out of the window
- changes topic or says that he has finished after two minutes
- has a good pencil grip and appropriate body posture (does he lean all over the table top?)
- writes smoothly and easily. For example, does he form each letter individually? Does the margin travel across the page as he goes down the lines? Do letters go up and down off the line? Is he leaving gaps between words? Does he stick out his tongue or chew his lip as he presses hard on the paper?

It is surprising how much you can pick up as a result of discussing a topic and watching a child spend a few minutes writing.

Maths tests

Maths is a wide topic. It involves numbers, shapes, fractions, money, weights and so on and so on. It would take hours to cover a child's skills and knowledge in relation to every aspect of maths. What the EP is likely to do is to administer a written test and also a mental maths test. The WIAT written maths test comprises sums which get rapidly more difficult and include the four basic computations, decimals, fractions, square numbers and so forth. It does give an idea of what type of written sums the child is familiar and successful with.

These maths tests are not very fine grained and produce quite crude measures, but the combination can provide helpful information which, when taken in combination with the WISC, can highlight where the child's maths strengths and difficulties lie in terms of:

- number sense
- ability to deal with maths topics which include any form of spatial element (fractions, diagrams, charts, etc.)
- the ease with which concepts are applied and understood versus reliance on rules and procedures
- the ability to work through maths procedures in a detailed and accurate manner.

The assessment will not give a detailed account of what the child can do and achieve in every mathematical domain. What it should do is identify whether there are areas of maths where some attention should be given. The chapter on maths will elaborate on this.

After the tests

Most psychologists will give the child immediate feedback. This is unlikely to be facts, figures, scores or a 'diagnosis' but some positive comments on the things he has done well and some empathetic comments on the things which look difficult. It is interesting that once the EP can demonstrate to children an understanding of their areas of difficulty and of what must be hard for them, most, if not all, children are happy to open up and discuss their strengths and difficulties in a way that would have been unlikely at the start of the assessment. The older the child, the more detailed the feedback.

The parent interview

This is the time when parents and psychologist can get together after the psychologist has read the questionnaires and worked with the child. The psychologist should start by going over the parents' stated concerns and check what they would like to achieve as a result of the assessment. Obviously not all psychologists will work in the same way, but this is what I think parents should/could expect to get out of the interview:

- Feedback on the child's test results and the chance to discuss if this all seems to be in line with the child whom the parents know and love.

- Any implication arising from the assessment. Does it look as though the child is experiencing an area of specific learning difficulty? Does this accord with the parents' views?

- Outcomes. As a result of the above, what needs to happen next? What are the child's needs and how can these be met?

In an ideal world, once the assessment is completed and the report written and dispatched, the parents will have a 'road map' to guide them through the next year or two.

So, who should attend the parent interview? More often than not it seems to fall to the mother to deal with the psychologist. This is more to do with fathers' work schedules than lack of interest, but where possible it is helpful for both parents to meet the psychologist. There are two reasons. Parents are often not on the same page. Fathers tend to be the ones saying 'If he would just pull up his socks all would be well', while mothers often take a more sympathetic approach. In such cases it is useful for both to hear what the assessment reveals. A second reason is that unless both are present they may find it more difficult to come to a shared agreement over how to tackle any difficulties identified. The implementation of suggestions, strategies and interventions takes time and effort. It is better and easier if both parents understand the importance and can lend their support and energy to make it work.

There are some psychologists who always like to include the child in this session. Personally I have not found it helpful. Children over the age of 14 are offered the option, but my experience has been that while they may have been open and outgoing providing insights into their learning in the one-to-one situation with the EP, the moment we are joined by parents they can become self-conscious and less cooperative. They would much prefer to relax, eat lunch, watch a DVD, play a game or complete their homework than sit through a session where they are the focus of attention for their parents and the psychologist.

The presence of the child also inhibits parents from saying all that they might wish to say – at least it ought to!

The report

How soon can parents expect the report?

Parents should expect this to be turned around within three weeks. It is also reasonable to ask that you can treat this as a draft and that you are able to veto any information which you think is inaccurate or that you have divulged confidentially. It is not reasonable to ask the psychologist to change any professional views or conclusions. You can ask the psychologist not to distribute the report to other people until you have read it and given your permission.

Will it be full of jargon?

Psychologist reports vary. Some communicate better and more naturally than others. Inevitably there will be some jargon, but as part of deciding who to take your child to see you could ask if you could see a sample report (with names and addresses removed). This will enable you to see how understandable it is.

Will it include advice?

You may also want to find out whether advice and suggestions will be included and whether these will be targeted very specifically for your child. If you see a sample report you can check if there are five pages of very general suggestions or whether the psychologist has made the advice as relevant as possible to the child concerned. As a parent you want specific advice that is well targeted. Most parents are likely to implement the three most important recommendations and ignore everything else if there are too many and they are not prioritised.

Should the school be allowed to see the report?

Absolutely yes, yes, yes. If the report clearly identifies an area of specific learning difficulty and includes suggestions as to how the child can be supported in class and in school it is vital that the report goes in. I strongly suggest that parents send a copy to the school and ask for a meeting to discuss the contents some time in the following few weeks. That way parents can ask what the school thinks, what they are planning to do about it and when it will be possible to review the child's progress.

The psychologist's report inevitably ends up in a filing cabinet. This means that when your child changes class at the end of the year and finds himself with a new class teacher or multiple new subject teachers and a new head of year, it is highly possible that none of these teachers will know about your child's particular difficulty and specific educational needs. Parents should feel confident to make an appointment to see the most relevant person some time early in the autumn term and show them the report. Discuss the progress so far and ask his form tutor, head of year or the school's special educational needs coordinator (SENCO) to make sure that all teachers are made aware of his specific difficulties.

Will my child be labelled and stigmatised as a result of an assessment?

It is quite natural for parents to worry that a psychologist's assessment may be detrimental to how their child is judged. However, there is much more acceptance that different children learn differently, that strengths and difficulties vary and that a specific learning difficulty label does not relegate the child to the back of the class. Any 'good' school will be pleased to have strengths and difficulties identified, particularly if they are accompanied by sound and helpful suggestions for supporting the child.

Many parents are particularly concerned if their child is about to sit an entrance exam for a new school. Should they reveal that an assessment has been done and that their child has some areas of difficulty? Should they keep quiet and only mention it if he is offered a place? This is a very personal decision and there are no right and wrong answers; however, there are two relevant points I must make:

- Do not squeeze your child into the wrong school. If he has an area of specific difficulty do not do all you can to ensure that he scrapes in by the skin of his teeth and then feels miserable and inadequate for the next seven years.

- If you show the school his report and they accept him they are, by definition, taking responsibility for him. You can expect his needs to be accommodated, and if there are ever any difficulties because of his specific learning difficulty you will not be held responsible because you withheld information. They will know what they are taking on right from the start.

What if I do not agree with the psychologist's conclusions?

It is entirely possible that you are right and the psychologist has misread the situation. However, it is also possible that the psychologist is right and you are burying your head in the sand. I remember explaining to a set of parents that I thought their son was showing many of the signs of attention deficit disorder. They had other views and made it clear that they felt the assessment had not been useful. They thought that his school was to blame for the difficulties he was experiencing. Three years later the mother phoned up. She said that they now thought that my 'diagnosis' was correct and asked whether I could send them a copy of the report that I had written at the time.

It can sometimes be hard to accept the truth about our children, particularly if information is not presented in a sympathetic manner. But however much you may dislike what you may be told, do try not to reject it out of hand – stand back from the situation and try to see how other people may view your child.

I have been aware from time to time that I am the third or fourth person to be asked to be involved in assessing a particular child. These are the parents who are willing to shop around until they get the answer they are comfortable with. This is certainly not good for the child.

I think my child had an off day and he could have done better

Parents do not always think through how important it is that their child is feeling fit, well slept and properly fed and watered when he comes for assessment. I have seen children who have been brought in sick and who have thrown up in my waiting room. I have seen children who have come direct from Heathrow straight off an overnight flight. I have had numerous children who yawn and lie on the desk and then tell me that they were not in bed until midnight the previous evening. This is not fair on the child and any test results are likely to be compromised. To be fair to the parents they may have made the appointment many weeks, if not months, ahead and are determined not to miss their slot, but more often than not little connection seems to have been made between the child's performance and his physical state. But do remember if you want your child to perform at the optimum level try and get him to the psychologist's office in a relaxed, healthy and happy frame of mind.

What shall we tell him about the assessment?

Tell him that he is going to spend time working with someone called a psychologist who sees many children and that it is the psychologist's job to work out what each child is good at as well as what difficulties each child might have in school. It is also the psychologist's job to find ways of making things easier and to find out what help would be useful for each child. You can tell your child that he will be doing some reading, writing and maths. They will do some tests together which most children really enjoy.

What about exam concessions, such as extra time and use of a laptop?

For children who experience specific learning difficulties the criteria for special provision such as additional time, use of a laptop, use of a scribe or short breaks during the exam are set out by the Joint Council for Qualifications (JCQ) on an annual basis and there are regular changes. Their pronouncements apply to pupils who are taking GCSEs and A-levels. The criteria have become more stringent over the past few years. The child in question needs to show that in one or more of the relevant areas he is functioning at a level which is well below the average mark. A report should be completed by an EP or a special needs teacher with the right qualification.

Some children are given special provision for their 11-plus and 13-plus exams and this is generally dependent on having an EP report which states that without special provision the child will be disadvantaged relative to other children. Some receiving schools are happy for the child to have extra time but others are not. To date, no criteria have been agreed, so it is really down to the individual psychologist to decide if a recommendation for special arrangements is justified.

At university the same allowances are given. Whether a student qualifies for these allowances will depend on the specific university. The best way to find out is to speak to someone in the special needs department.

Can parents get help with the cost of a private assessment?

It can be expensive getting a private assessment done, and in addition many parents cannot afford ongoing specialist help if it is prescribed. So, what are the options?

Well, as you will see, I have listed useful organisations relevant to the various difficulties described in this book, and a good first step might be to get in touch and find out if there is anything helpful in your area. There are, for example, some centres which will cover or help with the cost of assessment and specialist teaching if the pupil needs it and if the family is on a low income.

What is available through your child's school or college and from your local authority?

Let's start by looking at what schools are charged with doing. All schools have a legal requirement to publish information about their arrangements for identifying, assessing and making provision for pupils with SEN (special educational needs) within their school or college. The SEND Code of Practice 2015 outlines how this should be done and covers children and young people from birth to 25 years.

Responsibility starts with the individual teacher, so this is who you should first talk to if you have concerns about your child's progress. Let's assume that you have already discussed your concerns with your child's teacher or with the school's SENCO and that additional or modified support has already started. Once help or a particular programme is in place, staff must keep records, monitor progress and review things with parents on a regular basis. If progress is limited then consideration should be given to the best way of changing or increasing help. At this point the school may seek the advice of an educational psychologist (or other relevant professional) who may carry out an assessment or may just observe your child in class and then make suggestions. If your child is in a private school you will foot the bill, but if he or she is within the state system then there is no charge.

Once the school has given its best shot at helping your child and if he or she still seems to need more support, then the school is in a position (and has the right supportive paperwork) to request that the local authority carry out a formal assessment. If the LA thinks that there is sufficient evidence it will agree to carry out an assessment and if, as a result of the assessment, it transpires that the pupil does indeed experience SEN then the LA will issue an education, health and care plan. These are referred to as EHC plans and have replaced what were previously known as statements of special educational need.

Can parents also request that the LA carry out an assessment or does it have to come through the school?

Current legislation allows for parents to approach their LA and request a formal assessment of their child's special educational needs. Young people also have the right to request an assessment.

If the LA agrees to go ahead it will then collect evidence from a range of sources (including an EP assessment and report) and on the basis of this evidence decide if an EHC plan is warranted. The EHC plan is a document which sets out the pupil's needs (educational, health and social), specifies the resources required to meet these needs and names appropriate schools.

The exact processes and procedures can vary from area to area, though the legal framework remains the same. To find out exactly what happens in your area you can first obtain a copy of your local authority's 'local offer'. This is a document which explains all that parents will need to know about provision and assessment; it also outlines how to deal with disagreements, complaints and tribunals.

If parents require more help they can, through the LA, make contact with their local information, advice and support services (IASS; formerly known as parent partnership services). This is an impartial and confidential service for parents and is very useful. For parents who are worried about their child's education, who just do not know which way to turn and are desperate to find the right help, it can be a godsend to find an informed ally who can help to steer them through the paperwork and meetings and can explain just how things work within the local authority.

How do you know if your child might meet the criteria for an EHC plan?

According to the 2014 Code of Practice a pupil is deemed to have a special educational need if he or she:

- 'has a learning difficulty or disability which calls for special educational provision to be made for him or her'
- 'has a significantly greater difficulty in learning than the majority of others of the same age'
- 'has a disability which prevents or hinders him or her from making use of facilities of a kind generally provided for others of the same age in mainstream schools or mainstream post-16 institutions'.

As you will see this is open to interpretation and disputes can and do occur. It can be very clear if a child has a profound disability, but areas of difficulty such as dyslexia and dyspraxia are much more contentious. The bright child who is bumping along may definitely not be working to the level that reflects his intelligence but he may nevertheless be at or just below the average. He most definitely will not qualify.

What is the purpose of an EHC plan?

The purpose of an EHC plan is to make appropriate provision to meet the special educational needs of the child or young person, to secure the best possible outcomes for them and, as they get older, to prepare them for adulthood. The EHC plan will outline their needs and specify the provision required.

What kind of educational provision may be made available?

The past two decades have seen a rise in the number of children with SEN who are given specialist support to enable them to access the curriculum within a mainstream school. There are many good reasons for this. However, some parents may feel strongly that they would like their child to attend a specialist school where staff are familiar with his or her area of difficulty. There are some excellent special schools both state and private. There are, for example, specialist schools for pupils who are dyslexic, who have specific language issues or who experience ASD. If, for example, your child is assessed and is found to have literacy skills which are two or more years behind the average (despite good teaching), then you may want to fight for a place at a school which has huge experience of helping such children and whose aim is to get him back to mainstream schooling as soon as possible.

Does a local authority assessment take long?

The whole process from requesting an assessment to the production of an EHC plan can take some time. The LA must respond to a request for assessment within six weeks. If they agree the request then assessments must be carried out, reports gathered in and collated and for them to be considered by the LA. This tends to take months rather than weeks. If a negative decision is made and the pupil's difficulties are not considered significantly marked to warrant an EHC plan or if parents disagree with any aspect of the EHC plan – such as provision or named school – they have the option to make an appeal to an SEN tribunal.

If your child has already had an independent assessment carried out by an educational psychologist, speech and language therapist, an occupational therapist or a doctor, or indeed any other relevant professional, you can submit these as evidence to be considered by the LA.

Many parents can find the form filling and sheer tenacity required to get through this procedure truly daunting. To them I offer the following advice:

- Start from the position that all those you are dealing with who are working within the LA do really want to help and to do the best for your child. Do not be afraid to contact them on a regular basis to find out how things are going, but try not to get frustrated with them if things seem slow.

- Try to be as organised as you can with the paperwork. Keep copies of all reports and other correspondence so that they are easily accessible.

- Be persistent, keep in touch on the phone and, if necessary, nag.

- Make use of any relevant support groups or organisations.

Once your child has an EHC plan you may think that your job is complete but you are not there yet. The important thing is that any recommendations are put into action. Just having an EHC plan does not mean that life in school will suddenly be better. Recommendations must be implemented and parents will continue to need to stay on top, keep involved and attend all review meetings.

KEY POINTS

Independent educational psychology assessment:

⇨ It can be useful to get an EP assessment, however small and niggling the concerns. The process will help to clarify the problem, identify any underlying causes and provide suggestions as to the best way forward.

⇨ The assessment process involves the EP in the collection of background information, work and administration of tests with the pupil, feedback with parents and a written report.

⇨ It is important for parents to provide as much background information as possible so that the EP can get an idea of the big picture. Honesty is generally the best policy. Information from school is also an important part of the process.

⇨ The child should be prepared for the assessment and know what to expect. He or she should arrive feeling well and having had adequate sleep the previous night.

⇨ Tests given are generally an IQ test, literacy and maths tests and further 'diagnostic' tests if necessary. In addition, the EP will note how the pupil works and approaches tasks. The EP will look at school books and discuss strengths and difficulties with the pupil.

⇨ The pupil assessment is followed by the parental interview. This can provide valuable information and gives the opportunity for the EP to feed back and explain any findings and for the parents and EP to discuss the best way to proceed and to help the child.

⇨ A report should be expected within the following three weeks. Parents should provide a copy of the EP report for school staff.

⇨ This should be followed up with a planning meeting so that any suggestions can be considered and their implementation arranged.

Assessment arranged by the child's school and/or LA:

⇨ All schools and education establishments are legally required to publish their arrangements for identifying and assessing pupils with special educational needs.

⇨ Responsibility starts with the pupil's class teacher and/or with the school special educational needs coordinator.

⇨ If the ongoing application of special provision followed by review indicates that the school is unable to meet the pupil's educational needs with their current level of provision then the school may request that the LA carry out a full assessment with a view to obtaining an education, health and care plan.

⇨ An LA assessment can also be requested by the parents or the pupil.

⇨ If this is successful and if it results in an ECH plan, the LA has an obligation to ensure that adequate provision is funded and put into place.

⇨ Parents need to remain involved at all stages and must keep a close watch on the adequacy and application of provision.

Chapter 12

THE WISC-IV

UNDERSTANDING TEST SCORES
AND SPIKY PROFILES

All the tests mentioned in the previous chapter on assessment are known as 'normative' tests. This means that they compare a child's performance with that of other children. The assumption is that intelligence, reading skills, spelling skills and so on are normally distributed.

What does normal distribution mean?

Let's take height as a good example of normal distribution. Some people are very tall, some are very short and the rest fall somewhere in the middle, with the largest number of people around the average. Similarly, a few people are extremely clever, a few are very slow and the majority are somewhere in the middle.

If a very large number of people are given an IQ test their scores will form a curve (known as a bell curve because of its shape), as shown in Figure 12.1.

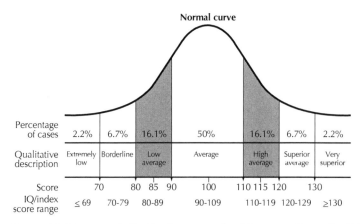

				Normal curve			
Percentage of cases	2.2%	6.7%	16.1%	50%	16.1%	6.7%	2.2%
Qualitative description	Extremely low	Borderline	Low average	Average	High average	Superior average	Very superior
Score	70		80 85 90	100	110 115 120		130
IQ/index score range	≤ 69	70-79	80-89	90-109	110-119	120-129	≥130

Figure 12.1 A normal distribution curve for IQ scores. From the Wechsler Intelligence Scale for Children® Fourth UK Edition

As you will see 50 per cent of the population will achieve an IQ score of between 90 and 110 (the average range) with 25 per cent below and 25 per cent above.

So, how useful is a single IQ score? Is it a reliable measure or does it change over time? This form of distribution works well for a single measure such as height, weight or shoe size, but isn't there more to intellectual ability? It is very reasonable to query whether a single IQ score can really represent a child's ability. What about the fact that many children have strengths and difficulties? Can it be reasonable to define a child with one score which it has taken the psychologist between one and two hours to elicit? And, anyway, do these tests actually measure general ability and how reliable are they?

These are valid questions, particularly as getting an IQ score can take on great importance for children and parents. All the tests given are highly reliable in the sense that if a child is retested his scores remain remarkably stable over time. However, I think it is important to be very circumspect about labelling a child with a single IQ score and in particular those children who are having any difficulties with learning. The reason for this is as follows.

A full IQ score is obtained when the child's results from ten individual tests are added together and averaged. Many children whom I have assessed have achieved very variable scores on the individual tests, so the average tells us little about how they actually function. In contrast, the individual tests tell us a great deal about their strengths and weaknesses.

I have certainly found the WISC to be an immensely useful assessment aid. It provides excellent data when we are looking at a child's strengths and weaknesses in relation to attributes that are central to their performance in the classroom.

Interpreting the scores to gain greater understanding

As mentioned before, the test is made up of ten subtests which are grouped into four indices:

- *Verbal Comprehension Index* (VCI) – this is composed of subtests measuring verbal abilities utilising reasoning, comprehension and conceptualisation.

- *Perceptual Reasoning Index* (PRI) – this is composed of subtests measuring perceptual reasoning and organisation.

- *Working Memory Index* (WMI) – this is composed of subtests measuring attention, concentration and working memory.

- *Processing Speed Index* (PSI) – this is composed of subtests measuring speed of information processing, hand–eye coordination and attention.

The first two indices – the VCI and the PRI – do successfully pick up on a child's level of intellectual ability, while the second two – the WMI and the PSI – are measures of how efficiently he can process, and respond to, incoming information.

The three tests which make up the VCI tests sample different aspects of verbal reasoning. Together they can show how well children can make verbal connections and how well they have understood information about the world around them. Children who excel in these tests are those who in the long term (all things being equal) do well in school exams. They most probably write well and are capable of good self-expression.

A child's performance on the three tests which make up the PRI are a good measure of his capacity to manage non-verbal concepts. Children who do particularly well here may be our engineers and architects of the future. They should find maths concepts easy to master. Those who have difficulty on the test which looks at spatial skills are often those who find some aspects of maths (fractions, graphs and diagrams) difficult to deal with.

The WMI has little to do with how clever a child is and all to do with immediate memory. Chapter 2, Working Memory, explains what this is and the way in which working memory affects how easily a child copes in the classroom. Poor scores here set off warning bells. The child with poor working memory is more than likely to have some difficulties to contend with. The child with good working memory is likely to be 'on the ball', to be quick off the mark and to be the one who you rely on to take in what you have said, remember it and act on it.

The PSI tests also have little to do with intellectual ability per se. They sample hand–eye coordination and visual processing speed and can also reflect any difficulties with concentration and attention. Poor scores on these tests often go with poor concentration and attention and/or with dyspraxic difficulties.

Many of the children whom I have assessed have produced spiky profiles. They are intellectually capable and have done well on the first two indices. For these bright children difficulties in the classroom are due to poor working memory and/or poor speed of information processing. Parents can be thrilled to find that their child excels on the first two tests. These scores reflect the fact that he is essentially a bright young thing. However, if his working memory and/or information processing skills are even relatively weak, there is a high chance that he will be struggling to demonstrate his good ability within the classroom and his school achievements will be below the level that might be expected. *Expectations need to be set accordingly and he needs to develop compensatory strategies.*

When there is a great discrepancy between the scores on each index it has not been the practice of the psychologists who have worked with me to give a full IQ score.

So, what we see is that the WISC is a useful tool to help elicit a child's strengths and weaknesses, but in reality unless his test profile is fairly even (i.e. the four indices' test scores are within ten points of each other) his full IQ score is not going to tell us much about his future performance. Used appropriately it can give good, solid data. Test results should not, however, be seen in isolation. They are just part of the assessment mix.

One last word of caution. The WISC is not a fair test to use for children whose English language skills are weak or who may be culturally or socially deprived. Performance is, up to a point, dependent on experience.

KEY POINTS

⇨ An IQ test is a normative test and compares the testee with others who are within a similar age range.

⇨ The WISC-IV comprises ten subtests, which are subdivided into four indices.

⇨ Performance on these ten subtests can give very useful information about a child's areas of strength and weakness.

⇨ A single IQ score should be interpreted cautiously, particularly when the individual test scores are discrepant and show marked strengths and weaknesses.

⇨ The WISC is not a fair test for some children. It is not fair for those who are culturally or linguistically disadvantaged.

SECRETS OF SUCCESS

If you have got this far and think that your child may indeed experience a specific learning difficulty or indeed a range of co-existing difficulties here are some important pointers to help you to take your first steps to successfully support your child.

Stop, think and plan.

➠ Do not panic, but do take this seriously. Your child is going to need your love, patience and understanding for some time to come.

➠ Remember you are your child's very best resource. You may be advised to seek the help of other professionals such as an occupational therapist or a speech and language therapist. Their input may be very helpful, but you need to be involved and to follow up on suggestions.

➠ If you have other children, a job and a busy life, you will need to sit and think carefully about your schedule and how to fit in the help that your child needs. It is my experience that parents who can manage to provide consistent, calm and low-key support over a long period are the most helpful.

➠ Even with the best help in school and from others outside school, you need to be involved. This does not mean that you have to teach him yourself if it doesn't suit the two of you, but you will need to keep an eye on progress.

➠ Do not feel overwhelmed. Set small achievable goals for yourself, as well as your child. Reward yourself as well as your child when you have achieved these.

Find out all you can about his specific difficulty and his pattern of strengths and difficulties.

➠ Read, talk to others and go on courses.

➠ Find out about your child's strengths and needs. An assessment is a good first step in looking at what he finds hard and what he does easily.

➠ Find out if there are any support groups in your area.

➠ Find out what any national organisations have to offer. See the resources list.

Think of the ways in which you can help him to remain confident and happy.

➠ Try and see the world through your child's eyes and you will be more likely to be able to help him.

➠ Never, ever talk about his difficulties to others when he can hear. I just cannot stress this enough.

➠ Give him every opportunity to do the things that he does well and to have time to master them to a point that will give confidence, enjoyment and raise self-esteem.

Build good relationships with school staff and liaise well with them.

➠ Develop a good rapport with school staff.

➠ Do not be afraid to be demanding on your child's behalf.

➠ If you get an educational psychologist report, do share it with the school.

➠ Listen to advice from teachers, psychologists and specialists and implement suggestions if they seem right and sensible.

Harmony at home.

➠ It is not unusual for one parent to take on responsibility and for the other to opt out or to feel that an undue 'fuss' is being made. Even worse, sometimes one parent thinks that all will be well if only their child would work or concentrate harder. It is important to try and resolve this issue and to share the same goals for your child. Parents need to be united.

➠ Ensure that other family members are all 'on the same page'. Make sure that grandparents, uncles and aunts understand the difficulties and support both you and your child.

➠ Stick to a routine. For many children who are reluctant to settle down to the things they are not so good at it can be helpful to make practice/homework/extra lesson times as routine as possible. If they are at the same time each day or on specific days, it can lead to less discussion. This does mean that a routine should be developed during term time.

➠ Restrict extra-curricular activities. It is tough that it is the very children who are struggling and having to work extra hard in school to keep up who are the ones that need to put in additional work at home. It is probably wise to ensure that they are not subjected to a huge number of extra-curricular activities. They are likely to be tired after a day of school, and rushing out to music or ballet or gym each night of the week is really too much.

➠ However, it is also important that the child with a specific learning difficulty does get to do the things that he is good at. It might be playing an instrument, riding a pony, playing football for a club or doing martial arts. It is important for these children to feel that they have an area of expertise which is theirs. As far as is possible try and make sure that his younger brother does not do the same activity, particularly if there is any chance that he will overtake his big brother.

➠ Do not feel embarrassed by your child's difficulties. I know that some parents feel it reflects badly on them. Many of the parents of children with significant difficulty have made a point of telling me about the achievements of their other non-dyslexic children. It has seemed to me to be their way of saying 'I can be a good parent'. I sympathise. We put great store on academic achievement and want to feel that our children are succeeding.

There will be ways in which your specific learning difficulty child will make you as proud as all the others. Just remember to value all that he does well and to let him know that you believe in him.

Part 2

THE PARENT TOOLKIT – TIPS FOR TEACHING

Chapter 13

TEACHING TIPS

Teaching our own children can be quite a challenge. We care desperately about their progress and really want them to succeed. It is always so much easier to be patient and positive when teaching other people's children! However, parents are a great resource, and if it is at all possible to find a way of working together with your child in a harmonious and happy way then so much the better. We have already looked at specific suggestions for how to help pupils who experience any one of the difficulties covered in Part 1 of the book. The tips in Part 2 are more generally relevant.

First let's start with the belief that all children of whatever ability and with whatever learning difficulty can and will learn. If there really is no progress then the teaching, not the child, may be at fault. Use a different approach.

Progress may often seem slow in some areas but do not despair. It's better to be a good tortoise than a manic hare. Do not push your child to do too much one day and then do nothing with them for the following month.

Learning does not necessarily follow an even trajectory. Spurts and plateaus can occur. It is likely that if there is a plateau in one area, the child will have been making progress in another.

One universal feature of children with specific learning difficulties is that performance varies from day to day. In his book *The Secret Life of the Dyslexic Child*, Robert Frank, who is himself a dyslexic professor of education, says that some days he gets up and knows that things will fall into place and other days he knows that there is no point in even beginning with certain tasks that are affected by his dyslexia. It is important to recognise that because your child coped well one day does not mean that he is not trying or being deliberately obstructive if he has greater difficulty the next day. Sometimes it may be better not to push.

Think about how you teach

It often seems that it matters not so much *what* a child is taught, what programme or what method is used, so much as *how* the child is taught. Above all, an enthusiastic and engaged teacher is more likely to get the best from his or her pupils. A sense of fun and a sense of humour will go a very long way to making sure that a child enjoys new learning. (This also applies to any tutors, specialist teachers or other professionals who parents may engage to teach their child.) If you become frustrated it is time to give up or to walk away.

Start from what your child knows and can do

The New Zealand educationalist Marie Clay, who developed a reading programme called Reading Recovery, set out exactly how a half-hour lesson should proceed. Each lesson or practice session, she suggested, should start with 'Roaming round the known'. I love this idea and I do think that it has much to commend it. If you start out with an activity or task which your child has mastered, it provides a sense of confidence and achievement. It is far more likely to get the child engaged and focused than starting with something which is on the cusp of being too hard. Once you have warmed up with the known then you can introduce something new or something that your child has not yet mastered.

I remember one young dyslexic child who was very difficult to 'engage'. The game I spy was used as a way of getting him to reinforce his knowledge of letter sounds. The analysis of sounds within words was hard for him, so before his mother challenged him with 'I spy something beginning with b' she would start off with 'I spy something yellow' or 'red' or 'on the kitchen wall'. He loved doing this, and by the time she threw in a 'starting with m' he was engaged and wanting to 'get it' and to outwit his mother.

Let him have some control of the agenda

Ask your child to tell you what he thinks he should be practising or learning; this will help to involve him and get him to take some ownership of his learning. It is so often mum who seems to be pushing the homework, revision or reading practice up a steep and resisting hill.

Little and often

It is more effective if teaching or practice is done on a little-and-often basis than if it is done for a long period on a less frequent basis. Practice or rehearsal of newly learnt facts or information is also more effective if the initial practice period is close in time to the initial learning. The period between each practice can be gradually lengthened. You will find more details about this in the chapter on memory.

Multisensory learning

There are different ways of presenting new material and things to be learnt, but children with a specific learning difficulty do benefit from a multisensory approach. This means being creative about the range of ways you can get them to process information. Can they see it, hear it, sing it, say it, smell it, feel it, do it? The more ways they can experience learning the more likely they are to take it in. Make use of their processing strengths.

Divide tasks into steps

Some things lend themselves to being 'sliced' into a series of steps. Perhaps your child has been told to do a particular project at home or simply told to revise. If he has not been told how to do these things he may well feel helpless and consequently frustrated and cross. You can help by showing how a task may be tackled step by step. This will often reduce any panic and anxiety.

Demonstrate how finding solutions to tricky problems can be fun

Parents can show through their own behaviour that all problems can be solved (calmly and happily). Indeed problems can be fun even if a good solution is not immediately obvious.

Allow him enough time

Children who experience an area of specific difficulty often need a little extra time to sort out their thoughts and then to find a way to communicate them. Parents should give sufficient time before they jump in to tell or do on behalf of the child.

Measure progress

It can be encouraging to find a way of measuring overall progress. You and your child might set a target or targets. It could be that he will learn five new sight words, will learn to tie his shoelaces, or will read two books on his own. He can keep a daily record of how well he has done. Try and see if you can slice progress into small increments. With the sight words this might be recording how many he has done correctly at each practice. With the reading it might be keeping a record of how many pages or chapters he has managed. The kind of records a child keeps when doing Kumon maths is a good example of measuring progress.

One aim of setting targets and measuring success is that your child will see and experience a link between his effort and his progress. It is a great moment when children see that they *can* learn and that they *can* achieve but that it does require them to work at it. The way in which you respond and give praise will also make a difference. It is best to link successes to the effort made and the work put in rather than to the child's ability or intelligence.

Rewards

Hand out stars or other rewards when he does what has been pre-agreed. If he is sitting down to homework at 5.30 with the correct books he may be able to put a star onto his star chart. Perhaps ten stars can be traded for something he wants to buy or do. Do not take stars away – find an alternative sanction if you need one.

If you issue an ultimatum or threat (it's almost inevitable that this will happen from time to time), you must follow through. There is no point in saying if you haven't fetched your reading book within five minutes you will forfeit television for a week unless you mean it and implement it.

Dealing with emotions

What about a panic or anger? Many children who are having difficulty in school come home frustrated and exhausted. They may very well have had to suppress emotions, anxiety and irritations in school, and once home they are safe to let it all out. It might be kicking the cat, winding up a sibling or throwing a wobbly when mum makes a simple suggestion. Try not to respond similarly. You can deal calmly (and firmly) with the behaviour, but it is important to acknowledge to your child that you can see he is unhappy and that you empathise. Help him to articulate his frustrations. Perhaps you can work out a better way for him to let off steam. A good go at a punch bag may be one solution.

Finally, try not to compare your child with difficulties with his siblings or friends who do not have difficulties. He already knows he has difficulty and his confidence is easily dented, even if he appears robust and bouncy.

KEY POINTS

⇨ All children, whatever their difficulties, can and will learn. If things are very slow or seem to be stuck, change the teaching.

⇨ Progress is rarely even.

⇨ Make it fun and interesting.

⇨ Start from what he knows – roam around the known.

⇨ Allow him some control of the agenda.

⇨ Teaching is best if it is little, often and multisensory.

⇨ Divide long or difficult tasks into smaller steps.

⇨ Set targets and measure progress.

⇨ Acknowledge and defuse frustrations and anxiety.

⇨ Do not compare him with peers or siblings.

Chapter 14

TIPS FOR READING

It does seem so unfair that for the majority of children learning to read happens almost like magic and yet for our dyslexic or poor readers it can often appear to be an epic challenge. It takes most children at least two years to progress from learning how to sound out short regular words to becoming fluent readers with instant word recognition. It is going to take the dyslexic child considerably longer.

There are two ways in which the young reader starts to make sense of the words on a page. She either has to learn to sound out each word or she has to learn to recognise the whole word visually. Both approaches play a part, and most children rely on a combination of both to get off to a successful start.

Phonemic awareness

The absolute key to unlocking the reading process is the knowledge that each letter has a particular sound and that these sounds can be blended together to form a word. For many children making this connection is a real eureka moment.

The dyslexic or poor reader is often disadvantaged because she is expected to sound out (match letter sounds to letter symbols) while still having poor ability to discriminate the small sounds in words. This is known as poor phonological awareness.

Most children will automatically learn to discriminate the speech sounds of their home language. All they need is normal hearing and exposure to speech. Indeed, our young children's hearing is generally particularly acute and sensitive to speech sounds. There are, however, some children who will need more focused support to ensure that they are ready for reading. This will include the children who suffer from frequent colds and catarrh and who, as a result, have glue ear. There are others who may have difficulty and who may eventually be diagnosed with auditory processing disorder. Finally, we know that poor phonological processing does seem to be indicative of dyslexia.

In view of the importance of this ability it is a vital place to focus efforts.

There are many songs, games and activities which can be slotted into everyday activities. Here are some examples, and more can be found in the games section in the appendices.

- I spy with my little eye something beginning with... This can be extended to 'words ending in' or 'words rhyming with'. (It is important to use letter sounds and not letter names.)
- Ask her to tell you which of three words start (or end) with the same sound and which is the odd one out.
- Ask her to give you a word that rhymes with...
- Give her a word and clap out the syllables together.
- Sing and clap out words together.
- Teach nursery rhymes.
- Teach tongue twisters.

Activities such as these can be fun and can be done on walks or car journeys, during meals or at bath time. Any word activities you can find which will help your child to be familiar with the sound systems of our language are well worth doing. It is not possible to overstate the importance of this.

How can you support your young reader in the early days?

If you have a child who you think may be at risk of reading difficulty or if she already seems to be struggling with the basics then it is time to give some consistent and well-planned support.

Try and fit in a reading session several times a week. I started by suggesting five times a week and then realised that for most parents this can be hard to organise, but do try and treat it as a priority. The sessions do not have to be more than 15 minutes long. Do not expect miracles, just be patient and be positive. Secrets to success are little and often and fun. I know fun may feel like a tall order, but check out the section in this book which gives tips on motivation for help and inspiration.

Remember that early reading and spelling are closely linked. Reading requires the young reader to decode words, while spelling requires her to encode words. Both activities will be difficult if she has a problem hearing the sounds in words, so you could initially work on both at the same time.

A good reading session might comprise:

- an activity which builds on phonological skills or knowledge

- an activity which teaches new, or reinforces already learnt, sight vocabulary

- time spent reading and/or spelling. This might be listening to her read, reading to her or reading with her.

Teaching phonological skills and knowledge

Let's start by discussing how to help your child to build up the knowledge of letters and letter sounds. One click onto Amazon brings up a vast range of materials designed for parents to use at home. There are games and activities to teach the alphabet, letter sounds, phonics and blending.

In school, children in nursery and reception class are beginning to learn letter sounds and will also start a phonics programme. It would definitely be worth checking out what scheme her school is following so that you can use and reinforce the same materials and approach. A well-structured scheme will also set out the best order in which to introduce letters.

- You will need to decide if you are teaching the letter name as well as the phoneme and grapheme. If you do include the letter name, be consistent. You could point out a specific letter, for example 'd'. You can introduce it by saying this letter is called 'dee' and it makes the sound 'dah'. *(A phoneme is the smallest unit of sound. There are approximately 44 phonemes in English (it depends on different accents). Phonemes can be put together to make words. A grapheme is the written representation of a phoneme. Graphemes can be made up from one letter, e.g. p; two letters, e.g. sh; three letters, e.g. tch; or four letters, e.g. ough.)*

- You also need to be consistent in the use of upper and lower case letters. It is usual to start off with lower case and introduce upper case at a later stage when the child is familiar with the lower case.

- Once she has learnt even just a few letter sounds she can start to blend these to form words. Simple regular consonant-vowel-consonant words are best.

By Year 2 (when children are six or seven), it is generally expected that they should have gained sufficient knowledge and basic skills to become good readers, so we see that gaining the basic skills to enable young readers to take off and become fluent generally happens over a two- to three-year period.

If your child is struggling and is not moving so fast as her peers, do not despair. Take things at her pace and be prepared to have to spend more time on working systematically through a programme. Once individual letters are mastered she will start to learn double vowels and initial and end blends. She will learn to 'chunk' words into groups of letters, so, for example, when she is sounding out 'animal' she will say 'an-i-mal' rather than 'a-n-i-m-a-l'.

You can use:

- magnetic letters which will stick to the bath or to the fridge. These are fun and easily available

- homemade letters which can be written on card or stuck on a big bit of paper in pasta or any other material

- alliterations. If, for example, you are working on the letter s you could match the letter to a picture of a snake and make up a sentence to go with it – Sammy snake comes slithering sneakily into the sunshine.

How to help your child to build a sight vocabulary

It can be a help in the early days of reading to learn to recognise a good number of words. Whole-word recognition on its own does not give children the tools which they need to tackle new and unfamiliar words but it can give early readers a boost if they have a bank of words which they can recognise by sight. This should be done in parallel with phonic work. Perhaps your child has already brought home a bundle of flash cards, which she has been asked to learn to sight read.

Here are a few tips for making this type of learning successful. We will look at choice of words and methods of learning.

- *Choice of words.* If you are deciding what words to use remember that it is best to start with words that look very different. You can talk about the features of visually distinctive words such as aeroplane (this is a long word with one up and one down stroke). Add in words which are very meaningful to the child (his name, his siblings' names, etc.). Do not introduce words that sound the same, such as where and were, and weather and whether. Mix nouns with high frequency words (the latter are more difficult to remember – see the chapter on spelling tips).

- *Methods of teaching.*

  » Whole words can be used as labels on objects around the house, such as bed, table and fridge. It is very likely that some incidental learning will happen.

  » Words can be written on individual cards. Start with just a few words; you could make several copies of the same word. These can be spread face up on the table and you can ask your child to identify one with a certain word on it. If she is correct, she can keep it; if she is unsure which word it is or is incorrect you can read it out loud and put into a pile, which you will keep. Once all the cards have been removed and are either in her or your pile you can start again. Spread out the pile of words that she did not recognise correctly the first time and repeat the process until she has managed to collect all the words. If this is all a bit too laboured just stop and continue another time.

  » You could also play Pelmanism with words and pictures so that she can match together picture-picture, picture-word and word-word.

  » Introduce new words very slowly, making sure she is not overloaded, and give her every opportunity to succeed.

  » Make sure that she engages with the task itself and is not looking to you to see whether she is correct or not. Some children get very adept at reading adult body language to see if they are picking up the right card. If you remain impassive she will have to start to look at the word and find strategies for remembering it.

  » The more successful she is the more confident and motivated she will be, so do not start off with 20 words all looking alike. Start with five or less words and ensure that they are visually distinctive and sound different.

Reading with her and to her

Parents have a vital role to play in ensuring that children learn to love books and to see them as a source of information, interest and joy. She needs you to read with and to her. She needs you to ensure that she can access books. This will entail you reading aloud as well as providing audio books.

I have sometimes met and worked with children who have spent years struggling to gain reasonable literacy skills. It has always felt sad when it has been apparent that this 10-, 12- or 14-year-old sees books as a source of misery, just something she has to use in order to learn to read. For these children the reading activity has come to mean reading practice and not something which can be done for pleasure or information.

Listening to her read

Make it as easy as possible for her. In the chapter on tips for teaching I mentioned Marie Clay's roaming round the known. When you and your child start a reading session, spend a few moments talking about the book and go over the story so far – what does she remember and what does she think might happen next? If you have scanned ahead you can introduce the vocabulary that you have seen is coming up. That way it will be at the forefront of her mind when she starts to read.

Whether she is 7 or 12 she needs to engage with and enjoy the book and to become confident of her ability to read. This means finding a range of books which she enjoys and which she doesn't want to put down.

The biggest secret weapon I can tell you about is paired reading. This is without doubt the very best way of ensuring that reading sessions are friction free and fun for all. Details are provided later in this chapter.

She is reading quite well now – should I continue to listen to her reading?

It remains important to share books even after she has taken off and is romping through Harry Potter on her own. There are times when children happily read books that they do not fully understand. It can be helpful if a parent can engage their child in discussion about the book that she is currently reading. This will obviously entail the parent reading the book themselves but it is worthwhile to do this from time to time.

Parents who read themselves and who evidently find it a rewarding activity are modelling the value of books, papers, magazines and so forth and are demonstrating that reading is done for pleasure as well as information.

Help during secondary school

We will look first at ways in which parents might help a child who is still really struggling and whose reading skills remain several years below age level. We will then look at support for the moderately weak reader who is able to read but who is neither an avid, fast or very fluent reader.

The struggling reader

There are a small number of children who, despite good specialist teaching, just do not make the necessary progress. These are likely to be what I can only describe as the children with extreme dyslexia. Any parent with a child who is reading and spelling at a seven-, eight- or nine-year-old's level at the time of transfer to secondary school will be extremely worried. An outline of the steps which parents may take to access an appropriate educational environment for this child is given in Chapter 3, Dyslexia, and advice on how to get help from your local authority are provided in Chapter 11, An Educational Psychologist's Assessment. What I will do here is to consider compensatory strategies and ways in which parents can try to lift some of the burden.

- She needs help to access literature. She needs easy access to the information that others are getting automatically from reading; for example, from skimming the newspapers, or absorption in a novel. Find ways in which this can be achieved. This will probably involve much reading aloud to her. Continue to seek books which are of interest to her but where the vocabulary and structure are not too complex.

- Use a paired reading technique to help with any texts she has to read for homework.

- Read onto a recording device and then listen to it to see whether listening to her own voice makes it easier to take in the information than just reading it.

- Help her to make use of technological resources and gadgets with voice recognition.

The moderate reader

Once she is in secondary school she will be expected to read for an increasingly wide range of purposes and will require help to learn how to modify the manner in which she is reading. For example, she can skim read to extract particular bits of information and read more slowly in order to fully understand a complex topic.

She will need to learn specific techniques when reading as part of her exam revision activities. For example, she should learn to highlight things to be remembered (Chapter 24, Habits, Strategies and Study Skills, gives more details).

Difficulty with reading comprehension

There are some children who for a range of reasons can read a page and at the end have absolutely no idea what they have been reading about. It may be that the child is still putting so much effort into decoding unknown words that there is little 'brain space' for her to think about what it all means. It may be a case of poor attention and concentration; she may find it difficult to keep on track. It may be due to a language processing problem or even poor working memory. Whatever the reason there are a number of strategies you can use to help support the development of good comprehension habits. It is important that children learn the habit of actively thinking about what they read, as they read it. Strategies to support comprehension include the following:

- Suggest that she reads a paragraph, then stops, thinks and highlights key points.

- Ask her a question prior to reading and get her to skim the text to find the answer.

- Work on prediction. An adult could read the introduction of a story and the child could then think of one, two or even three predicted outcomes.

- Ask her to read a short story or newspaper article and explain it in her own words.

- An alternative way of dealing with a chosen article might be to analyse it for structure. What kind of opening sentence has the author used – is it interesting and attention grabbing? How many points have been made in the article, how has it been concluded and how has the author pulled it together?

- She could learn to use a 'visualisation' technique in which she is encouraged to make a mental image of whatever she is reading about. The idea is that the content can more easily become a comprehensive whole rather than a series of sentences.

Visualisation

Here are three steps which you could go through as you teach your child to get mentally engaged with the text she is reading.

- *Show her what you mean by visualisation.* To do this read aloud from a simple book which gives easy opportunities to visualise what you are reading in your mind's eye. It could be a Roald Dahl book or something else with good word pictures. Stop after two or three sentences and tell her what you could see in your mind as you read.

- *Get her to practise.* She could shut her eyes and try to conjure up an image as she listens to you read to her. Stop after two or three sentences and talk about it.

- *Discuss.* Ask her what pictures she has been able to see in her mind. If she is finding it difficult then talk with her about the images that you have formed. You could talk about turning the story into a film in her head. Remember to be positive and encouraging even if she has difficulty to begin with.

Paired reading

- *What is it?* Paired reading is really very simple; what happens is that an able reader (often the parent, but it could be a sibling or classmate) reads aloud in unison with a less good reader.

- *Does it help children learn to read?* This all sounds a bit too easy. Can it really help children to learn to read? The answer is yes; young children who read on a regular basis using this system do make good progress and thoroughly enjoy it. A further advantage of the system is that it is a great way of supporting poor readers to access texts that they might otherwise find a struggle.

- *Where and when should it happen?* Choose a quiet and comfortable place to sit together. If at all possible try and stay away from the rest of the family so that you are not interrupted or disturbed. (For the reluctant reader this special time when she has your undivided attention can be very motivating.) Choose a time of day when she is happy to read. Do not ask her to read just when her favourite television programme is on or when she is tired.

- *How long shall we read for?* Read together for anything between 5 and 15 minutes. It is better to spend a short time reading on a regular daily basis than to spend 45 minutes once a week.

- *What will you read?* Let her choose the book that you will read together. If she chooses one that you think she will find too hard, don't worry or tell her to go and change it. Let her give it a go, and if it is too hard she will choose better the next day.

- *How to get started?* Start with some discussion about the content of the book. If you have already started a book, recap what happened the previous day. Scan ahead and informally see if you can introduce any new vocabulary that she will meet as you read. Ask her what she thinks may happen next. The purpose of this discussion is to facilitate the reading process. If she can predict the story or has just heard the vocabulary then she is more likely to make successful attempts at unknown words.

- *Now read together.* You and your child will read the book out loud together. And I mean together, with your voices in unison. You may think that unless she is struggling to sound out words on her own she will not be learning, but the evidence is that learning happens and reading improves. If you read together you will read more than she would if she were reading on her own. This means she covers more text and is exposed to more words. It also means that she can follow the story and will not lose the sense of what she is reading because of endless painful interruptions as she struggles on her own to decode an unfamiliar word.

- *Read at her pace.* It is important to read at her pace. Allow her to read a fraction of a second ahead of you (when she is reading words she can manage), but when she struggles, takes too long or misreads a word just say the word for her and make absolutely sure that she repeats it. Resist the urge to make her sound it out.

- *See it, hear it and say it.* Make sure that she looks at each word. Either one of you can point a finger at each word as it is read. It is best if she does this. It is important that she sees, hears and says every word.

All this may feel rather odd and uncomfortable to start off with, but do persevere, and soon you will get the knack of reading at the right pace and doing so in a way that she finds helpful and enjoyable.

After a period of reading together your child may feel sufficiently confident to read on her own. She can use a non-spoken sign to signal that she would like you to stop reading. She could, for example, squeeze your arm. If she misreads a word or is still struggling after five seconds then say the word and make absolutely sure that she repeats it, then continue to read together. She can signal both for you to stop reading and also if and when she would like you to start again.

When a parent and child read together in unison the parent voice acts like the stabilising hand at the back of the two-wheeler bike which the child is just learning to ride. With your hand in place she can pedal upright and soon gets the feel of riding solo.

The beauty of this system is that she can then access books of her choice without fear that they will be too hard. Reading together you can keep the pace up so that it is easy to keep track of meaning without laboriously sounding out difficult words.

Is this suitable for all children?

You can use this technique with children of any age. It is great for the young child who is making positive progress but who needs many hours of reading practice to help her become an automatic reader. It makes reading relaxed and fun.

It is brilliant for children who are experiencing difficulties. I know that many parents do find reading with their slow reader very distressing and frustrating. We care deeply, we want to see rapid improvement and we can be desperately worried on their behalf. Frustrations start when that darling child disappears upstairs to get her reading book and fails to reappear for 15 minutes. You may have lost the reading slot you were going to fit in between fetching one child from his fencing lesson and starting to cook the dinner. Frustrations continue when you finally sit down to listen to her read and she manages to sound out an easy word on the first line but then fails to read it again and again even though it appears five times on a particular page. If we are honest, many of us will own up to getting irritable and less than positive with our poor readers. It's not good or motivating for them either.

But, with paired reading, your poor reader will fetch the book quickly because she knows it's going to be fun and there will be no stopping and struggling with simple words because you will supply them. No one needs to feel frustrated!

It is particularly useful for the teenager who is a slow reader or who is still struggling. For these children the reading required in order for them to complete their homework may be the final straw after a long and tiring day at school. Parents may, however, be reluctant to read the necessary texts aloud to them but find it more productive and constructive to read aloud with them.

One final plug for paired reading is the way it enables even the weakest reader to read for fun and for meaning. This is, after all, the purpose of reading, but sadly I have encountered a good number of poor readers who have got to the point where they see reading as a miserable task which they have to do in order to learn to read.

It really is important that parents do all they can to ensure that their poor readers continue to think of books as a source of interest, entertainment and information.

KEY POINTS

⇨ Reading builds on a firm base of phonological knowledge. Work on phonological skill and awareness before focusing on actual reading.

⇨ Spend plenty of time on the basics.

⇨ Make sure that she is following a very well-structured multisensory programme. Get advice on this.

⇨ Make sure it's fun.

⇨ Practice should be little and often. Chip away and don't give up.

⇨ Do not compare her with others.

⇨ Make sure that her vocabulary continues to develop despite lack of reading exposure.

⇨ At secondary school ensure that the very poor reader has help to access texts through assistive technology or by reading with/to her.

⇨ Support the development of reading comprehension as well as reading accuracy.

⇨ Use paired reading to ensure that she is accessing a wide range of literature.

⇨ Make use of assistive technology.

Chapter 15

TIPS FOR SPELLING

Spelling is a subset of writing and we use our visual, auditory and motor skills in the process. We rely heavily on what a word looks like to check that we have written it correctly; if we are unsure how to spell a word we may slow down and try to sound it out. With practice, these words become easier and eventually the spelling of them becomes automatic.

It can take time to develop good spelling because in English we have so many exceptions to the rule. Many of our words are not spelt as they sound and all this must be learnt. So in addition to needing a good visual memory, good phonological awareness and good kinaesthetic skills, we also need to have a good memory. We need to store knowledge about spellings in our long-term memory and have the ability to retrieve this knowledge rapidly and easily as we write.

Difficulties in any one of these areas may have an impact on the speed and ease with which children learn their spellings. It is important to remember that learning to spell does take longer than learning to read, so regular, positive, consistent help is going to be the best approach. But how specifically might parents involve themselves in helping?

The purpose of this chapter is to look at ways in which parents can support their child's spelling skills and development. These tips are no substitute for a good book on the teaching of spellings (and there are many user-friendly and admirable books on the market), but it sets out suggestions and ideas which parents may find useful. The chapter covers:

- selecting words to be learnt
- techniques for learning new spellings (primary and secondary)
- over-learning
- the weekly spelling list
- spelling rules.

Selecting words for spelling

Parents may want to start a spelling programme at home to help their child improve his spellings. It may not be clear where to start or how to approach this task. A useful first step is to select the words to be learnt. Here are several ideas or approaches that could be used either on their own or in tandem:

- Look back at the child's school work and pick out the words which he frequently uses and which are spelt incorrectly. If these can be corrected then the child's written work will immediately start to look significantly better.

- Work through a list of 200 of our most high frequency words. These are easily available in publications or online.

- Select some words that relate to topics being learnt in school.

- Ask the child what he would like to learn. There may be some words which he is longing to write accurately or which have a particular meaning or resonance for him.

- Think about how you decide to group words.

- Combine words from the same word family. Word families are groups of words that have a common feature or pattern – they have some of the same combinations of letters in them and a similar sound. For example, at, cat, hat and fat are a family of words with the 'at' sound and letter combination in common. It is thought that the 37 most common word families in English are: ack, ain, ake, ale, all, ame, an, ank, ap, ash, at, ate, aw, ay, eat, ell, est, ice, ick, ide, ight, ill, in, ine, ing, ink, ip, it, ock, oke, op, ore, ot, uck, ug, ump, unk.

- Combine words with similar roots, prefixes or suffixes. For example, gener-ally, fin-ally, natur-ally.

- *Do not* present words at the same time which sound the same but which are visually different or which have confusing letter sequences. For example, hear/here, sion/tion, form/from, salt/flat.

- *Do not* present words which look the same but sound different, such as come and home, or hair and bear.

A note about high frequency words

The list of the most commonly used words begins: a, and, he, I, in, it, of, that, the, to, was. These words are followed by: all, as, at, be, but, for, had, have, him, his, not, on, one, said, so, they, we, with, you.

These may look short and easy but children find them considerably harder to learn than naming words and words for things which can be visualised. None of these useful little words above brings a picture to mind, and for that reason they can be more of a challenge to learn. It might well be prudent to mix them in with some more concrete words (dog, cat, tree).

How to do the initial learning

The first method parents might try is LOOK, SAY, COVER, WRITE, CHECK. This is a tried and tested method and does seem to work well. It works on the premise that it is better for children to write whole words from memory than to copy letter by letter. Here is how it works:

- LOOK very carefully at the target word; does it have unusual features or are there any words within the word? Ask the child to shut his eyes and memorise the word. Look at the word again, then shut eyes, say it and write it in the air with a finger. Then look a further time.

- SAY it and COVER it.

- WRITE it.

- CHECK the word. Uncover the target word and ensure that the child checks that the word is correct. If not, it is important that the whole word is written again and not just the incorrect letters.

This procedure can be repeated, and as he becomes more familiar with the word a short delay might be built in between looking and writing. Once the words are learnt they can be dictated in a list or incorporated into a dictation.

There are other ways in which a child can be helped to learn a difficult word. Some methods suit one child but not another, and this is likely to depend on the individual differences in the way they process information. Experiment with your child to find out what suits him best.

Learning techniques

Primary-aged children

- Turn it into a picture, for example Figure 15.1.

Figure 15.1 Turn it into a picture

- Trace it several times in different colours to make a 'rainbow' word. Do this in joined-up writing, saying each letter name as you write it. You will have to write it quite a few times.

- Make up a funny mnemonic for the whole word or for part of the word, for example 'does' = Dad Only Eats Sweets, or 'Thursday' = u r sick!

- Look for a little word in the big word, for example 'hospital'.

- Write the word in big letters and look carefully at the shape. How many *tall* letters are there? How many letters with *tails*? When you think you have a good 'picture' in your head, mentally take a 'photograph' and 'put it' on the wall. Then 'read' the letters out aloud several times.

- Think of another word with the same pattern and learn them together, for example 'could', 'would', 'should'. (You might have a mnemonic for them such as o u lovely duck.)

- If there are any silent letters, say them in your head, for example 'Wed-nes-day'.

The mnemonic method definitely does not work for all children. One child (who was dyslexic with poor auditory memory) wrote the word 'besse' in his English book. His teacher asked him to read it out and he confidently read the word as because. Suddenly the penny dropped. He had been taught the mnemonic Big Elephants Cause Accidents Under Small Elephants (BECAUSE) but had remembered it as Big Elephants Squash Small Elephants!

Secondary school-aged pupils

Let him try out some of the following ideas and see what works.

- Beat out syllables and write them as he says them.

- Say the names of the letters in a particular rhythm.

- Understand the derivation of words. For example, tele means far, vision means see.

- Find words within words. These may need to be pointed out. Cap/a/city for capacity or we/at/her for weather.

- Reinforce spellings by learning more than one word with a similar pattern. For example, sound, round, found or please, ease, release (as with primary-aged pupils).

- Exaggerate the pronunciation of words and make it sound funny.

- Make up rhymes or phrases to remember tricky spellings (possesses possesses five s's).

- Spell it out and stress it. I had a real problem with awkward until I learnt to spell it out letter by letter with an emphasis on the letters which are in bold – **aw-k**w-**ard**.

- Understand the structure of words and the use of root words, suffixes and prefixes. Build on the root word. For example, appoint, disappoint, disappointment, disappointed.

Spaced learning

Whichever method works best for your child try to ensure that he spells the word again:

- a few minutes later

- an hour later

- that evening

- each day for a week.

Spacing the reinforcement of learning in this way maximises the efficiency of the learning.

What is multisensory teaching/learning?

It is now common practice for children who are found to be dyslexic to be prescribed a 'well-structured, multisensory spelling programme'. We know that getting the child to engage more than one sense can aid learning.

Seeing and hearing are of course vital, but finding ways of incorporating touch and movement can also help to reinforce the learning process. Tracing letters and words in the sand, making letters out of different materials such as sandpaper or pasta stuck onto a large piece of paper and making letters and words with the whole body (walking or jumping in the shape of the letters) while saying the letter or word all help to reinforce the learning process and to make it more likely that next time it will be called up from long-term memory.

What is over-learning?

There are many children (particularly those with a poor working memory and those who are dyslexic) who have difficulty in retaining newly learnt spellings. They may work hard to learn the ten words which they are given by their class teacher each week. They may do well in the weekly spelling test but then all that has been learnt seems to evaporate overnight or indeed ten minutes later when the child uses one of these newly learnt words in a story or essay and immediately spells it incorrectly. All the effort that went into learning those words now seems a sad waste of time.

There are no short cuts or miracle cures here. But there is a solution, and that is over-learning. What we mean by this is that new words must be gone over and rehearsed many, many times to ensure that they are well and truly embedded in long-term memory but in a way which enables the child to access them fluently and easily when necessary. The difficulty is that this takes more than a week.

Over-learning will require parent and child to work together to:

- select the words to be learnt

- apply an appropriate learning technique for the initial learning

- practise them on a regular basis until they are learnt to a level where they are spelt rapidly and 100 per cent accurately.

The regular practice is what constitutes 'over-learning'. Once parent and child have selected words and gone through the initial learning to the point where the child is able to write the word to dictation the following process can be implemented.

- *Select criteria for success.* (What will he be able to do which will demonstrate that he has learnt the words to a satisfactory level?) The aim is for the child to be able to write the words accurately and at speed without having to stop and think. It is usual to aim for 100 per cent accuracy. The speed at which each word will eventually need to be written will depend on several factors such as how long the words are, the age of the child and the ease with which the child can write. An average speed of something between three and six seconds a word might be realistic.

- *Make the materials needed.* Provide the child with a sheet of A4 paper, which has been divided into a grid with 30 spaces. To do this turn the page to landscape and draw five evenly spaced lines across the page and five evenly spaced lines down the page, stopping on the bottom line. The space under the bottom line can be used to record the date of the dictation, the number of words spelt correctly and the time taken. Once the parent has drawn up (or used a computer to generate) a grid, it can be photocopied (or copied) as many times as wanted.

- *Dictate and time.* If, for example, ten target words have been selected then set the stopwatch and dictate all ten words three times each in random order. The adult can adjust the speed of dictation to fit in with the child's progress. Once the final word is written in the last space, stop the clock and make a note of the time taken. If there are 30 words and the criteria for success is, for example, five seconds a word, then the child will have met the criteria for success once he is able to fill the grid in 150 seconds (two-and-a-half minutes). It may take some time to reach this goal.

- *Corrections.* It is important that the child does the corrections himself because that way learning will occur. Give the child a copy of the correctly spelt words and ask him to check the words which he has written. He can tick them if they are right and correct them if they are wrong. The whole word should be rewritten as part of the correction process, not just the letter or letters that were wrong.

- *Recording success.* At the bottom of the page the child can record how many were correct first time round.

- *Practice.* Repeat the procedure on a daily basis until the words are 100 per cent correct at speed. Continue with this process until the criteria for success have been met for three consecutive days. At this point the daily practice should have well and truly helped to get the words stored successfully in long-term memory but in such a way that they can be retrieved when needed.

- *Check.* Check that these words have been retained both one week later and a month later. If any errors occur put the offending words on one side and ensure that they are revisited.

The beauty of this system is that the child is competing with himself (and does not risk comparison with other better spellers), and if his results are recorded on a daily basis it is easy for him to see that his spelling of these words is getting faster and more accurate. This can be highly motivating and we all know that nothing succeeds like success. The other bonus is that it does not need to take very long.

Once these ten words have been learnt, the process can be started again with a new batch. It is important to revisit the first group of words a week or so after they have been ticked off. If the child has difficulty in remembering any of them, pop them back into the practice sessions until they are reliably learnt.

Should your child be exempted from the weekly spelling test?

If your child is one of those who works hard to learn his weekly spellings but who has totally forgotten them by the next day, is it not more useful for him to spend the term learning a limited number of words so well that they become totally automatic? Is it not better that he spells a few words correctly at all times rather than fails to learn a new set of ten words each week (130 over the term) and, at the end of term, finds that none of them have been reliably remembered or accurately used in writing tasks?

There is definitely a case here for discussion with the teacher. The poor speller could either:

- work on the words which are personally most relevant and take a separate weekly test

- be exempted from the weekly test in the knowledge that a specific programme is being followed at home

- do the weekly test without the benefit of having tried to learn the words but also without being made to feel bad if many of the words are wrong.

Most sympathetic teachers will be able to see the sense in this, but it is important that the child is not 'let off the hook' and does continue to do a short period of spelling practice or learning on a daily basis.

Spelling rules

Spelling rules can be taught and applied in tandem with any of the ideas above. There are simple rules, such as magic e, which can be taught to quite young children, but there are others which are more difficult and would not be suitable until they are older.

The fact is, however, that those for whom spelling does not come naturally will have to spend time and effort learning the rules and the exceptions until they become reasonably well automated. They most definitely need help with this.

The key to teaching and learning spelling rules is to be very systematic and not to rush. There are some excellent publications that parents can use, which are easily available. The trick is to find one that is as user friendly as possible and sets out what there is to learn in a clear and easy-to-follow manner.

Topics covered include rules such as the magic e, when to double a consonant, when to change y to i, how to build words through prefixes and suffixes, plurals (leaf, leaves; tomato, tomatoes), silent letters, disappearing letters (tiger, tigress) and dropping an l (all ready, already).

If you have never experienced any problem with spelling it may come as a surprise to discover all these rules and exceptions! I must admit to having been unfamiliar with them until I observed a specialist dyslexia teacher working with poor spellers.

General tips

- Try and keep it fun.

- Ensure that spelling is seen as important but not to the extent that the child is inhibited in using words he is not sure how to spell.

- Learn the alphabet really well. Not only should children be able to recite the alphabet starting from any given letter but it also helps if they can gain a visual image, which will facilitate and speed looking up any information given in alphabetical order.

Give them letter tiles or cards and see how quickly they can arrange these on the table in front of them.

- Keep a dictionary or an iPad to hand.

- Keep an alphabetic notebook and add words the child finds tricky or troublesome.

- Play word games, do crossword puzzles and have spelling competitions such as hangman.

- Make sure you know how the word is pronounced as well as how it is spelt, what it means and how it is used.

- Encourage the use of a spelling aid – spell check for those who are working on a computer and an electronic device such as the Franklin spell check for those writing by hand.

- Make use of computer programs such as Word Shark.

KEY POINTS

⇨ English spellings can be tricky because of the many exceptions to the norm.

⇨ Parents can plan a spelling programme, which they can implement at home.

⇨ Parent and child must first select the words to be used. These could be words often spelt wrong, high frequency words, words relating to topics or curriculum subjects and words which are meaningful to the child.

⇨ Establish how accurately and fast these words will have to be spelt to be judged as well learnt.

⇨ A look, say, cover, write, check method can be used for initial learning.

⇨ There are many mnemonics that can also be used to support initial learning.

⇨ Practice should be spaced. The intervals between practices can be gradually lengthened.

⇨ A multisensory approach is important for pupils with spelling difficulties.

⇨ Over-learning helps to get new words into reliable long-term memory.

⇨ Regular practice periods should be maintained until the criteria for successful learning have been met.

⇨ The weekly spelling test may not be useful for a child with weak spelling. Discussion with the class teacher may be useful to decide how to help the child use time spent on spelling to maximum benefit.

⇨ Spelling rules are vital for the older poor speller.

Chapter 16

TIPS FOR WRITING

For many children, and indeed adults, putting pen to paper can be a painful affair. From the eight-year-old who has to write up a project to the postgraduate student writing his thesis, the process of organising information and getting it on the page can cause anguish and sometimes meltdown.

The two key elements I shall consider in this chapter are structure and content. I know only too well from writing this book (a first for me) that both can be a challenge. I also know from the children I have assessed and from discussions with their parents that for certain children the process of getting thoughts onto the page can present their biggest hurdle.

Writing is a complex business and brings together many skills that experienced writers may take for granted. These are skills that develop slowly as children progress from reception class through to A-levels and university.

Writing involves organising and planning the content, sequencing ideas and selecting vocabulary. Then there is spelling, grammar and punctuation to worry about. Conventions about where on the page to start will have to be remembered as well as when to indent or start a new paragraph. Finally, it all relies on the physical process of putting pen to paper and forming letters and words. There is a lot to learn.

There are a huge number of publications and websites focusing on ways to help your child communicate in writing. My purpose here is to provide just a few ideas. These are by no means exhaustive but perhaps they will be a jumping-off point. Of course, these suggestions need to be adapted to meet each child's current level of operating.

Different stages

Nursery, reception and infant school

Writing will of course be short and sweet as your young child starts his journey as a writer. I recently saw the photo of a three-year-old who had written her name all on her own. She looked triumphant as she held it up to the camera. Her expression was one of great pride and satisfaction. She had done her name independently and succeeded.

In the first instance, children will use the words that they feel that they can confidently write. Sophie's mother wondered if her five-year-old daughter lacked imagination when she saw in her 'writing book' that she had written, 'I like mummy, I like daddy, I like teddy.' What Sophie's mother had overlooked was the fact that Sophie had few words that she could confidently spell and that she was simply practising what she knew.

So, the first task for young children is to develop a written vocabulary which will eventually enable them to communicate ideas and thoughts. We can make the task easier for them by providing some structure:

- Suggest that the child does a picture and then writes a caption.

- Divide the page into blocks so one idea can go into each section. He might like to start with a picture in each block which he can then write underneath the picture.

- Provide sentence starters so that he can just finish the sentence.

- Provide any written vocabulary that he wants or asks for so that he can copy it.

Junior school

As he becomes more proficient at writing and develops a larger written vocabulary he will be able to write a simple story, diary or account of an event. This is when content starts to become an important element in the process.

Knowing or thinking what to say can be a stumbling block for some young writers. Parents can help through talk and discussion. Before children have to write a story, a diary or even a letter or email they will benefit from lots of chatting and talk around the topic. Once ideas and vocabulary are generated, more help may be required with structure.

Parents can now provide a more sophisticated level of scaffolding or structural support for writing. They can make a framework:

- Record his ideas; ask which he wants to use and help him to turn each into a sentence. Sentences can be numbered or given titles so that he can work systematically through.

- Suggest that he answers a series of questions based on the ideas generated. Where is the party? Who is there? What happened? How does it end?

- Talk about stories having a beginning, middle and end.

Parents can motivate the young writer by thinking up some genuine reasons for writing; a letter or email to a grandparent or godparent can add purpose and also enjoyment, particularly if a reply is received. He could help make out the shopping list or even write a story for a younger sibling. Help him to write and illustrate a large format story book for a smaller child. He can either use a word processor or hand write the text.

As children progress through primary school they will start to write for many different purposes. At each stage, parental involvement can be effective if attention is given to helping first with structure and then with content. If this is a project, the structure might be determined by a series of questions or a narrative where the structure might be worked around the story line. For example, if it is a project on the northern lights, questions might be: What are they? When and where can you see them? How are they formed? What do they look like?

If it is a thank you letter, the structure might be as follows:

- Thank you for the present/stay...

- Then something about the present (maybe what you liked) or the best bit about staying.

- Then a new paragraph about what you have been doing recently or what you are planning to do soon.

- Then you can finish.

If it is a story then it might be divided into main events or follow a structure such as setting the scene, introducing the characters, what happens and how it ends.

Secondary school

As pupils progress through secondary school the need for structure will increase. The type of writing required will continue to expand to cover more purposes. One of the clearest structures children will learn is how to write up a science experiment (aim, hypothesis, equipment, procedure, risks, results, discussion and conclusion). This provides a good example of using very specific headings and then completing, or filling in, the content. For all children, but particularly those who find it hard to write:

- talk is still really important – if he cannot say it he will still not be able to write it

- brainstorm ideas and get these written down. Brainstorming removes the pressure of thinking and writing simultaneously.

Keep a file of the ideas which are not used this time. If ideas are not forthcoming, provide some headings: 'Things I like to do'; 'Places I have been'

- record ideas. When ideas are shared verbally use a voice recorder. Students can then listen to the recording and use what they have said for their writing.

Aids to organising, sequencing and planning what to write

A graphic form of organiser is a good way to start planning. These are visual representations of the information which can be included in the writing or the information which still needs to be included. Examples are mind maps, Venn diagrams or family trees. There are a number of good computer programs designed for this purpose.

Create a framework for the first draft. Take the ideas which have been sorted onto a graphic form and decide how these can be used. Take account of the purpose of the writing.

Communicating well verbally can help with the process of communicating in writing

Ask your child to read a short story from a daily paper and then ask him to tell you about it. This might be something that can be done at home at a mealtime when there is an appreciative audience. It should remain fun, and if it is to be fair then a second person should also have to read and talk about something of their choice. The process of explaining or relaying information to an audience in a clear and concise manner can be difficult, but it is often an excellent way to learn to process information and communicate effectively. The idea is for the child to become more confident in discussing and explaining things verbally; if he learns to do this he should then find it easier to put thoughts onto paper.

Analyse the ways in which good and experienced writers structure their writing

With your child, analyse a newspaper article for structure and to see how the author has put it together. What kind of opening sentence has been used? Is it interesting and attention getting? How many points have been made in the article? How has it been concluded and how has the author pulled it together?

Keyboard use

The subject of using a keyboard to write has been addressed in the chapter on handwriting but needs to be considered here too. For many pupils the use of a laptop to complete written work has proved to be a godsend. It is not just those children who have poor handwriting who benefit. It certainly seems that when typing is automated it frees up the brain to focus on content and structure. For many children who have struggled to express themselves in writing it also seems to help them to lose some inhibitions. The knowledge that they can edit seems to enable them to get it all out and onto the page without worries. I have certainly met and worked with teenagers who can write the most wonderful prose using a laptop but whose handwritten work is not only difficult to decipher but also lacks fluency and quality.

Proofreading

Accurate proofreading is a challenge for many adults as well as children. There are, however, a number of strategies which parents might consider teaching their child. These will need to be used appropriately for stage and age.

- Do not proofread immediately or you will only see what you intended to write.

- Read it aloud. This helps to show where the full stops and commas should be and it helps to identify any omissions, wrong words or strange grammar. It also helps to see if it all makes sense.

- Mark the words that need correction. Read the whole text and then start to correct. Use a dictionary if necessary.

- Check handwriting. Is it legible for others to read? Does it need to be rewritten by hand or would it be better typed?

All the while it is worth remembering that learning to write and putting thoughts on the page is a complex business and there is much to coordinate. It takes time, patience and practice to succeed.

KEY POINTS

⇨ Writing brings together many skills: planning the content, sequencing ideas, selecting vocabulary, spelling, grammar and punctuation.

⇨ In the early days, children can be helped through prompts, ideas and scaffolding.

⇨ Ideas can be generated through much talk, discussion, events and experiences.

In secondary school:

⇨ Writing style changes for different purposes.

⇨ Generating ideas still needs talk, experiences and discussion. Ideas can be recorded.

⇨ Mind maps can be used to help organise content.

⇨ The writing of good writers can be analysed and discussed.

⇨ For some pupils the use of a keyboard is very liberating.

Chapter 17

HANDWRITING TIPS

Schools may differ in the way that they teach handwriting and in the importance they place on this skill, as well as the time devoted to it. Regardless of these differences, handwriting does need to be taught and it is not just the school that can influence outcomes; parents also have a role.

There are three key objectives. If children are to communicate effectively in their written work then their handwriting should be legible, fluent and carried out at a reasonable speed.

Letter formation

It can be helpful to guide young children into forming letters correctly from very early on. It is easier to do this than to have to correct bad habits later. There are plenty of simple books on the market that will take parents through the conventions of correct letter formation.

For example, for circular letters, such as a, c, d, e, g, o and q, start at one o'clock and follow round in an anti-clockwise direction. Upright letters nearly all start at the top and come down: b, h, l, k, n, p, r, t, u.

Young children can start by doing letter patterns which lay the foundations for correct formation well before they start formal writing. They can, for example, trace along a line of circles, uprights or an unbroken line of w's or u's or lower case e's in a special book. They can paint letters in bold colours. They can trace them in the sand. There are many ways in which they can start to get these patterns into muscle memory which will in turn help to automate the process.

If your child is already writing and you notice that he is forming letters in an unusual manner, you could first speak to the class teacher to find out what method is being taught in school. Find out if there is a handwriting scheme and see if you can access a copy. See how this is implemented in school and ask how you can reinforce things at home. Correct letter formation facilitates cursive (joined-up) writing.

Figure 17.1 How to complete different types of letters

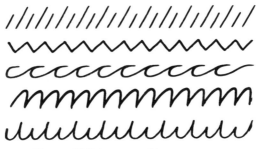

Figure 17.2 A range of letter patterns

Pencil grip and the use of different writing materials

It is much harder to write fluently with an incorrect pencil grip. The correct one is a tripod grip whereby the pen or pencil is held between the forefinger and thumb while resting lightly on the middle finger. It is considerably harder to write fluently with other grips. To get children started off in this position may require parents to experiment with pens, pencils or crayons of different thickness. It is also possible to buy triangular pencil grips which will slip over the pencil and grip onto it where the child holds the pencil. This also ensures that the child holds the pencil shaft in the correct place and not too close to the top or bottom, as well as placing the fingers in the right triangular position. Some children may find this harder than others.

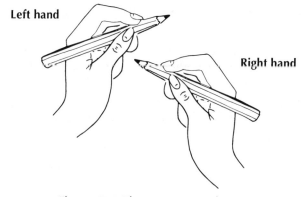

Left hand

Right hand

Figure 17.3 The correct pencil grip

Correct body posture

The physical process of writing involves the coordinated movement of fingers, hand and arm as well as the rest of the body. A child is going to find it easier to adopt the correct posture if the table and chair are the right size and height. The ideal position is with both feet squarely and firmly on the floor. The paper can be turned slightly to right or left depending on whether the writer is left or right handed. There should be ample room on the pen side so the child's hand is not cramped or brushing into a neighbour or other obstacle.

Figure 17.4 The correct body posture

Using the optimal writing tool

Pencils should not be too hard. Fountain pens should be kept as a goal and a treat for when a good level of skill has been achieved. They are not easy to handle because of the variable friction of the nib on the page, though the Lamy pen is, in my view, excellent (for children and adults). Biros and ballpoint pens are not conducive to great handwriting either. A roller ball, such as a Berol pen, is good for most children. The friction is even and it flows smoothly and easily; it is clean and does not smudge.

What can go wrong?

Already we can see that there are a number of potential areas where a child may experience difficulty with writing if instructions and opportunities to practise have not been forthcoming. There are other things which may also affect writing legibility and fluency:

- a move from one school to another and a change of style
- poor fine and gross motor skills
- physical disability
- poor vision
- low motivation.

Indeed, difficulties may result from a combination of factors.

What can parents look out for?

As writing skills progress there are a number of things which parents can keep an eye open for in relation to the quality of the writing. Your child's writing may contain the following:

- a mixture of printing and cursive writing on the same line
- writing which slants in one direction and then another
- letters which differ in size
- letters which wave up and down off the line
- inappropriate and mixed use of upper and lower case letters
- a margin which creeps across the page
- words which are squashed up against each other
- irregular gaps between the letters.

Some children tend to write very slowly or spend hours trying to produce a perfect result. This can involve endless rubbing out and anxiety. Any of these difficulties may be indicative of an area of specific learning difficulty.

Physical difficulties

The following are signs of physical difficulty:

- a tendency to flop over or lean on the desk rather than sit upright
- a tendency to be fidgety while writing
- other associated body movements, such as a wiggling foot or mouth movements
- the pen being gripped very tightly
- difficulty in performing simple repetitive hand or finger movements.

Children with poor core strength and stability are likely to find it hard to maintain an upright position and these are the children who end up with their head on the table. They can find writing extremely tiring. Some children have difficulty in relaxing or mobilising their shoulder or arm and this can impact writing. Some have a stiff hand or simply have very poor hand control.

Some children cannot disassociate the movements of other parts of their body as they concentrate on writing. It might be that their mouth moves in unison with their writing or that a tongue appears as they concentrate. These physical oddities and difficulties with writing are very common for pupils who are dyspraxic.

Poor vision

If a child has any form of impaired vision it may affect handwriting. Alice was visually impaired, and her field of vision was restricted. In order to keep her writing within her field of vision she made it very tiny. Her teachers did not understand this and she was frequently told to write larger.

Very slow writing

This can need some careful unpicking. It may be a result of problems relating to the physical aspect of writing; however, it could be difficulty in planning and thinking about the content, it could be lack of motivation or anxiety, or it could be a combination of all the above.

Who and what can help?

If difficulties with writing seem to stem back to something physical, if, for example, there is a very tight pencil grip, if the whole process looks really awkward, if posture is poor and if he 'hates' writing and is getting tired, then seek the advice of an occupational therapist or a physiotherapist. They can judge if there is an underlying physical problem and can also provide therapy and suggest activities and exercises which will help ameliorate the weakness. They will also know if the use of special equipment such as a sloping desk or wobble cushion would be helpful.

Poor or slow handwriting may affect homework and may also be causing problems for a child in school. The key aim is to try and ensure that poor writing does not become a barrier to learning and performing. It can be frustrating for the bright child to find that he cannot get his good ideas down on the page within the allotted time or to find that he constantly gets negative feedback about the quality of his writing rather than the quality of the content. His work may be deemed as inadequate, too brief or too untidy or messy. This can be dispiriting for the child who has put his heart into the content (also see the chapter on dyspraxia).

It is certainly worth liaising with school staff to see if you can get teacher involvement in finding solutions. For example:

- Can homework be moderated? There can be a dilemma for parents if their child cannot get homework completed in the suggested time limit. Should the child spend three times as long as everyone else or can he concentrate on producing his best within a time limit?

- One solution might be for the parent to act as scribe, particularly if the content is more important than the presentation. That way the child will be able to focus on ideas, information and what he wants to communicate. Check if the school will allow this.

- When writing activities are taking place in the classroom, it is helpful if the teacher is clear about how much is expected. Perhaps the child could be asked to do a short but interesting page of writing. If it is within his capability at least he can earn a star or good verbal feedback and gain a feeling of satisfaction.

- It is also more motivating if the pupil has a sense of the purpose of his writing.

- Are there other ways in which the child can communicate his answer or ideas? Could he use a picture form or voice recorder?

Children can be helped to understand that the quality and legibility of their writing can be legitimately variable. We all use different scripts for different occasions. None of us do our best italic script for the shopping list.

Writing and dyspraxia

Poor or illegible handwriting is a key indicator of dyspraxia. The younger child is likely to have difficulty with the physical aspects of writing, and the older child may continue to have poor handwriting but is also likely to find it hard to plan and organise the content (see the chapters on dyspraxia and study skills). For these children typing is a godsend.

Keyboard skills

Typing is the very best solution for some children. For the pupil with writing difficulties due to dyspraxia or other related physical difficulties the initial process of learning to type may be arduous and painful; however, perseverance pays off, and I have yet to meet a student who did not feel liberated by touch typing.

Once the process of typing becomes automated it seems to free up the brain to focus on the other higher-order processes involved in completing a written assignment. Spelling seems to improve. The immediate feedback which comes when misspelt words are highlighted is one factor, the ease with which the pupil can read things back helps, and corrections can be easily made without making the text look even worse.

Many poor writers are able to write neatly and reasonably rapidly for a brief period but cannot sustain this. Their hand begins to ache or the writing deteriorates and slows down. They do not experience such difficulties when typing.

Students enjoy the fact that they can throw their ideas down fast and then edit. As Abigail said in the chapter on dyspraxia, the summer holiday break which she used to learn to touch type was time very well spent.

Children who have been identified as having a physical impairment or dyspraxia can be given special dispensation to use a laptop for exams. This includes GCSEs and A-levels.

There is a school of thought which suggests that teaching typing with all fingers is unnecessary and that many children can text and type just as fast with two or in whatever way they have taught themselves. As a touch typist I find this hard to believe but have not run trials to see whether they are able to type as fast as the typist using both full hands. In any case, I would advocate aiming for full use of all fingers.

I have quite often encountered parents who say that they do not want their dyspraxic child to learn to type until he or she has learnt to write better. These skills are not mutually exclusive and it seems unnecessary to make the dyspraxic child's life harder than it already is by waiting until handwriting is perfect. Typing can be started by the age of eight or nine years.

Finally, writing can be an art form. A short course on calligraphy or italic writing or even a visit to see old manuscripts might just open up a child's mind to the pleasure and enjoyment of learning how to produce an attractive style of script.

KEY POINTS

For the younger child in primary school:

⇨ find out if the school is following a particular handwriting scheme

⇨ ensure that letter formation is correct

⇨ make sure that he is sitting correctly and that the table and chair are at the right height

⇨ provide the most appropriate pencils and pens.

If the handwriting of a child of any age is poor:

⇨ analyse handwriting for different kinds of error

⇨ consider any particular causes of poor writing, for example poor physical control, poor vision, too much focus on content

⇨ consider the best ways of supporting your child through moderation of work and homework, scribing for him or using a voice recorder

⇨ seek an occupational therapist's assessment

⇨ encourage the acquisition of keyboard skills at the appropriate age and stage.

Chapter 18

TIPS FOR MATHS

The aim of this chapter is to help parents to think about the way they address maths with their children. Many parents can feel panic rising at the mere thought of maths. Their own experiences may have been miserable and on top of that the way maths is taught today can seem incomprehensible. The terminology may seem alien and the methods taught confusing.

Despite all this you do have the knowledge and skills to help make your child's experience of maths both fun and accessible. You can help to boost your child's confidence as a mathematician and you can help your child to make connections, to engage in systematic problem-solving activities and to find the links between maths and real-life situations. You can help to ensure that he has a grasp of the mathematical concepts which underlie the maths processes and procedures he will be taught.

The suggestions and ideas in this chapter are accessible for any parent, even the most maths averse. Just remember, you know more than you think you know; after all, in addition to your own working life you are running a household, paying the bills and calculating the best deals and the amount of fabric you need for new curtains!

This chapter does not aim to show parents the nuts and bolts of how to teach their children long division or calculus or to cover the national curriculum. There would be far too much to cover, and anyway others with specialist knowledge have already done a much better job than I could. There are some brilliant resources to guide parents through the thickets and bamboozling jungle of algebra, geometry and trigonometry. Some are listed at the end of the book.

What is the point of maths?

We need to ensure that children can see that there is a point to maths and that it is not just endless pages of identical sums that need to be got through. But perhaps a reminder to ourselves is needed first:

- Maths can be fun. Children can be helped to engage enthusiastically with many maths activities through games, challenges and puzzles.

- Maths helps you to solve problems like calculating best deals and how many packets of crisps you need to get for your birthday party.

- Maths is important for future lives and careers. A good foundation in mathematics is fundamental to many areas of study and practice, from engineering and architecture to science and accountancy, and, of course, includes computer science and software development.

- Maths is the language we use to quantify the universe, and it is as essential to our understanding of our physical and metaphysical world as language.

Your six-year-old may not be ready to appreciate the full beauty and benefit of maths but will love to have opportunities to explore maths activities (without a clue that he is doing maths). By the time your teenager is choosing his subject areas it would be good if he was aware of the way in which maths permeates life in the 21st century. He may not be fully aware of just how much maths is involved in a great many professions and occupations. He may need to be reminded of this fact, or helped to work out where maths is needed, when he is moaning that it is all pointless and that he will never, ever, be needing geometry again after he finishes this year's exams.

So whether we like it or not, maths is important, and since there is really no way of getting around that fact we may as well do all we can to help children discover the pleasure that mental engagement and challenge can bring as well as enable them to do their best without fear of failure or sense of inadequacy.

Maths involves understanding – it is not just about following procedures. You can do much to ensure that your child enjoys and engages with experiences that will help his understanding of maths so that he is not left following a monotonous formula.

We need to start at the beginning. Maths is cumulative and good strong foundations are all important. There is much that parents can do to lay these mathematical foundations.

Numbers and counting

Parental influence is much in evidence even before children set foot into the nursery or infant class. The basis to all mathematics is numeracy. Numeracy is the ability to count and to manipulate and work with numbers. In the early days there is no such thing as too much counting! Counting out items with your child one by one, whether they are stairs, beads, fingers, people or whatever, will help establish one-to-one correspondence. In the first place it's important to link counting and numbers to concrete objects, whether it's how many socks to go into the wash, sorting beans or Smarties into groups of twos, threes or tens, or playing with a giant abacus. The abacus is a great visual aid to seeing that 1 and 9, 2 and 8, 3 and 7 and 5 and 5 all make 10.

As children get an understanding of numbers, counting can get more complex. Try counting in twos, fives or tens. As they get older, counting can become more sophisticated. It can go up in 100s or 150s – whatever number you choose. Children need to learn to count on from a number and to count from one decade to the next. As they get more proficient they can count down in ones, twos or threes.

Dominoes is a good game for early recognition of number patterns. Card games also present many opportunities for recognising numbers as well as for rapid addition, sorting and sequencing. Poker can rapidly become a favourite. A dartboard (with magnetic darts) brings challenges with scoring. A game of table tennis needs the ability to track the score and to know when the server will change.

Practical activities such as helping to lay the table will involve informal multiplication. How many mats are needed? How many knives or spoons?

From nursery through to primary school there are a multitude of activities which are helping children to learn and consolidate their ability to manipulate and manage numbers.

Most children seem to have an innate capacity to comprehend numbers; they will readily learn to count, to group and order quantities and to estimate what the answer to a question might be. There are some children, however, for whom this does not seem to come naturally. These are the children who are now thought to experience dyscalculia (see Chapter 5, Dyscalculia and Other Maths Difficulties) and they will need a great emphasis on these early number activities to really help them get a 'feel' for and an understanding of numbers.

Mathematical language

It is important to attach language to counting and other maths activities. For example, help the child to become familiar and to understand the concepts of more than, less than, add and take away; focus on the mathematical vocabulary which will emerge within the maths curriculum. A conscious look at the many and varied words which we use to denote a single operation such as 'take away', 'subtract', 'less than' and 'minus' is also important. These are the words that can cause confusion in the classroom.

Maths language is not restricted to number. Help the child to learn the vocabulary of shape, size and quantities. Always remember that the words must link to experiences, objects or actions.

Visual/spatial experiences

One great mathematician described how, as a child, he had few toys, but because his father was a builder he was surrounded by bricks. These were his playthings. He claims that they were influential in the development of his mathematical brain and mathematical thinking.

The opportunity to handle and to play with toys that have a spatial dimension, such as Lego, is vital. If the only way to encourage your daughter to play with Lego is to get pink Lego, then get pink Lego. Building bricks and any type of construction toy will also enhance a child's understanding of how things fit together and the different properties of shape.

In Chapter 5, Dyscalculia and Other Maths Difficulties, I outline the importance of spatial awareness in relation to many maths activities. Pupils who have poor visual/spatial capacity frequently struggle with fractions, decimals and geometry and can find it difficult to deal with graphs, maps and coordinates. These pictorial representations are more easily grasped if the child has a real feel for the concrete. So, plenty of opportunity to play with and to get a real feel for concrete objects can feed into the ability to work in the abstract and to understand the symbolic representations which will crop up in maths.

Children can learn from playing with jigsaws, tangrams, Rubik's Cubes and objects which are made of parts which can be arranged and rearranged. Even a square of card can be cut into symmetrical parts and given to the child for reconstruction. This kind of play can work for an individual child or small group working together.

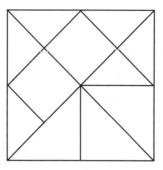

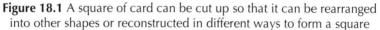

Figure 18.1 A square of card can be cut up so that it can be rearranged into other shapes or reconstructed in different ways to form a square

Understanding volume and capacity

Children will absorb much from playing with water and sand. They will tip water from container to container and learn about volume and conservation. They will discover if the tall thin container holds more, less or the same as the short fat container. This experimental, exploratory play should continue into primary school but can become more sophisticated. Again, add in appropriate vocabulary to reinforce knowledge. Ask questions such as: How many cups of water will it take to fill the watering can? Which container will hold the most sand? How much water do we use in our household each day? As they get older and start to want to help in the kitchen, use the time cooking together to help further knowledge of weights and measures. Cooking also provides a wonderful opportunity to reinforce the importance of planning ahead and of good organisation.

Patterns and relationships

Maths also involves patterns and relationships. In fact, pattern is really at the heart of mathematics, and any serious mathematician would tell you that maths is the study of patterns or that it is a set of connected ideas.

Each times table follows a pattern. If, for example, you give your child a series of numbers, say 2, 4, 6 and 8, can he work out the relationship between each number? Can he see that if you add 2 to 2 you get 4, if you add 2 to 4 you get 6, if you add 2 to 6 you get 8 and that the rule is to add 2 each time? The trick is to find the rule which will tell you what will come next. Children can enjoy looking for the rule they need to apply to complete a sequence or to repeat a pattern.

Try giving him materials such as coloured pegs on a board or a box of buttons, or even a ball of string and some scissors, and ask him to play around and come up with his best idea for playing with or using these materials. What patterns can he make? How might he describe this pattern? He may even be able to pose a maths question or a set of rules based on his play. Learning experiences in which children come up with their own ideas and thoughts are very valuable.

Sorting and grouping

Can he sort by colour, size, shape or by number of corners? He can help to sort items for laundry, or the animals on his play farm. Sorting can present special problems. How can he deal with problems such as when it's necessary to fit some items into more than one category? Maybe he is sorting farm animals according to whether they are brown or white, but what is he to do with those that are brown and white? Sooner or later he will hopefully create his own Venn diagram.

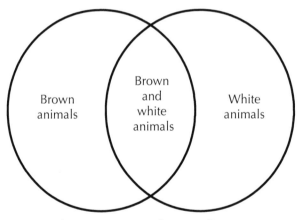

Figure 18.2 A simple Venn diagram

The average household has immense scope for finding practical activities which will enable children to build up experience, language and concepts which will help him once formal maths learning is under way.

Make use of experiences

Get him involved in adding up (or estimate) your shopping as you go round the shop or to check your change. Get him to work out best value. Can he help you work out the cost of a holiday or a train journey?

Use visual aids to help him with time

Mark birthdays and events onto a wall calendar. Put up a weekly timetable. A timeline on the wall of his bedroom can help to give a mental image of historical events.

Problems, challenges and puzzles

In her book *The Elephant in the Classroom*, Jo Boaler tells the reader about Sarah Flannery, a young woman who became European Young Scientist of the Year for inventing a 'breathtaking algorithm'. As a child, Sarah and her siblings loved the puzzles which their father would regularly give them. These were puzzles which challenged their thinking, encouraged their curiosity and made maths interesting. Boaler goes on to stress how important puzzles can be to mathematical development, 'especially if children are encouraged to talk through their thinking and someone is there to encourage their logical reasoning'. Start with something such as: 'How many adding sums can you make that end with the answer 21?' This could be extended to include multiplications. Give him a number and ask him to make up a question to which it is the answer. Can he make up more than one question? Or find a source of good problems such as the one below (answer at the end of the chapter).

The two-jars problem: Given a five-litre jar and a three-litre jar and an unlimited supply of water, how do you measure out four litres exactly?

Questioning and talking it through

When a child writes a story it would be a strange parent or teacher who looked at it, put a cross against it and told the child that it was wrong. We would be more likely to comment on the good points and discuss ideas for improvement or extension. Maths, however, tends to be correct or incorrect. It can be disheartening for a child to get a cross and told to return to the drawing board. It can be more fruitful to talk with the child and to ask him to explain how he had done the sum, what he had been thinking about and how he had worked it out. That way it may be possible to see if he has been going along the right track and where he may need a steer to a better solution. He might have been very close to the correct solution.

Unlike the class teacher who is trying to support 30 or more children, parents have the luxury of sufficient time to investigate how and what their child is thinking. Good questions can guide a child's thinking. What do you think would happen if...? Can you think of another way to do...? Questions will help you to find out what he knows and what he needs more help or practice with. Ask him to explain things to you; after all, teaching is the best form of learning, so see if he can put things into his own words. It is as important (or possibly more so) to listen carefully as it is to talk or explain.

Stay relaxed

Any interactions around maths should be kept light and relaxed. Getting things wrong is not a problem. If we never got things wrong we would never learn. This is a message children need to hear, and their experiences must show that it is true.

It is not just during the primary school years that hands-on, practical experiences are of great value. The time when this was really brought home to me was during the year I spent studying for my Postgraduate Certificate of Education. I was fortunate to have a great maths tutor. The maths curriculum was brought alive with numerous maths games and challenges. We played games illustrating probability and chance; we carried out activities which enabled us to find the rules that governed algebraic formula. We cut things out and rearranged them until tessellation (an arranging of shapes which fit together) and geometry were seen in a new light. We had the satisfaction of experiencing many 'aha' moments when the light dawned and connections were made. For the first time I really wished that I had had more and better maths of this kind in my formal education. It most certainly underlined for me the very real value of practical, hands-on experience coupled with challenge. For the first time ever I found myself totally engaged in thinking and wanting to find the solution, to see the pattern and work out if a formula would fit. The frustration of not being able to get to the right answer was replaced by the challenge and delight of trying to work things out. It was an experience that we owe all our children in the maths classroom.

Parent involvement during secondary school

There are 20 million more jobs, we are told, for people who are mathematical problem solvers. It has never been more important to encourage our teenage pupils to stick with maths. Issue number one may be convincing your child that maths is a subject worth working at. He may not be aware of how widely it is applied in this day and age. Do you have friends or colleagues whose work involves maths who can inspire him about what they do? Even if he really is not likely to be taking

A-level maths, it's still important to find ways to link maths to real-life situations so he can see the value of the subject.

Fortunately there seems to be a move towards making the teaching of maths more relevant and engaging. Let's hope that, with your encouragement and that of his teachers, your child has come through primary school feeling confident and capable where maths is concerned.

But, now you and he have secondary school maths to get engaged with! This may definitely seem to be a step too far. Parent involvement at this stage can be difficult because teenagers may not want parents fussing over maths homework, even though they may be stuck and frustrated. Also, because they may be stuck and frustrated, they are not going to be easy to work with.

However, there are a few rules of engagement which may help to make it all manageable.

Prepare ahead

Check the curriculum. Read up on methods. Yes, this is a challenge, but there is a great deal of readily available information which parents can draw on so that they understand what their children are learning. I have listed some helpful books and websites at the end of this book. It is simply frustrating for the child if the adult has to laboriously look things up while he is left to fiddle with his protractor.

Keep an eye on homework

Parents should keep an eye on homework as this may be the first place where it is evident that something is going wrong or has not been understood. It is easy to blame the teacher when a child is having a hard time with maths, but teaching maths to a class of 30 children can be a real challenge. There is so little time to devote to an individual child who has got a bit stuck or just cannot understand what they are meant to be doing. Remember also that in primary school your child's class teacher is not a maths specialist. If you think that there is a real problem do discuss it with school staff.

If he is stuck, do not give the same verbal explanation six times with increased volume. Can you think of coming at it in another way? Can you use physical materials and different forms of representation? Pictures, diagrams…talk to him and ask him what he thinks. Can you see where he is coming from?

Take sufficient time for explanations. Some children only need a 'hint' and they can work things out for themselves, so do not go on and on if he is no longer listening. Observe your child and see how you and he can work together in a way that does not frustrate either of you. You are his role model.

If you do indeed feel panic rising or some other negative emotion, it is time to stand back and decide how to handle it. There is no point in transmitting these feelings to your child. There are several ways in which you might manage the situation:

- Talk to his teacher and find out the curriculum for the term or the year. Find out what methods will be taught and what is expected. Ask if there are any publications which could help you. You could check the national curriculum for maths. It is easy to access online.

- Carve out time to support and help your child. Make sure that he is not doing maths homework and asking for help just as you are cooking the dinner.

- If this is just too much then enlist the help of another relevant adult either within the family or neighbourhood and make sure it is someone who has better maths skills than you do and who has the ability and attitude that will ensure that your child feels positive and enjoys the sessions.

- Whatever you do, and this is the advice of many maths experts, never say to your child 'You must be like me, I am hopeless at maths' or 'Never mind, I could never manage maths either'.

- Please remember that girls are no less capable than boys. There is no inherent gender difference relating to maths ability.

Rote learning

I am going to end this chapter with a few words about rote learning. It may seem to fly in the face of all that I have written so far about the value of experience and hands-on exploration of maths. However, even though the value and importance of rote learning is a little controversial, there are many advantages to learning times tables and basic number facts until they are absolutely automatic and known so well that the answer can be found without thinking or without using any mental energy.

This automatic knowledge proves immensely helpful when children are engaged in more complex computations. If, for example, a child is doing a four-step problem and one part requires him to multiply 5 by 7, it is quick and efficient if he just automatically 'knows' that the answer is 35 rather than having to stop and work it out. Working it out takes time and mental space. While he is working it out he may well forget what the overall sum is about, particularly if he has poor working memory.

Some children need more practice than others but this kind of learning can so easily be done on a car journey or sitting on the bus. Times tables can be sung and chanted. Times tables can be written up on the child's bedroom wall. Quizzes can be fun but make sure you do not drill and kill. Try and ensure that it is not all verbal. Work to your child's strengths. Is she better at remembering verbal information or is she better as visualising and learning from writing, chart, picture or diagram? Always make it fun and do not rush the child who needs to go over and over the same material many times before it really 'sticks'. Over-learning can be of particular help to children who have poor working memory. Finally, don't forget that learning can be helped if you take a multisensory approach. Let her hear it, say it, feel it, sing it, make it, do it.

The Kumon maths approach can also be used to reinforce basic facts. The fundamental success of Kumon is that it is repetitive. The child does the same worksheet over and over until it is done accurately at speed. Daily improvement is highly motivating for the child. The child can see learning and success. He is only competing with himself and yesterday's performance, so he need not feel that others are better. If he keeps a record of his performance he can see his improvements.

Even good mathematicians can experience difficulty in getting times tables and number bonds to stick. It's important to remember that difficulty in these areas does not equal a bad mathematician. Your child with the poor memory may have a good grasp of maths concepts, good spatial skills and be a great problem solver. Not only is it important that parents do not equate poor learning of number facts with poor mathematical ability, it is vital too that these particular children do not start to think of themselves as being hopeless at maths.

KEY POINTS

⇨ Parents often know more than they think they know.

⇨ Maths is fun, helps to solve problems, is important to adult life and it is the language we use to describe the universe.

⇨ Maths needs firm foundations based on experience of handling materials along with parental involvement, discussion and introduction of maths language.

⇨ Maths involves an understanding of numbers, visual/spatial information, volume and capacity, patterns and relationships, and an ability to sort and group.

⇨ Children build understanding through concrete experiences, the use of visual aids and engaging with problems, challenges and puzzles.

⇨ Good questions and talking things through can enhance a child's understanding.

⇨ Parents should stay relaxed and make sure that their involvement is not a cause of friction.

⇨ Parental involvement with maths at secondary school may be more of a challenge for some; however, those who can should remain involved.

⇨ The secret to success is to plan ahead, keep an eye on homework, take sufficient time to help, liaise when necessary with school staff and enlist help if things are not working out.

⇨ It can be useful to rote learn times tables and number facts, particularly for pupils with poor working memory. The automatic knowledge of times tables will reduce memory load.

Answer to the two-jars puzzle from earlier: Given a five-litre jar and a three-litre jar and an unlimited supply of water, how do you measure out four litres exactly? There are many ways to find a solution but here is one.

Fill the five-litre jar. Pour the water from the five-litre jar into the three-litre jar until it is full. You have two litres of water remaining in the five-litre jar. Dump the water out of the three-litre jar. Then pour the two litres of water from the five-litre jar into the three-litre jar. Now fill up the five-litre jar completely. Pour water from the five-litre jar into the three-litre jar until it is full. Since there were already two litres of water in the three-litre jar, you have poured exactly one litre out of the five-litre jar. So, there are exactly four litres remaining in the five-litre jar.

Chapter 19

TIPS TO HELP HIM HANDLE LIFE'S KNOCKS AND SETBACKS

It can be absolutely heart wrenching when that child with a specific learning difficulty comes home distraught or tearful. Parents can feel deeply protective; these children are so often misunderstood or made to feel inadequate. When parents hear about treatment that seems unkind or unfair it is not unreasonable if their first reaction is one of hurt and anger.

Whether he has been left out of a group, put on the bottom table, felt humiliated in class or any one of the many things which can go wrong, it is quite reasonable if a parent's first reaction is emotional. It is tempting to want to cry with your child. Parents may feel like marching into school and letting rip at the bully or the teacher or any other perpetrator of the problem.

Indeed, most of us would rather suffer ourselves than see our children unhappy because of some event in school. Although we care passionately, it is not always easy to decide how to help them learn to handle life's knocks and setbacks. Let's start by looking at possible first steps when things have gone wrong.

Take a breath

Do not let your feelings show (if you cannot handle it, how can you expect your child to cope?). You might get your child a drink and sit somewhere comfortable. You are the rock and the repository for these unhappy feelings.

Listen to him

Let him tell you all about it and listen well. Don't brush his worries under the carpet or overreact. You are getting your child's perspective and this will help him to sort out his feelings. It is important for your child to feel that you are listening, that you are there to support him and that you emphathise.

Get the full picture

It is important that you get an understanding of what has really happened. You might want to write down what your child says. You might ask questions and get him to go over it again.

Move on to solutions

Once your child has had a chance to tell his story and has been empathetically listened to he may:

- feel better and want to leave it there

- be able to think of ways in which he could manage better if this happens again

- decide to try and tackle the problem himself. He might like to ask the teacher if he can talk to her about his worries.

If he wants to deal with things himself you could help him to brainstorm solutions. You can make suggestions. You could ask him what he would like the teacher to do.

Your knowledge about the kind of person your child's teacher is may colour your thoughts and decisions about how you and your child are going to handle the situation.

The important decision for you and your child is whether:

- he will manage things on his own. This may or may not include raising the issue with the teacher himself

- you will together arrange to discuss the problem with the teacher

- you, the parent, will raise concerns with the teacher.

Decide with him if you are going into school on his behalf

If you decide that you will go into school, make sure that your child knows that you want to work with the school (the teacher, the head or whoever) to resolve the issue.

There is a big difference between saying that you will be talking with his teacher to find out why he feels this way rather than saying you will be talking to (accusing) his teacher to find out why the teacher did this to him or didn't prevent that from happening.

Make sure he knows that you expect to be able to work with his teacher

However angry or upset you might feel about what has happened or however unfair it seems, it is not helpful for your child to think that he can come home and wind you up with tales of school. After all, you only have half the story. Until you speak to the teacher you will not get the full picture. Children feel more secure if they feel that home and school are unified.

KEY POINTS

⇨ Listen to your child's concerns calmly and without distress.

⇨ Hear what he has to say and empathise.

⇨ Try and get the full picture.

⇨ Move to solutions. What would he like to happen? What can he do? Does he need your help?

⇨ Make a plan.

⇨ Make sure that he knows you will work with his teacher or other member of school staff.

Chapter 20

TIPS FOR POSITIVE LIAISON WITH SCHOOL STAFF

It is not only when a child comes home unhappy with a specific concern that parents might need to tackle a difficult issue with a classroom or subject teacher. Parents may, for example, be worried about the quality of teaching or about their child's slow progress. Alternatively, the school may ask the parents to come into school to follow up on something which they are concerned about.

At times this can feel distinctly nerve-racking. For many parents, particularly those who themselves experienced difficulty in school, going to meet with a teacher instantly makes them nervous and puts them on the defensive. For others, any criticism of their child will act like a red rag to a bull. Neither the timid nor the belligerent approach is likely to lead to the best outcomes. So how should parents proceed?

Below are nine steps which should help to lead to success and which should ensure that parents are viewed and treated as effective advocates for their child rather than hysterical and impossible parents. These steps apply whether it is the parent who has initiated the meeting or the teacher.

If parents have been asked to come into school because there is a concern about the child's behaviour or learning, most of these steps still apply. Do ask what the meeting is about beforehand so that you can prepare yourself.

Steps to success
Step 1
Discuss things with the teacher concerned and do not, in the first instance, go directly to the headteacher or other more senior member of staff unless you feel that the circumstances are very unusual or serious.

Step 2
Remember, teachers are people too. Teachers are sensitive and easily hurt. It is difficult to rebuild bridges once they have been broken. Think

about how you would like to receive the feedback you wish to convey to the teacher. You will get a better outcome if the teacher is feeling positive and is willing to engage with you. If you upset or antagonise her, communication is much less likely to be successful. Do not make accusations and place the teacher in a position of defence either by note, email or in person.

Step 3

Unless it is an emergency, schedule an appointment with the relevant teacher. Do not lodge a complaint out of the blue at the start of the school day! As a teacher it can feel very unpleasant being at the end of a complaint for which one is not in any way prepared. It does not make the teacher feel warm and positive about the child who is the cause of the attack and does not lend itself to quietly working on solutions.

Remember, too, that at the end of the school day your child's teacher will be tired and will also have more work to do before going home. Catching her as the children leave the classroom is not a good moment for an unscheduled meeting, particularly if the subject to be discussed is in any way difficult.

Step 4

Be respectful. Go into the meeting with a positive manner and with the expectation that you both want to work things out for your child. Keep a light touch. Approach the teacher with the view that she has your child's interests at heart and that she is a professional who cares about your child. Assume that she will be your ally. It may be that she is unaware of what has caused your child to be distressed. She has many other children to look after.

Step 5

Start with a positive. If you want to get the best from the teacher do start out with a positive comment. She may be feeling anxious about this meeting. Tell her what your child likes about her classroom or what your child has enjoyed doing under her watch. Show appreciation, but it must be authentic. Then explain that you hope that she can help you understand what is causing your child some difficulty, distress and unhappiness.

Step 6

Be specific about your concerns and keep it child orientated. You could tell in your child's words what the issue seems to be. Explain what your child 'feels' rather than launch into an attack about her behaviour or a description of what seems to have gone wrong. Then allow time for the teacher's perspective.

Step 7

Listen and hear. Be aware that the teacher may have a different perspective to your child and that it may be just as valid as the picture that your child has painted. Keep an open mind. Consider both sides of the situation.

Step 8

Clarify the situation and seek a solution. After listening to the teacher, see if together you can clarify the problem and consider ways to support the child. Try and agree what actions are necessary and what role each of you may play. If necessary or appropriate, set a date to review how things are going. This step is of particular importance whether the meeting has been initiated by the parents or by the school. In both cases home and school have a responsibility to find solutions.

Step 9

Be grateful. This may not come easily if you do not think that the teacher has been helpful or sympathetic, but it never does any harm to be polite.

Let's look at likely or different outcomes

At best you may come away from the meeting feeling that it went wonderfully well. You may be delighted with the teacher's response and feel that the situation has been cleared up. At worst you may come away feeling that no progress has been made. Most likely the outcome will fall between these two extremes. Again, there is a range of options open to parents.

You can escalate the issue and take it to the headteacher. Headteachers do have a habit of defending their staff, so beware, and if it is a really sticky issue perhaps you should consider having a third party present to help adjudicate. Do have a clear idea of what outcome you want. If the teacher has been unhelpful you may have decided that it would be in your child's best interests to change class.

At no stage do parents have to be unpleasant or challenging. Parents can express their views in terms of: 'I think we all want Mary-Jo or Simon to have the best year possible but the current situation is interfering with his/her education.'

How to be a good parent and build up credit

So far we have looked at how to handle difficult situations and issues. But let's step back and see if there is anything which parents can do to start to build a good and trusting relationship with their child's classroom/ subject teacher or headteacher before any problems arise. There may well be a moment when a parent needs to be bothersome and demanding on their child's behalf and it will be helpful to have banked a store of goodwill and to have established a good relationship.

Parents can play an important part in supporting teachers. It is the small day-to-day things which count, and it is not who can bring in the biggest and best present at Christmas which teachers really appreciate.

Here is a simple list of things parents can do which really can help to support the smooth running of the school day:

- Check the school bag for messages and notices. These can so easily stay crumpled in the bottom of the bag for days or until they are out of date.

- If communication is now electronic, check the relevant website for school information.

- Respond promptly to messages.

- Ensure that children take the right equipment into school on the correct days.

- Be aware of report cards and sign progress notes.

- Make use of any home–school liaison methods in use, for example homework hotlines.

- Ensure that homework is done and handed in on time.

- If there is an open door policy, make use of it but do not abuse it.

- Attend open days/evenings.

Good, positive and personal feedback is also hugely appreciated. If there is something your child has particularly enjoyed in school or if the teacher has gone out of her way to be helpful then let the teacher know that you have noticed and appreciate it.

These may seem small things but, with 30 or more children in the class, cooperative parents can really make life easier for the teacher, enabling them to focus on the teaching. The involved and cooperative parent is already ahead if any difficulties arise and need to be tackled.

KEY POINTS

⇨ When there are issues to be resolved parents can do much to ensure that interactions go smoothly and positive outcomes are achieved.

⇨ Make an appointment and be specific about any concerns. Keep things child orientated.

⇨ Treat your child's teacher with respect and start with the assumption that he or she wants the best for your child.

⇨ Listen (and hear) as well as talk.

⇨ Seek a solution (or action plan) and agree a review date.

⇨ Things are likely to go best if you already have a positive relationship with your child's teacher, so ensure that you are cooperative and supportive on a day-to-day basis.

Chapter 21

TIPS TO ENHANCE LANGUAGE AND COMMUNICATION SKILLS

'Mastery of language affords one remarkable opportunities.'

Alexandre Dumas

This chapter considers ways in which parents can enhance the language and communication skills which are of such importance in the classroom. We will look in particular at listening, talking and awareness of the needs of the audience. These sophisticated skills develop over time, and at every stage children can be encouraged and supported.

Listening and hearing

Once children are in formal school they do need to be able to listen well. A huge amount of the school day is taken up with listening – to the teacher, to peers, to audio media. It has been suggested that many children spend as much as 50 to 70 per cent of their time in school listening to their teacher.

However, whether or not a child is inattentive or has poor working memory, he can be helped to become a good or better listener. The process of listening involves hearing, attending and understanding. We may be able to hear well but we do not necessarily listen effectively. One task is to help children gain an awareness of the need for active listening.

There are many activities that you can integrate into life at home which will help him to be aware and conscious of the act of listening and to learn to really process what he is hearing. Listening games can be introduced from quite an early age.

In addition to the samples below you will find more games to encourage listening in Appendix 2.

- True and false. Get him to listen to statements and to ring a bell if it is true or to shake a rattle if it is false. 'The sky is red.' 'Badgers hibernate in summer.' 'Ice is cold.'

- Tell a continuous story where each participant must start from the beginning and add a bit.

- Practise listening for key words. Tell a story and ask the listeners to listen out for certain words.

- Listen for particular information, for example within a story.

- For older children try playing the Radio 4 game 'Just a Minute'. In case you do not know the game, it goes like this. The first participant starts to talk about a topic. It could be rabbits, fairy cakes or balloons – whatever. The aim is for the speaker to talk for a minute without repetition, hesitation or deviation. Listeners can challenge the speaker if they think that he has repeated a word (except for words in the title), hesitated or that he has deviated from the subject. If it is a correct challenge then the challenger takes over and tries to continue with the subject for the rest of the time available. Players gain a point for a correct challenge, two points for being the speaker when the time is up and five points for speaking for the entire minute without being correctly challenged.

There are other more general activities which parents can use to encourage awareness of listening. The first thing is to try not to say things more than once. Wait patiently until your child realises that you are expecting a response. You may need to stand over him, but sooner or later he will get the message. When you have gained his attention, see if he can recall what you said. It is so often the case that when our children ignore what we say we repeat it several times at an ever-increasing volume. They learn to tune it all out until fever pitch has been reached. Try to reverse this trend and train up more responsive listeners.

The child with poor working memory does have genuine difficulty in retaining more than a particular amount of information in his immediate memory. The answer here is to make sure that you do not overload him with too much information or too many details. Keep requests short and simple and expect a response. For other suggestions see the chapter on working memory.

Encourage good talking

Children need to talk to become good talkers. Expressing views and thoughts or telling anecdotes or just telling mum what happened in school does not always come easily and fluently. Some children seem to start their sentence several times before they get going, others may struggle to find the word or words they need. Some children are naturally more gregarious and talkative than others. The quiet ones may have given up the struggle to get a word in edgeways. But, learning to talk well and to express oneself is something that can be learnt through experience.

Here are some suggestions for helping them to 'get it out':

- Be interested and attentive. We all know if someone is not really paying attention to what we say and if their mind seems to be somewhere else. It can be discouraging, especially if we have just revealed something sensitive or of great importance to us. If the listener appears interested and to value what we say we are more inclined to open up and to chat.

- Encourage your child to talk. Some children are much chattier than others. Start open-ended conversations such as 'How was your day?' rather than using closed questions such as 'Was your lunch good?' which may simply elicit a yes or no answer.

- Give your child time and encourage him to think before he speaks.

- Give him time to express himself. You may need to be particularly patient as you wait to hear what he wants to say. Some children do take longer to find the words or to work out what they need to say to make themselves understood. Many children that I have worked with have started a sentence several times before they finally get it out.

- Hear him out. Do your best not to cut him off midstream just because you know what's coming next or because you disagree or do not value his opinion.

- Value what your child thinks. Ask your child for his views and opinions. Share your own views.

- Extend conversations. You might want to pick up on a particular element of the conversation and ask further questions, or you might reflect back.

- Reflective listening. If he has just been telling you that life is tough in the playground and you think he has more to say but he comes to a halt, you can show that you are interested and still listening by reflecting back what he has said. You could for example say, 'Oh, so you are finding the playground a bit uncomfortable – can you tell me more about that?' Then leave him enough time to continue.

- Help to clarify experiences and thoughts. As you listen you can feed back what your child has said to you in your own words. Your wider vocabulary may help your child to express himself better, and your understanding of his situation may give him greater clarity.

- Share your own thoughts. Ask what he thinks about a dilemma you may be facing: 'Shall I get blue or green fabric for the new cushions?'

Social communication

This aspect of language is to do with understanding the (unspoken) conventions of language and communication. We adapt the way we use language to meet the needs of our audience. We are able to read between the lines. We are able to understand jokes and innuendo. We have learnt what it is socially acceptable to say to whom and under what conditions. We are able to read the body language and facial expression of the person we are talking to. We can see if they are looking engaged, bored or desperate to go. All of this develops gradually from the age of about four years.

These aspects of language and communication are not so often articulated and some children will need to have these things made more explicit than others.

It is children who are on the autism spectrum who have the greatest difficulty with these aspects of communication. Children who are dyspraxic can also find it hard to read body language and facial expression; this lack of sensitivity to the more subtle aspects of communication means that they too can, at times, find themselves at odds with those around them. They may go on too much, they may appear rude or insensitive to others, and they may inadvertently be annoying to their peers. Children with ADHD may also have communication difficulties. If they are impulsive they may butt in, take over or fail to follow the thread of conversation.

Some children do not have any area of specific learning difficulty but may just not be naturally adept at social interaction. There are downsides to poor communication, particularly if it leads to unpopularity or an invitation to bullying. Fortunately, it can often take very little to improve the situation.

At the age of 12 Vicky was disliked by the other children in her class. The more unhappy she became the more annoying she seemed to them. Vicky was negative about life and quick to cry. No one wanted to be landed with her as a partner or to have her in their group. One day she asked why no one liked her. A couple of the girls in her class explained to her what they found annoying and suggested how she might behave instead. Vicky tried things out and in a very short period of time she had managed to change everyone's perception of her and they started to enjoy her company. Vicky became happier and a virtuous cycle began. Soon her unpopularity was a thing of the past. These two girls in Vicky's class had given her some informal social skills training. As soon as Vicky changed her behaviour, others responded differently to her.

Children who are not naturally adept with these practical aspects of communication could do with some help to learn to:

- consider what they would think if someone else said this

- listen to what others are saying and to build on it

- listen when they have asked a question and not immediately change the subject

- be aware that talking incessantly on one topic just because they find it interesting does not engage their audience

- think about what is suitable for their audience

- be aware if what they are going to say is kind, true and necessary

- pick up non-verbal cues such as body posture and facial expressions

- consider if they are being positive or constantly moaning and being negative.

How can children be helped with these aspects of communication? If the problem is evident then it might be helpful to start with a speech and language therapist. They are trained and adept at working on these skills either individually or in small groups.

In most cases this should not be necessary and parents can just be aware of the need to help explain and coach their child in these skills, to talk through what seems to be happening and to make suggestions as to what he might try out, then see what happens if he behaves slightly differently.

Appreciation of language

Both spoken and written language can be very powerful. A moving book or poem, a rousing speech or a clearly structured argument can all influence those who are exposed to it. However, it is probably not until secondary school that most children will awaken to the full possibilities of language – both written and spoken – to convey ideas and feelings, cause an impact and make a difference. The way something is expressed can evoke emotions and awaken an understanding of a complex or difficult subject.

Eleven-year-old Edward was entered for a City & Guilds speaking exam along with the rest of his class. He learnt from this experience that if he wanted to make an impact, cause laughter or just make sure that he was heard he had to think through what he wanted to say, wait for the right moment, use good timing and express himself clearly. His high mark in this exam has added greatly to his self-confidence as a verbal communicator.

Many children have found that their confidence and ability to talk well have been helped by engaging in a debating society, joining a drama group or being part of a philosophical enquiry group. Debating and philosophy will provide some framework or rules which they can apply when building an argument or making a point. Drama group shows how it is possible to step outside the restrictions of being oneself and find out what it feels like to try a different approach or style of communicating.

It is often not until secondary school age that children are really set alight by reading and by literature. Many of today's well-known authors have found their inspiration in the literature of those who went before. It can be an exciting moment when a teenager reads something which awakens within him the power and possibilities of language.

It may take a while to find inspiration, so it is important that children are exposed to a range of books, films and theatre which they might not normally encounter. We do look to school to do much of this and there is nothing like an inspiring English teacher, but parents can ensure that they play their part too. Discussion, analysis and comparisons can enhance and deepen the child's experience of the book or event. It is hoped that something will really catch your child's imagination.

Language, thinking, vocabulary and experience

The way that we see the world and the words we use to describe it are closely entwined. The more words we have at our disposal the better we will be able to express ourselves with clarity. We can use language to regulate and order thoughts. The right words help to clarify and crystallise thought. If we wish to clarify our thoughts we will often talk through an idea or concept.

The importance of a good vocabulary runs right through from toddlers to university students. Vocabulary makes a difference. Good and enthusiastic readers are likely to pick up new words on a regular basis, and reading does appear to be the main medium for extending vocabulary. The vocabulary of poor readers often lags quite significantly behind the vocabulary of the voracious reader. To offset this, parents can continue to read to the reluctant or slow reader and make sure that plenty of good audio books are available.

What about bilingual children?

There seem to be more pluses than minuses for the child who grows up in a bilingual household. The first obvious advantage is that he will have effortlessly acquired a second language; this is something which those who have struggled with French or German in school will really envy! There is one important rule. It has been found that children can learn most effectively, in the early days, if each parent – or other adult in the household – sticks to conversing with the child in one language only. So if the family speaks English and French then it is best if, for example, dad speaks French and mum speaks English to the child. It is not unusual for bilingual children to be a little delayed in either one or both languages. This is hardly surprising when we consider that they are learning twice as many words as other children. Their vocabulary in one language may appear to be small compared with their peer group, but if you add together all the words they know in two languages their vocabulary will outstrip the monolingual child. One further plus is that children who are learning two words to represent one item ('chair' and 'chaise' can both be used to represent the ideas of that thing you sit on with a seat and four legs) will be aware at a younger age than their monolingual peers that a word is an arbitrary symbol which can be used to represent a 'thing' or an idea or a concept. There is some evidence that this speeds up conceptual thought.

The second language user in secondary school

Although children can generally acquire a second language for day-to-day use without too much difficulty, it can take up to seven years to develop the sophisticated language required to deal with abstract concepts such as those involved in maths and science. Thus children using their second language within school may be disadvantaged if they have not been learning for long. They may appear to be fluent speakers, but have considerable difficulty with the deeper processing and understanding of abstract concepts.

KEY POINTS

⇨ Good language skills underpin academic success.

⇨ Children need help and encouragement to listen and to talk well.

⇨ Social interaction and communication skills can be taught where they are needed.

⇨ An appreciation of language and the power of language can be fostered through literature, debate, philosophy and performance.

⇨ A good vocabulary is paramount.

Chapter 22

TIPS FOR MOTIVATION

How do we engage the child with a specific learning difficulty in the learning activities which he or she finds so difficult but which are so necessary if progress is to be made? In this chapter we will look at some of the things we know about motivation and see if there are ways in which this knowledge can be used to good effect. The aim is always to encourage children to become actively involved in their learning.

We know that intrinsic motivation (i.e. the motivation which comes from within) is fuelled by two important factors:

- Feeling competent. We are considerably more likely to be motivated to do things which are within our capabilities. If things are too hard then we tend to feel demoralised and to give up. If they are too easy we are bored. This applies to both physical as well as mental activities.

- Autonomy and freedom of choice. We are also more likely to be motivated if there is a degree of choice and if we have control over the agenda.

We can immediately see the difficulties! Children with specific learning difficulty are constantly asked to engage with activities where they feel less than competent and they frequently have absolutely no control or choice over the agenda. However, there are a number of strategies that parents can employ to help with these situations.

Provide challenges at the optimal level
This is key to success. Things which are too easy are dull, and tasks which are too difficult are quickly given up. So, if things are too easy or difficult, modify them.

Provide opportunities for your child to be in control
Try and involve your child in making choices about how and when he completes work. If parents are very controlling and directive it will

reduce their child's feelings of competence and autonomy. These are both important to intrinsic motivation.

Encourage children to set their own goals

Involving children in goal setting will help them to take ownership of the task. This is particularly important for children who seem to have opted out and see learning situations as something that is done to them. If, however, goals have to be imposed from outside, parents can help their children to work out how they might best meet these goals and provide opportunities for them to do so.

Allow time

Children need time to try things out. Parents who intervene too quickly with examples and solutions will reduce their child's feelings of independence and autonomy.

Be consistent

It is unreasonable to expect a child to take responsibility for activities such as homework if the daily routine is constantly changed. The reluctant reader is unlikely to become a self-starter if his mother or father bribes him to read every day for five days and then forgets all about it for the next two weeks.

Try to replace blanket praise with some good quality descriptive feedback

This is one of the most effective ways that parents can encourage intrinsic motivation. It is very easy to provide unspecific encouragement and praise, for example, 'Well done, good essay' or 'Great game of football/netball'.

It is better if your feedback can be detailed, positive and descriptive. For example let your child know just what it is that he is doing well – which aspect of the essay was good or in what way he played well. He may have used paragraphs appropriately, or his story may have had a great start, middle and end. He may have made good use of his team mates. He might have been particularly attentive or might have scored a good goal following some hard practice.

The important thing is that this type of feedback helps the child to feel competent, it informs him about what was good and could lead on to discussion of what still needs work and improvement.

Praise and feedback must be honest

It is not helpful to praise a child for poor work when he is obviously not trying and not doing well. Children are quick to pick up on phoney or obviously manipulative praise. It can feel very patronising and is a certain motivation killer. The trick is to catch them when they have made an effort. It may take some close observations but keep alert to finding something you can genuinely use to build on. It might be something like: 'Well done, your pencil grip is getting better. I like the way you are managing to keep the pencil between your thumb and forefinger. See how it helps your writing.'

If your child has made no effort and the results are bad he will be as much aware of it as you are and should be able to handle very direct feedback. Just be sure to link the lack of effort to the poor result and not his lack of ability or talent.

Associate success with effort

If children learn to associate success with effort, involvement and sticking with a problem then they are considerably more likely to maintain motivation and to feel good about themselves as learners when they succeed.

Avoid associating a child's success with his general ability

If a child believes that he has done well because he is clever he may be reluctant to stretch himself or to have a go with something that is difficult or challenging. He may fear that failure will indicate that he is not, after all, clever. Failure will then further erode his motivation and self-esteem.

Try not to become reliant on rewards and punishments

The extensive use of rewards, threats and punishments may work while they are in place, but when you remove them the chances are that your child will be less motivated than before. There is nothing wrong with the odd carrot to get a child started but do not rely on it.

Always talk positively about your child within his hearing

If a child overhears a parent or grandparent talking disparagingly about him, his motivation to do well in whatever area they are discussing is more likely to shrivel than to grow.

Avoid negative comparisons

Do not compare a child's work with that of a sibling or class mate. If a child is told that he is inferior to his brother or sister or that he is at the bottom of the class he is more likely to give up than to try harder. Indeed, it is an excuse for not trying. Why bother when you know that you are not capable?

KEY POINTS

⇨ Intrinsic motivation, which comes from within, is fuelled by feelings of competence and autonomy.

⇨ Pitch tasks for your child at the right level and involve him in goal setting.

⇨ Give him time to try things out before intervening or taking over.

⇨ Give positive and informative feedback in preference to blanket praise.

⇨ Associate success with effort.

⇨ Do not rely on external motivators.

Chapter 23

TIPS FOR CONFIDENT LEARNERS

Confidence is not a single concept. It is quite possible to be a confident sportsman and an insecure mathematician, or a confident actor but socially shy. Even confidence with learning may vary between subjects. It may depend on the teacher or the peer group or the child's capacity to achieve. This is likely to be particularly true for children who have areas of specific learning difficulty.

Although confidence for different activities and situations may vary over time, children do have an image of themselves and of their worth which is more constant. Children gain this picture of themselves through the mirror that others hold up to them. The way in which peers, teachers and parents react and respond will make them feel good, capable, clever and wanted, or the reverse.

One important aspect of the parent role is to help children to believe in themselves, to feel that they are of value and that they can succeed.

In this chapter we will look at ways in which parents can help their child to:

- build inner confidence
- develop the competencies which will enhance confidence
- gain confidence through reflection.

Building inner confidence

A child's self-image will be shaped by the way in which her parents treat her as well as through her experiences in school. Does she feel, for example, that she lives up to her parents' expectations? Does she feel that they are proud of her and that they love and value her, or does she feel she is a failure and disappointment? Does her teacher value her work? Do other children like her? Has she been the victim of bullying? The way a child perceives herself will feed directly into her self-confidence.

Children pick up very quickly on what their parents think of them. They are acutely aware of whether they please you, annoy you or exasperate you. The catch 22 is that it is so much easier to enjoy and give positive feedback to the confident and happy child. But all children need to feel that they are special, that they are of value and that they are unconditionally loved.

- A strong, loyal family who tell good stories about one another will engender confidence. Do have fun and enjoy your children. Engage with them in a way that shows enthusiasm and happiness. Don't look miserable, sad and exhausted. Children quickly feel that this is their fault. Build in time to play games, laugh together and enjoy their company. Step outside the daily routine and make time for adventures and light-hearted engagement. If children perceive that parental childcare is a burdensome chore they will feel that they are a nuisance and not a life-enhancing pleasure.

- Children need to feel that they have their parents' approval. Nothing beats the experience of receiving parental affirmation and pride. Children need to feel special, that they count and that they are of value. They need to feel that their parents believe in them and that they can turn to their parents for emotional support and encouragement. If parents cannot do this for their child who else will? I know, there are moments we may not feel deeply proud; children can be embarrassing, and their performance or behaviour may, at times, leave much to be desired. But keep looking for something you can praise and for some area where she has made progress or shows aptitude.

- Give unconditional love. You love them, but this does not always mean that you love their behaviour. Distinguish between your child as a person and any behaviour you may feel is not acceptable or good. A child should not be called terrible or ghastly, but her behaviour (which she can change) may be described as terrible or ghastly.

- Value who she is, not what she is. What she is could become a label which she feels provides a form of value. She does not need to gain attention and value because she is asthmatic, dyslexic or especially pretty.

Building confidence through achievement and the growth of skills

Much of this book is about supporting children to learn successfully and to increase their competence in all the areas which impact on their school progress, so you will find just four key points here.

- *Mastering skills.* Whether it is learning the alphabet, swimming for a club or learning to knit, a child's confidence will grow when she sees that she has mastered another skill. But do not expect her to run before she can walk. It is easy to put a child off if too much is expected. Introduce activities at the appropriate stage and let learning take place at her pace and in manageable increments.

- *Being stretched.* When we are pushed out of our comfort zone we can feel stressed and anxious, but the degree of satisfaction when we cope and succeed can make it all worthwhile. When 14-year-old Alice and seven other teenage girls hiked 110 miles of the Appalachian Trail with all necessary supplies on their backs they had moments when they despaired, cried and felt they would never make it. But as they completed the walk and were met by the camp supervisor they were brimming with pride and confidence. They had done it. This growth of inner confidence was not just a fleeting emotion. It fed into future activities and provided Alice with the confidence to stretch herself in other areas.

- *Coping with life.* It can be a good moment when a child copes with a difficult or challenging situation on her own. It is difficult to set up situations that will achieve this result, but it is almost inevitable that you will need to trust your child to deal with challenges. Both you and she may be a little out of your comfort zone. I can vividly recall my first solo outing on my pony. It was not all plain sailing, but I coped, and was very proud when I got home and my mother had trusted me to manage.

- *Helping others.* Providing help and support to others is another way that can aid the confidence of some children. The emotionally damaged and disturbed children who I taught in special school could be hostile, uncooperative and aggressive. But they were at their loving, kindest and most helpful best on the days that we shared an adventure playground with physically disabled children from another special school. Here they could offer help and support without any fear of the rejection they were so used to experiencing; here they recognised other children with difficulties and needs which rivalled or exceeded their own. This principle can apply in other situations. The slow reader may gain confidence when she helps a younger child. The socially shy child might blossom if she has to care for a smaller child in a social situation.

Gaining confidence through reflection

We all know how easy it is to feel undermined, that others are better than us, that we are useless and that we haven't made progress or cannot learn. There will be times when children take a knock or find their peer group difficult. There will be times when the challenges each child faces become greater. It might be increased expectations in school. It might be the move from primary to secondary school or the shift from GCSEs to A-levels.

It is important to listen and to acknowledge your child's anxieties and concerns, and it may well be that she has a good reason for feeling worried. If this is the case a plan needs to be made to support her to deal with the problem. If, however, it seems to be a case of wobbly self-worth, there are other things which might help. A reality check may help to shift her perspective.

- Help her to list five strengths and five achievements.

- Encourage her to list five things which she likes about herself.

- Can she write down the good things others would say about her?

- Self-approval. Look back with her over a particular period – it might be a day, a week, a month or a year – and consider what she has achieved and done well. Ask her what she is proud of. Endorse what is true. Can you, her parent, look back over a similar period of time and tell her about the things that you are happy that she has achieved?

- Goal setting. Can she set one, two or three goals which, if achieved, would make her feel better about herself? How is she going to set about achieving these? What will she need to do? Can they be broken into small steps? When and how will she review them?

How can parents deal with external factors which impact on their child's confidence?

It can be difficult to decide how to deal with situations which are impacting on your child's confidence if they are outside the home and outside your usual remit. What can or should you do if your child's confidence is taking a knock because of the way in which a teacher is treating her or because she is experiencing bullying or other difficulties with her peer group?

A good start is to support her by listening to and acknowledging her concerns and feelings. You may give advice or help her to think of ways to deal with the situation. If this is insufficient to help her to cope then your intervention will be necessary. You will need to raise these issues in school and see if some resolution can be found (see Chapter 20, Tips for Positive Liaison with School Staff).

If a group of children in the class are making things difficult for your child you will need to work with the school staff. If your child's confidence and self-esteem are really suffering, maybe a change of class could be discussed.

If your child is unfortunate enough to be in a group in which there is a bully or a group of bullies and is not getting the necessary support to change things, then it is important that she is not left to suffer indefinitely. If a change of class is not possible it may be necessary to make an even more dramatic change and to consider an alternative school.

KEY POINTS

⇨ Confidence is not a single entity – it can change from situation to situation.

⇨ Inner confidence and self-image come from the way in which a child is loved and supported.

⇨ Confidence can be built through the mastery of skills, coping and succeeding with activities that stretch and are on the edge of a child's comfort zone.

⇨ Parents may need to intervene if their child is losing confidence because of problems relating to school work or friendships.

⇨ Parents should step in rapidly if their child is being bullied. In the first instance discuss this with the school.

Chapter 24

HABITS, STRATEGIES AND STUDY SKILLS

The ideas in this chapter build on (and may repeat) much that has already been said and suggested. The overall aim of this book has been to help parents to understand and support their child's learning; every chapter has suggestions relevant to the area of difficulty under discussion. This chapter is a little more general and emphasises the importance of good habits, strategies and study skills from Year 1 through to university.

Give them the tools

In this concluding chapter we will look at the ways in which parents can help their children to become efficient and effective learners and performers. We will focus on setting good conditions, the organisation of materials and time, and the importance of learning and using good study skills.

Study skills are all about 'how to' study. Whether it is writing an essay, revising for an exam or planning a task there are systematic approaches which make the task manageable, make it more likely that it will be done well and which help to remove feelings of panic and frustration. Good skills will help to make the student feel competent.

As children progress from one key stage to the next, more is expected of them. Work gets harder, and the skills they need become more complex and sophisticated. The jump from infant to junior school or from junior to senior school brings new challenges. Pupils need to learn to work in a time-efficient and focused manner as they approach their GCSEs. The demands of A-levels will stretch them further, and by the time they enter university or other forms of apprenticeship, training or higher education they should be proficient in a wide range of skills to ensure successful independent study. At each juncture there is a step change in what is needed, and children can waste time and become frustrated if they are not sure how to tackle the topic. You can ensure that they have the tools.

And, what is more, it has been found that good study skills can raise a pupil's exam results by up to two grades. None of this is brain surgery but neither is it self-evident. Children need to be taught.

We tend to think of study skills in relation to GCSEs, A-levels and higher education, but it's never too early for parents to model, shape and encourage good learning behaviours. Children need to build strong foundations for their organisation, learning and study habits. Good habits start in primary school.

Primary school

Creating the right conditions for good learning

Whether children are in infant school or secondary school we need to start by paying attention to both their physical state and the conditions in which we are expecting them to learn.

Children will learn best if they are fit, well, happy and relaxed. If the child is working at home check that he:

- has had time for a snack or a drink
- is getting enough sleep
- is getting plenty of exercise
- is relaxed and calm (deal with any anxieties)
- is not bothered by any family issues.

Make use of good routines:

- Work out when his flashcards, homework or revision can be fitted in.
- Think about how this will impact on the family schedule. Do you need to make changes to help him?
- Are you encouraging him to start to take responsibility for time planning?
- Ensure that reading, music or other practice is, in the early days, non-negotiable. If a short practice period becomes automatic, much time wasted in discussion, pleading and even threatening can be avoided.

Early time management and organisation:

- Draw up a weekly timetable with him and make sure it is colour coded and prominently displayed so that he knows which evenings he may need to do homework and when he needs to pack his kit for swimming or games.

- Ensure that he learns to check his bag as soon as he comes home to look for school letters, home–school liaison books, work assignments and so forth. Similarly, make good use of any internet links with school or teacher.

- Find a regular place where he can keep his school equipment or kit. He should take responsibility for getting swimming or games kit out the night before it is needed.

- Help him to make sure that his pencil case is up to date and contains all that he needs.

Learning techniques

Young children can be helped to apply the best techniques for their age and stage. Study skills can be scaled down, and even six-year-olds can be helped:

- *Use scaffolding to help with their written work.* Use simple structures for writing. For example, when your child has to write a story and may not be sure where to start or what to write, help him by talking with him. Ask questions – who is in the story, where does it happen, what happens? You might write the first few words of each sentence so that he just has to finish it. As he gets older he will begin to learn that writing his diary needs a different style to writing a story or writing up a science experiment and that a simple formula can be applied.

- *Early research skills.* Work with him to find out how to look things up in books and on the computer. He may need to work on his understanding of alphabetical order. He may need help with how to make a note of new information and how to use it.

- *Learning and memorising.* What are the best ways to retain information? He is likely to have to learn times tables and spellings. Help him to work out how he remembers best. Does he learn best through listening or looking or doing? (Remember, we know that the more senses that can be used together the better the learning will be.) Anything to be remembered should be fully understood and attended to (chat about it, question it, go over it); it should be revisited following a short interval so that the chance of remembering is high. Further practice slots should be actioned but the gap between them can be extended. So, practice after half an hour, after a further two hours, after half a day, after a day, after two days and so forth (only extend the gap if he is accurate).

Simple rules for work completed at home:

- Get all the materials needed ready and to hand.

- Be realistic about what can be achieved. Set targets. Help your child to learn not to overbook.

- Divide tasks into achievable chunks.

- Take breaks. We can concentrate well for 20 to 35 minutes. Then a walk or change of activity is useful. This is another good habit to adopt.

- Choose the best work environment. Does he need to be in the kitchen where you can see what he is doing? Does he work best with a background noise or does it have to be totally quiet? Is he distracted if it is too hot or too cold?

- Use appropriate technology to help.

Link effort to results

During this period children should begin to see a link between the efforts they put in and the results they get. This is an important development. If children consider that how well they do is a measure of how clever they are, they are left high and dry when they do badly. However, if they are aware that they have considerable control over outcomes, then they can pick themselves up, dust themselves down and have another go. The experience of success after effort will reinforce their belief in themselves and their capacity to achieve. You can help this by pointing out good work, but make sure that you link it to the time spent on it and the thought given to it rather than saying, 'Well done, great work, you are so clever.'

Secondary school and beyond

Do parents really need to be involved with their children's school work when they move on to secondary school? Once children are into their teens it is all too easy to let them get on with things on their own; indeed, we are aiming to create independent learners.

But what about our children with specific learning difficulties? Can they be left to muddle through? In my view the answer is definitely not. Parents should do their best to stay involved. This is not always easy, as many teenagers will have got to the point where they really do not want any more parental interference and they may be unlikely to ask for intervention or help.

Despite any possible resistance, and whether or not your child experiences any areas of difficulty, parents do have an important role. Their task is to ensure that their child is working efficiently and has the appropriate tools and techniques to maximise their chances of success. These are often referred to as study skills.

But how can this be done? If you are unclear where and how to get involved, start by observing how your child sets about tasks and ask a few probing questions to see how he is doing things.

The ideas which follow are most certainly not exhaustive and some of them may not work or suit your child. They are, however, enormously effective when they do work and when the right method is found for a particular child.

There are many excellent books dedicated to the topic of study skills, which can provide you with many more ideas. Study skills, as a topic, has, over the past couple of decades, become mainstream. Although it feels a very short time ago that there was almost nothing on the topic you will find that the internet is now awash with useful sites. Amazon too has numerous titles which may appeal. In my view every household should have a good book on this subject!

However, a very important word of warning – do not hand a book, however good, to your child and expect him to diligently use it. Few if any of us change our behaviours because of something we have read. We are slightly more likely to apply something we have seen demonstrated, but if we are to change the way we do anything we really need a coach or teacher who will tell us about it, demonstrate it and then work with us to do it. Once we have practised a few times on separate occasions then the new behaviour may well become integrated into our day-to-day repertoire.

If you think that you are unable to work with your child as the coach or teacher then find someone else who can or find a relevant course for your child to go on. I cannot overemphasise the importance of good study skills for all pupils and particularly for those who experience any areas of specific learning difficulty. Now let's look at key areas.

Habits

Organisation

Most children will work best if they have a specifically designated and well-organised workspace. You might start by taking a look at where he works. Ask yourself a few questions: Is his workspace organised? Does he have a place to keep equipment? Where and how is he keeping his notes?

- *Workspace.* Your child's workspace should be comfortable and efficient. His notes, files and exercise books all need to have a dedicated home so that they are easy to find. He needs a good work surface, and any bookshelves, filing cabinets and drawers need to be labelled and accessible. If space is at a premium, he should at least have dedicated boxes or trays in which to house things in an organised way. He needs a good filing system both on his computer and for his notes. He is likely to need help with all of the above.

- *Keeping organised.* We can waste an awful lot of time looking for things. Often it's that piece of paper which tells you what you are meant to be doing or has that vital contact number or homework assignment. The answer to this is a small notebook or any handheld digital device which will record the spoken word and can be kept in an accessible pocket. He can use this to record important information and things which need to be remembered.

- *Having the right equipment to hand.* A case or bag with all that he is likely to need – staples, post-it notes, plenty of A4 paper, ringbinders, scissors, rulers and so forth – can be extremely helpful.

Distractions

Distractions are not good! There is plenty of evidence that efficient multitasking is a myth. The brain can only pay attention to one thing at a time. If homework or study is interrupted with a text message, a phone call or Skype, the brain needs to switch attention from one activity to another. Each time that the brain must switch back to the study activity it takes time and effort for the brain to recall where it was and what it must do next. Distractions arising from phones, iPods, media and the internet should be minimised during work and homework periods – after all, we all know what a temptation they are.

If he simply cannot resist, the only thing to do is to remove the temptation.

There is much to be said for not allowing teenage children to have their own personal television or computer in their bedroom. It will cut down on distractions and will also ensure that you are aware of their internet usage.

The argument against this approach is that homework may often require an internet connection. I am sure that there will be divided views in all households on this, and parents and children do need to come to a workable solution together.

Time management

It is not just children who can find it hard to be good time managers, but life does run so much more smoothly when we have thought ahead, planned for deadlines and made use of lists and timetables. There are ways in which you can encourage the development of good time management.

- *Getting started on work assignments.* If he is a fiddler, encourage him to clear his desk at the end of each work session so that when he starts again he has a clear desk or table top in front of him with as few distractions as possible. A timer can be very helpful; he can set himself a time target to finish work. This may generate a sense of urgency and remove the temptation to deviate.

- *Timetables.* A weekly, termly and yearly timetable or planner can help to keep the secondary school pupil aware of what he is doing and when, how much time he has and how he can find sufficient time for homework, revision and all the other things he needs and wants to do. If he can see how many weeks he has before the end of term or the number of days before work needs to be handed in or exams are due to take place he can then plan and pace his work. The year is likely to seem much shorter when we start to chunk it into useable periods for specific activities. This can also generate a sense of urgency.

- *Sorting out what is urgent and what is important.* It can be helpful to make a list of absolutely everything that needs to be done, whether this is shopping or completing a piece of important coursework, and this should be categorised into activities which are 'urgent' and activities which are 'important'. Sometimes important activities are also urgent, particularly if these are left to the last minute! It would also be worth dividing out activities which will take just a few moments from those which are going to take a significant amount of time. It is important for him to decide which are his 'boulders', i.e. very important activities, and also those which are going to be time consuming. Boulders should be timetabled into his daily or weekly schedule. If a slot is created in which to complete his boulders, then he will be able to fit in the other less urgent or less time-consuming activities around them.

- *Getting down to work.* Some children may be brilliant at planning and organising – they may spend hours writing out their revision timetable, colour coding it, decorating it round the edges and putting it on the wall – *but* they may spend so long on planning that there is little time to actually get down to engaging with the work itself. These children need help to implement their carefully made plans. Some clear short-term targets could be motivating.

Skills

Effective reading

Children are required to read a wide range of texts as part of their educational curriculum. They will be expected to extract information, read in depth and search for new meaning; sometimes the text will be easy, or sometimes dense and full of unknown words or ideas. It is important for the pupil to learn how to vary the approach to different texts dependent on the task set.

We do not need to approach all books in the same way. A novel can be read straight off, but if it is a text or set book we should first find our way around it. The child needs to learn how to navigate the book before he starts to read. This kind of investigation may save much time and effort. He then needs to decide what he can get out of the book.

- What are the chapter headings?

- Are summaries at the start or end of each chapter?

- Is there an overview of what it's going to be about?

- What does he need to get out of the book? Is he extracting one small fact? If so, skim read until it is found. There is no need to plough through everything in detail.

- Is it material he is familiar with? If so, he can probably read quite fast but should not forget to stop and recap what he has read at intervals. He can use a highlighter pen to capture any important facts or details he is going to want to remember; he can mark the page with a small post-it sticker – that way he can find them easily.

- If it is new and complex material he will have to read at a pace that enables him to absorb and understand. He may need to read it more than once.

- What questions could he ask another reader who had just finished this chapter?

- Can he explain or recap what he has read to another person? (See also the section on reading comprehension.)

The key points here are to engage the mind, survey the whole book, help him to ask himself what he needs to find out, and decide whether this text will provide the information which he needs.

Research skills

Research skills include knowing where and how to find reliable information. We all need to develop a degree of scepticism and to question our sources. The internet is an amazing facility but brings its own dangers in terms of plagiarism, too much cutting and pasting, and not enough thinking.

Research skills will have started when your child was first required to produce a project. Maybe she used just one or two simple books and maybe you helped her to find questions to answer or headings to address. These will evolve to university level where students need to access journals, use library references, locate specialist texts and so forth. Many universities have excellent websites covering the kind of research skills needed for higher education.

Planning and structuring written work

Some children are bright, knowledgeable and can chat for ever on a topic that they are learning; they may, however, find it more difficult to get it onto the page. When we analyse the process it actually requires the assimilation of a number of separate skills and knowledge:

- *Planning, thinking, researching.* What does he know? What does he need to know? Does the title of the essay include a question? Encourage him to analyse the question and look for the verb.

Does it ask him to describe, define, compare, contrast, evaluate, etc.? If so, he should act accordingly.

- *Research.* Does he know where to find the information? What kind of source is needed? Once located he should read, understand and take notes. He should not forget to include references if they are necessary.

- *Writing.* This can be the hardest part. Sequencing and structuring information and arguments is a skill. The first question to ask is, what style or format is appropriate to the task? For example, a science experiment has a different convention to a story or diary or report. If it is an essay, does the title of the essay include a question? Is he sure that he has answered the question?

- *Mind mapping.* For many students it can be helpful to make use of software tools to assist the planning and structuring of written work. Notably:

  » Inspiration – a mind mapping tool for children of seven plus

  » Mind Genius for children of 11 years and over

- *University guides.* For undergraduates, many universities now have excellent guides as to what and how you should write for different purposes. For example:

  » report writing

  » science writing

  » dissertation structure.

Note taking

Check out your child's notes. Are they sufficiently comprehensive to enable him to work from them when it comes to learning and revising? The best notes are those done in the author's own words as a result of his own thinking. Notes taken verbatim in class may not have been understood. If they are to be useful they also need to be accessible and filed in such a way as to ensure that they can be found again. For effective note taking in lectures and lessons the child should:

- go to class prepared, taking the right pens and highlighters

- make sure he is taking notes in a book or on paper which is easily filed and stored

- make his own notes and not rely solely on notes prepared and handed out by the teacher; it helps mental engagement

- make sure that he is listening, paying attention and understanding. Note taking helps this

- try to precis and to use his own words. He should try and work out what is important. Hints come from what headings the teacher has used on overheads or written on the board

- note key words and write in short sentences

- highlight key concepts, using different colours to highlight subheadings.

The most important thing of all is for him to review his notes as soon as possible after the class (at least within 24 hours). At this point he can add details and additional notes where they are skimpy and make sure that he has understood.

Mind mapping is one technique for note taking that is highly effective for many students. It is a visual form of note taking that offers an overview of a topic and its complex information, allowing students to comprehend, create new ideas and build connections.

Studying for exams

Exams are coming up and you want to check that your child is on track. Talk to him about his revision timetable (let's hope he has one). Do you get the sense that he is keeping on top of this? Ask him to talk you through each subject. See if he can tell you about each of the topics he needs to cover. How is he planning his time for each? You should be able to find out if he needs help to organise his time. See if you can find out what he actually does during a revision session. Check back on a regular basis to see if he is keeping up.

- *Revision schedule.* Adopting an effective approach to revision will require your child to follow a series of steps. What subjects need to be covered? What are the topics within each subject? Does he have the information, books, notes and so forth to start to recap or does he need to gather more information? Can he list the missing elements and plan out where and how to fill them? A list of actions and the time needed can then be marked up on the timetable.

- *Note taking from written material.* He needs to read and understand the material and to write up the key concepts and ideas in his own words. The benefit of having his own notes is that, when he processes the material, he owns and understands the notes. The process of doing this helps ensure that information is remembered. He should not rely on teacher notes.

- *Revision techniques.* Once a set of comprehensive notes has been accumulated they need to be learnt. Long notes can be summarised into topic headings and kept as an aide-memoire on a card. He can test his knowledge and run through questions from past papers. He can work with a friend who is covering the same topic. Explaining things can be very reinforcing for some pupils. Thinking up questions to test the friend is also useful.

Learning and memorising information

Exams generally mean that there is much to be learnt and memorised. Some techniques are considerably more effective than others. The best techniques may vary from subject to subject. Can you find out if he is using good techniques for learning and memorising things? You could, for example, ask how he is handling maths learning: how does he learn formulae, number facts and methods? Can he summarise these techniques on two sheets of paper? You could ask how he is revising history, English or geography. Get him to show you his notes and talk about how he is progressing. How does he take notes? Has he got a good understanding of the topic and is revision systematic? What method is he using to learn facts and figures?

- *Memory techniques.* Once material to be learnt is fully understood it can be whittled down to a stack of revision cards that then need to be stored in memory in a way that makes it as easy as possible to retrieve. It is amazing just how much we can remember if we use our limitless imagination and link what we have to learn to things we already know. There are a good number of systems or tricks which can be used to help. Here are a couple. Let's imagine that you are trying to make sure that you remember all the different types of memory. You have divided the topic into six main headings:

  » long-term memory

  » short-term memory

  » episodic

  » semantic

» autobiographical

» procedural.

Then think of a word you can make with the six initial letters. In this case we could move 'lsesap' around to make the word 'lapses' (memory lapses). When you want to recall your categories for memory just call up the word 'lapses' and use it as a trigger to help you recall your six key topics.

Another technique requires visualisation. Take the six topic headings again. Shut your eyes and imagine that you are walking into a room you know really well. As you walk around the room place a topic in a particular location. Then when you are sitting in your exam and need to remember all you can about memory you can mentally revisit the special room and walk around finding the topics in the places that you left them. It will help if you associate each heading with something highly visual and unusual. Start by associating long-term memory with an item that is long, unusual and easy to remember. Place that item in the first location.

Exam techniques

How should the child use the time to best effect? He should read all the questions more than once and make sure he has really taken them in. It's natural to feel anxious at the start of the exam and before getting engaged with the writing. When we are anxious we do not always think best! He should decide which questions he is going to answer and how much time he can give to each. He can use the first half hour or so (depending on the total length of the exam) to plan out each answer. He might want to conjure up one of the mind maps he created when he was learning in order to help him to recall the details needed for his answer. He could create a mind map as a quick way of putting down the key points or key bits of information that he is going to include in his answer. He can leave these notes attached to his answer papers. If he doesn't manage to finish, the examiner can see at a glance what he was intending to do and where he would have ended up. He should know, before starting to write, just what he intends to cover and to convey to the examiner.

Exams and word processing

For many students this makes all the difference. Pupils with areas of specific learning difficulty can often type faster than they can write by hand, and the fact that it is easy to amend and to move text around can be very helpful. If this is the child's normal way of communicating it is likely he will be allowed to word process for internal and external (public) exams. Check this out.

Secrets of success

We have just looked, albeit briefly, at effective reading, research skills, planning and structuring written work, note taking, studying for exams, learning and memorising information, exam techniques, and exams and word processing. These all come under the umbrella of study skills.

You may have read this and thought that it all sounds interesting but you may still be wondering how you can actually encourage, help and ensure that your child picks up these skills and habits so that they become automatic and part of the normal routine. Well, here are the acknowledged secrets of success:

- *Choose the skills to be learnt.* The first step is for him (maybe with your help) to decide what study skills or techniques are best for the task in hand.

- *Apply these to actual assignments.* Make sure that when he starts to apply any of these new skills he does so on an actual assignment. It might mean initially spending extra time on homework so that study skills are integrated into doing whatever has been set, but this is time well spent because in the long run it will bring efficiencies and greater success.

- *Integrate the different skills.* Combine the application of specific skills together. This might mean that effective reading is combined with good note taking or that learning and practice periods are built into the weekly or daily timetable.

- *Review how successfully they have been used.* Try and build in a time for reflection on how useful and helpful the study skill has been. Are the outcomes better? What else might have been done?

Don't forget, your child will be more motivated to apply these techniques if he feels that he has ownership and is in control of how and when he does so, as well as seeing the benefit of putting in the initial effort to learn new techniques.

My final word in this chapter is to reiterate the importance of effective study. It is too important to ignore. If working with your teenage child is just too stressful, contentious or generally ends in tears, try and make sure that your young person is introduced to good techniques from an alternative source.

KEY POINTS

⇨ Children will do best, and improve outcomes, if they work efficiently.

⇨ The adoption of good habits and application of good study skills is central to the process. They can be learnt.

⇨ Study skills refers to how to learn and how to study, rather than what to study.

⇨ The primary school child can be helped by parents who take account of their child's physical state, the application of good routines, development of early time management and organisation, use of good learning techniques and application of a few simple rules.

⇨ Young children benefit from learning to see the link between effort and results.

⇨ Students in secondary school and further education can be helped to improve their habits in relation to personal organisation, management of distractions and use of time.

⇨ They can work on specific skills with regard to effective reading, research skills, planning and structuring written work, note taking, exam revision, learning and memorising, and exam techniques.

⇨ Study skills are most effectively applied if they are learnt on actual assignments, if the different skills are integrated and if there is a regular review of their effectiveness.

Appendix 1

EXPLANATION OF AGES AND KEY STAGES

<table>
<tr><th>Age</th><th>UK school year</th><th>UK key stage</th><th>UK tests/exams</th><th colspan="2">UK school/ institution</th><th>US grade</th></tr>
<tr><td>3–4</td><td>Nursery</td><td rowspan="2">Early years</td><td></td><td colspan="2">Nursery/ Preschool</td><td>Preschool</td></tr>
<tr><td>4–5</td><td>Reception</td><td></td><td rowspan="3">Infant school</td><td rowspan="7">Primary school</td><td>Pre-kindergarten</td></tr>
<tr><td>5–6</td><td>Year 1</td><td rowspan="2">Key Stage 1</td><td></td><td>Kindergarten</td></tr>
<tr><td>6–7</td><td>Year 2</td><td>SATs – Reading/ Writing/Maths/ English</td><td>1st Grade</td></tr>
<tr><td>7–8</td><td>Year 3</td><td rowspan="4">Key Stage 2</td><td></td><td rowspan="4">Junior school</td><td>2nd Grade</td></tr>
<tr><td>8–9</td><td>Year 4</td><td></td><td>3rd Grade</td></tr>
<tr><td>9–10</td><td>Year 5</td><td></td><td>4th Grade</td></tr>
<tr><td>10–11</td><td>Year 6</td><td>SATs – English/ Maths/Science</td><td>5th Grade</td></tr>
<tr><td>11–12</td><td>Year 7</td><td rowspan="3">Key Stage 3</td><td></td><td colspan="2" rowspan="5">Secondary school</td><td>6th Grade</td></tr>
<tr><td>12–13</td><td>Year 8</td><td></td><td>7th Grade</td></tr>
<tr><td>13–14</td><td>Year 9</td><td></td><td>8th Grade</td></tr>
<tr><td>14–15</td><td>Year 10</td><td rowspan="2">Key Stage 4</td><td></td><td>9th Grade</td></tr>
<tr><td>15–16</td><td>Year 11</td><td>GCSEs</td><td>10th Grade</td></tr>
<tr><td>16–17</td><td>Year 12</td><td rowspan="2">Key Stage 5</td><td>AS-levels</td><td colspan="2" rowspan="2">Sixth form/ College</td><td>11th Grade</td></tr>
<tr><td>17–18</td><td>Year 13</td><td>AS & A-levels</td><td>12th Grade</td></tr>
</table>

Appendix 2

GAMES AND ACTIVITIES FOR PARENTS AND CHILDREN TO PLAY

The following games and activities were originally compiled by the late Jean Augur (Education Director of the British Dyslexia Association), and appeared in her booklet *A Guide to the Early Recognition of Dyslexia*. They are reproduced here with the kind permission of her husband Frank Augur.

Games are a vitally important part of a child's development. Not only are they fun, but they also help to create the building blocks and skills employed in formal learning. They are especially useful for children who experience areas of difficulty and who may need light-hearted and engaging activities to reinforce aspects of learning where they may have difficulty.

It is absolutely crucial that games are fun or nothing will be achieved. If your child does not engage happily or is unwilling to take part, then try another game – something easier possibly. If you pitch the activity at a level where he or she can achieve success, things should go well.

Listening activities

- Put various objects in containers – sand, dried peas, pennies, buttons, etc. Shake the containers one at a time and ask the child to say what he thinks might be inside and describe the sound. Ask him questions such as: 'Is there one penny in here or more than one?' 'Is the sound hard? Gentle? Quiet? Loud?'

- Listen to everyday sounds, preferably with eyes closed. What can be heard? The telephone ringing, a clock ticking, hammering, voices? Listen to household sounds, such as the vacuum cleaner, a food mixer, the washing machine, the microwave. Listen to traffic sounds such as a motorbike, a lorry, an ambulance, a car.

- Record some everyday sounds like a tap dripping, the toilet flushing, the phone ringing. Play them to your child and see if he can recognise them.

- Ask the child to close his eyes and guess who is speaking. Is it his mother? Sister? Grandmother? Auntie?

Activities to help children to hear the way in which words are segmented

- Tap or clap a simple rhythm for the child to repeat. Gradually make the rhythm more difficult. Clap words with two or more syllables. Say the word as you clap it, for example black-board, hol-i-day, tel-e-vis-ion. Later, give the child a word to clap. Can he say how many beats the word has?

Activities to develop phonological awareness

- I spy. This game is too difficult for some children if the letter names are used. Therefore, take it in stages and play it several ways:
  - » Using the sound – I spy with my little eye something beginning with the sound 'b'.
  - » Increase the load – I spy with my little eye something beginning with the same sound as 'ball'.
  - » Using the letter name – I spy with my little eye something beginning with the letter 'b'.
  - » Using rhyming – I spy with my little eye something that rhymes with 'bat'.
  - » Ending sound – I spy with my little eye something ending with the sound 'b'.
- Sound a word in individual units, for example m-a-n, and ask the child to say the whole word – 'man'. Increase the number of sounds in the word, for example l-a-m-p, t-r-u-m-p-e-t.
- Rhyming. Start off the round with a word and ask each person to say a rhyming word, such as day-play-may-tray. The first to break the rhyme must start a new round, for example pin-tin-thin, etc.

Games for language and memory

- Simon says. Start with very simple instructions. Gradually make them more difficult, for example Simon says touch your left ear with your right hand.

- Say a group of words with an 'odd man out' in it: cat, dog, apple, fox. The child tells you or draws a picture of the odd man out. This can also be played with rhyming words such as cat, bat, fox and hat. Which word does not rhyme?

- I went to the market and I bought... Start with a particular group of things, for example fruit or vegetables, because it is easier for a child to remember related things. Later shop for random items, like a piano, a thimble, tablemats, a coat, etc. This game can also be played where each item must begin with a given letter, for example peas, potatoes, pancakes. Vary the game with other beginnings: I packed my case with... In my Christmas stocking I found... On my birthday I had...

- Songs involving memory and sequencing, for example Old Macdonald had a Farm, The Twelve Days of Christmas, Ten Green Bottles. Songs and rhymes involving days of the week and months of the year.

- Following instructions. Start with two only: 'Please pick up the pencil and put it in the box.' Gradually make the sequence longer: 'Go to the cupboard, take out a green exercise book, write your name on the front and bring it to me.'

Looking games, visual sequencing and visual memory

- Snap. Use pictures only at first, then perhaps introduce letters and words.

- Pelmanism. This is a card game in which all of the cards are laid face down on a surface. The object of the game is to turn over pairs of matching cards. The first player turns over two cards. If they are a pair she keeps them and has another turn. If they are not a pair she turns them face down again and the next player takes a turn.

- Dominoes.

- Sorting things into colours, shapes and sizes. Sorting pictures; for example, put all the pictures which begin with the same sound as 'table' in one pile and all the pictures which begin with the same sound as 'dog' in another pile.

- Happy Families.

- Look together at a picture. Cover the picture and ask the child questions about it. How many children were in the picture? How many people were wearing hats? Was it winter or summer?

- Provide pictures to talk about. Help the child to notice the details using prepositions in discussion: 'Is the man in the blue hat *in front of* or *behind* the lady?' 'Is the boy climbing *under* or *over* the gate?' 'Is the bus going *up* or *down* the hill?'

- Provide a tray of objects for the child to look at. After a few seconds cover the tray and ask the child to name all the objects she saw.

- Provide a tray of objects. Ask the child to look at them and then to close his eyes. One or more objects are then removed from the tray. Ask the child to open his eyes and say which objects he thinks were removed.

- Draw three shapes on a card, show the card to the child, cover it and then ask him to draw what he saw. Gradually increase the difficulty of the shapes and the length of the sequence.

- Show the child several pictures – three is enough at first – and ask her to arrange them in order to make a story. Encourage her to tell you the story or record it on a dictaphone. She may even be able to write it down.

- Bingo – looking only.

- Draw several related pictures and include a stranger, for example apple, pear, book, banana. Ask the child to point to the 'odd man out'.

- If the child knows his alphabet letters, put several plastic or card letters out on the table and ask him to look at them for a few seconds, cover them and ask him to write down or say which ones he saw.

- Ask the child to arrange her alphabet in the shape of a rainbow. Show her a card with three letters on it, for example SBX. Remove the card and ask her to take out the letters she saw and place them in the order in which she saw them. This is a looking activity. Do not say the name of the letters.

Kinaesthetic awareness

- Trace shapes, letters, words, simple pictures and so forth.
- Make letters with plasticine, modelling clay or pipe cleaners. Use chalk, paint and thick felt.
- Use felt tip pens to write very large letters. Make letters with the forefinger in a tray of dry sand.
- Feel and name letters made from felt or sandpaper with eyes closed.
- Feel and name wooden letters with eyes closed.
- Put various objects or wooden letters in bags and ask the child to name the objects or letters.
- Complete jigsaw puzzles.
- Thread a sequence of coloured beads onto a string and ask the child to repeat the sequence several times.

Games to develop physical skills

Do not neglect the physical skills, such as throwing, catching and kicking balls, and skipping, hopping and jumping. Many dyspraxic and dyslexic children find these activities difficult and will need a great deal of practice.

- Playground games, such as Follow my leader and What's the time Mr Wolf?
- The Hokey Cokey.

General activities

- Read poetry to your children, especially amusing or nonsense poems. Try making up jingles and limericks together.
- Mime a particular rhyme or incident and encourage the child to guess the mime. He can then choose something to mime in return.
- Play charades in groups.

- Take your child on outings to interesting places – the zoo, museums, the airport. A child who may be missing out on general knowledge because he is behind with reading can learn a great deal from such visits.

- Play board games, such as snakes and ladders, ludo and bingo.

- Watch television *together*. Television can be a useful form of learning if it is not allowed to be passive. Many programmes offer a great deal of scope for further discussion and activities. Older children enjoy factual programmes involving nature study and exploration, which can lead on to project work and interest files.

- Provide puzzle books – joining dots, mazes, word searches and simple crosswords are all excellent.

- Encourage your child to help in the kitchen – planning, organising, weighing and measuring are all good, and so too are cutting, rolling, whisking and, of course, eating.

GLOSSARY

Attention span
An individual's capacity to maintain focused attention in the course of an ongoing activity.

Audiologist
The professional who specialises in evaluating and treating people with hearing and listening difficulties.

Auditory processing
A natural process of taking in sound through the ear and having it travel to the language area of the brain to be interpreted.

Backward digit recall
A measure of verbal working memory involving the recall of digit sequences in reverse order.

Behaviour management
The use of specific strategies (rewards and/or punishment) to bring about change in the behaviour of others.

Blends
A consonant cluster such as bl, cr and nt at the beginning or end of a word. Both elements are pronounced.

Centile point
The score obtained by a particular percentage of the population on a particular measure; for example, the tenth centile point is the score achieved by the lowest 10 per cent of the population, and the 90th centile point is achieved by the top 10 per cent.

Central coherence
The cognitive ability to understand context and to see the 'big picture'.

Central executive
The sub-component of working memory that controls attention and coordinates activity both within the working memory system and between working memory and other cognitive systems such as long-term memory.

Chunking
A strategy that can be used to improve a person's short-term memory. It involves reducing long strings of information that can be difficult to remember down into shorter, more manageable chunks.

Cognition
The mental action or process of acquiring knowledge and understanding through thought, experience and the senses.

Cognitive
Describing intellectual activity; knowing as opposed to feeling.

Co-occurrence/co-existence
When a person (or pupil) experiences two or more areas of specific learning difficulty simultaneously or when an additional area of difficulty exists alongside a primary diagnosis.

Correlation
The relationship between two sets of test scores.

Criteria for success
Refers to the standards of achievement which will be reached in order to demonstrate that something has been learnt or mastered.

Cuisenaire rods
Set of coloured rods used for teaching number concepts and the basic operations of arithmetic.

Decoding

The ability to apply knowledge of letter-sound relationships, including knowledge of letter patterns, to correctly pronounce written words.

Descriptive praise

Involves noticing and praising exactly what the child has done right.

Differentiation

Tailoring instructions, work set or homework to meet the needs of a child's level of ability and educational needs.

Digit recall

A measure of short-term or working memory involving the presentation and recall of sequences of numbers.

Distractibility

The tendency to be distracted from an ongoing activity by task-irrelevant thoughts or events.

Education, health and care plan (EHC)

A document which sets out a child's SEN and any additional help that the child should receive. The aim of the EHC plan is to make sure that the child gets the right support to enable them to make progress in school.

Encoding

The process of changing one form of symbol into another, as in transferring the spoken word into the relevant written form in spelling or writing.

Expressive language

The ability to communicate with others using language.

Flash cards

Cards containing a small amount of information, held up for pupils to see, as an aid to learning.

Forward digit recall

A measure of verbal short-term memory involving the recall of a sequence of digits.

Glue ear

A common childhood condition where the middle ear becomes filled with fluid, which can cause an intermittent hearing loss.

Grapheme

A written symbol representing a speech sound (phoneme).

Handedness

The preferred hand which may differ for different activities or may be different from the preferred eye, ear or foot.

Hemisphere

One of the two halves, left or right, of the brain. The left hemisphere controls the motor activity of the right side of the body; the right hemisphere controls the left side of the body.

High frequency words

Common words that appear very often in written texts.

Hyperactive/impulsive behaviour

Elevated levels of problem behaviours relating to excessive motor and vocal activity, associated with ADHD.

IQ

Intelligence Quotient. A measure of an individual's general mental abilities based on several tests of knowledge and cognitive skills, expressed with respect to typical levels for a particular age (a score of 100 is average).

Kinaesthetic

Perception obtained through muscle awareness and movement. The feedback to brain from muscle receptors in limbs and body when a movement is made.

Kinaesthetic learning

Learning through doing, touching and experiencing.

Kumon maths

A method of teaching in which the student uses worksheets to follow a programme that becomes increasingly advanced and builds a solid foundation of skills. The programme progresses from counting to calculus and beyond.

Laterality

Pertaining to the left and right sides of the body. Mixed or cross laterality refers to mixed left- or right-side preference for certain activities.

Learning style

An individual's unique approach to learning based on strengths, weaknesses and preferences.

Long-term memory

Memory for experiences that occurred at a point in time prior to the immediate past and also for knowledge that has been acquired over long periods of time.

Memory span

A measure of the maximum amount of material that an individual can successfully remember on a test of working memory.

Mental arithmetic

Calculations that involve the retrieval of mathematical knowledge and possibly its application to particular problems that do not use external devices or memory aids.

Motor movement

Fine motor – activities involving small areas of the musculature of the body, for example writing and cutting.

Gross motor – activities involving large areas of the musculature of the body, for example skipping.

Multidisciplinary assessment

When a child is assessed by several different professionals who are liaising and working in collaboration. The professionals involved could be a speech and language therapist, occupational therapist, an educational psychologist, an audiologist and a behavioural optometrist.

Multisensory learning

Involves using each of the senses to aid learning. A multisensory learning activity might include listening, speaking, seeing, touching, doing and smelling.

National curriculum

The specification of the curriculum that must be taught from 5 to 16 years in state schools in the UK.

Neural pathways

The pathway taken by electrical signals that send information from one area of the brain to another or from an area of the brain to or from the body.

Number bonds

Different pairs of numbers that make up the same number. For example, 2 + 8, 3 + 7 and 4 + 6 which add to 10, or pairs that add to 20, 50, 100 and so forth.

Over-learning

The repeated practice of a skill or study of material to further strengthen memory and performance.

Paired reading

A shared reading exercise with a good reader and a weak reader who read simultaneously with their voices in unison. The procedure follows a clear structure and has been found to be very beneficial for poor readers.

Performance IQ

The IQ sub-score that relates to abilities on IQ tests that do not involve language.

Phoneme

Smallest unit of speech sounds which may correspond to a single letter (b, g) or digraph (sh, th, ai, oy).

Phonemic awareness

The ability to hear, identify and manipulate individual sounds – phonemes – in spoken words. Before children learn to read print, they need to become aware of how the sounds in words work.

Phonics

An approach to reading instruction where the emphasis is placed on the sound value of letters as a means of word recognition.

Phonological skills

Skills used to identify and manipulate the sounds of language.

Place value

The value of a digit depending on its place in a number.

Prefix

A word, letter or number placed before another.

Proprioception

Feedback to the brain about sensations in the body and unrelated movement from muscles to joint receptors.

Reading age

An individual's attainment in reading is expressed against the reading standard for the average child in a particular age group.

Reading comprehension

Understanding of text that an individual has read.

Reading Recovery

A well-established intervention scheme for children with reading difficulties. The programme provides daily half-hour sessions with specially trained Reading Recovery teachers for six-year-olds who are in the bottom 20 per cent of their class in terms of reading.

Receptive language

The ability to listen and understand language.

Reinforcement

Giving praise or a reward to a child in order to encourage that child to repeat the desired behaviour. This is based on learning theory, which suggests that behaviours which are reinforced are more likely to continue.

Reversal

The turning back to front of a letter, word or number. For example, d for b and was for saw.

Reward system

Can often make a positive difference to a child's behaviour by setting out clear rules and guidelines on how you expect your child to behave. Recognising and rewarding 'good' behaviour acts as an incentive to keep your child's motivation going and helps achieve the goal you're aiming for.

Scaffolding

Providing temporary support for an inexperienced learner in order to help them to complete a task or acquire a skill, and then gradually withdrawing that support.

Semantic

The meaning of a word, phrase or sentence.

SEN

Special educational needs. In the UK, recognition of SEN is associated with the necessity of differential provision for the child in school.

Sensory integration

The way the nervous system receives messages from the senses and turns them into appropriate motor and behavioural responses.

Short-term memory

The ability to hold information in mind for short periods of time.

Sight vocabulary

Words that have been memorised visually and can be read by looking at them rather than sounding them out.

Small step learning approach

Dividing tasks or activities into small, manageable steps.

Social skills/communication

The skills we use to communicate and interact with each other, both verbally and non-verbally, through gestures, body language and our personal appearance.

Spaced learning

Technique where learners are presented with a concept or learning objective, a period of time is allowed to pass (days, weeks or months) and then the same concept is presented again. This might involve a few repetitions, or many, depending on how complex the content is.

Spatial awareness

The ability to be aware of oneself in space. It is an organised knowledge of objects in relation to oneself in that given space. Spatial awareness also involves understanding the relationship of these objects when there is a change of position.

Special Educational Needs and Disability Code of Practice 2015

A document providing guidance for organisations and individuals working with and supporting children and young people who have special educational needs or disabilities.

Standardised test

A test which is administered and scored in a consistent, or 'standard', manner for all those taking the test. This enables comparisons to be made and to see how well each person taking the test does compared to others.

Tangram

A traditional Chinese puzzle made of a square divided into seven pieces (one parallelogram, one square and five triangles) that can be arranged to match particular designs.

Tessellation

An arrangement of shapes that fit closely together without gaps or overlaps.

Validity

The extent to which a test measures what it claims to measure. For example, does an IQ test measure intelligence?

Venn diagram

An illustration of the way in which separate groups (such as people who have dyslexia, dyspraxia and dyscalculia, or animals with wings and animals which are extinct) share something in common. Their commonality is shown by overlapping diagrams.

Verbal IQ

The IQ sub-score that relates to an individual's abilities on IQ tests involving verbal material.

Verbal memory

Memory for words or other verbal items.

Verbal processing speed

The time it takes to process and recognise familiar verbal information.

Verbal short-term memory

The sub-component of working memory that stores verbal information.

Visual acuity

The clarity of vision and sharpness of focus.

Visual processing

The process whereby light coming into the eye is turned into signals which travel to the brain where they are interpreted as visual images.

Visual tracking

The ability to maintain visual attention on an object as the object is moving or to maintain visual attention as the eye tracks along a line of print in reading or trying to pick out a particular letter.

Visuospatial short-term memory

The sub-component of working memory that stores information relating to vision, space or movement.

Visuospatial skill

The ability to perceive the spatial relationship between objects. The skills needed to complete a jigsaw puzzle or to understand an architectural plan.

Vocabulary

The number of words a child can recognise or use in speech or in written form.

Working memory

The ability to hold and manipulate information in mind for brief periods of time in the course of ongoing mental activities, such as computing a mental maths problem.

Working memory capacity

The amount of information that can be held in working memory. Each sub-component of working memory has its own limit.

LEGISLATION

Children with special educational needs (SEN) (GOV.UK): www.gov.uk/children-with-special-educational-needs/overview

Disability Act 1995: www.legislation.gov.uk/ukpga/1995/50/contents

EHC plans (IPSEA): www.ipsea.org.uk/what-you-need-to-know/ehc-plans

Equality Act 2010: www.legislation.gov.uk/ukpga/2010/15/contents

Rose report: *Identifying and Teaching Children and Young People with Dyslexia and Literacy Difficulties.* www.education.gov.uk/publications/eOrderingDownload/00659-2009DOM-EN.pdf

SEND Code of Practice: www.gov.uk/government/uploads/system/uploads/attachment_data/file/398815/SEND_Code_of_Practice_January_2015.pdf

The Local Offer for Local Authorities and Schools: www.thelocaloffer.co.uk/the-local-offer-by-local-authority

FURTHER READING

There is extensive research literature relating to all topics covered in this book. I made the decision not to include a long list of references for the individual studies and journal articles which have contributed to and shaped our current thinking about education and special needs; I am instead listing blog and book titles which provide further information for interested readers. These publications are but a small sample of what is available. Their inclusion does not imply a specific endorsement or recommendation ahead of all else in the market; however, the authors are well-respected experts in their fields. I have generally listed only one book per author, but many of these authors have several publications to their name, which readers may wish to follow up.

Introduction

Bishop, D. V. M. (2010, December 18) What's in a name? (Web log post). Accessed at http://deevybee.blogspot.com/2010/12/whats-in-name.html

Chapter 2, Working Memory

Alloway, T. and Gathercole, S. (2006) *Working Memory and Neurodevelopmental Disorders*. Hove: Psychology Press.

Baddeley, A. D. (1976) *The Psychology of Memory*. London: Harper and Row Publishers.

Baddeley, A. D. (1999) *Essentials of Human Memory*. Hove: Psychology Press.

Buzan, T. (2005) *Mind Maps for Kids: Max Your Memory and Concentration*. London: Thorsens.

Gathercole, S. and Alloway, T. (2008) *Working Memory and Learning: A Practical Guide for Teachers*. London: Sage.

Chapter 3, Dyslexia

Frank, R. with Livingston, K. (2003) *The Secret Life of the Dyslexic Child: A Practical Guide for Parents and Educators*. London: Rodale.

Hatcher, P., Duff, F. and Hulme, C. (2014, third edition) *Sound Linkage: An Integrated Programme for Overcoming Reading Difficulties*. Oxford: Wiley-Blackwell.

Ott, P. (1997) *How to Detect and Manage Dyslexia: A Reference and Resource Manual*. Oxford: Heinemann Educational Publishers.

Snowling, M. (2000) *Dyslexia*. Oxford: Blackwell.

Thomson, M. (2009) *The Psychology of Dyslexia: A Handbook for Teachers*. Oxford: Wiley-Blackwell.

Thomson, P. and Gilchrist, P. (1997) *Dyslexia: A Multidisciplinary Approach*. London: Chapman and Hall.

Chapter 4, Dyspraxia

Kirby, A. (2006) *Dyspraxia: Developmental Co-ordination Disorder*. London: Souvenir Press.

Kranowitz, C. S. (2005) *The Out-of-Sync Child: Recognizing and Coping with Sensory Processing Disorder*. New York, NY: Penguin Group.

Portwood, M. (1999, second edition) *Developmental Dyspraxia: Identification and Intervention – A Manual for Parents and Professionals*. London: David Fulton.

Chapter 5, Dyscalculia and Other Maths Difficulties

Babtie, P. and Emerson, J. (2015) *Understanding Dyscalculia and Numeracy Difficulties*. London: Jessica Kingsley Publishers.

Butterworth, B. (1999) *The Mathematical Brain*. London: Macmillan.

Butterworth, B. and Yeo, D. (2004) *Dyscalculia Guidance*. London: NFER Nelson.

Chinn, S. (2012, second edition) *The Trouble with Maths*. London: Routledge.

Hanwell, G. (2005) *Dyscalculia*. London: David Fulton.

Henderson, A. (1998) *Maths for the Dyslexic*. London: David Fulton.

Kay, J. and Yeo, D. (2003) *Dyslexia and Maths*. London: David Fulton.

Yeo, D. (2003) *Dyslexia, Dyspraxia and Mathematics*. London: Whurr.

Chapter 6, Attention Deficit Disorder with or without Hyperactivity – ADHD

Green, Dr C. and Chee, Dr K. (1997) *Understanding ADHD: A Parent's Guide to Attention Deficit Hyperactivity Disorder in Children*. London: Vermilion.

Kewley, G. D. (1999) *Attention Deficit Hyperactivity Disorder: Recognition, Reality and Resolution*. West Sussex: LAC Press.

O'Regan, F. (2007) *Successfully Managing ADHD: A Handbook for SENCOs and Teachers*. London: Routledge.

Chapter 7, Autism Spectrum Disorder

Frith, U. (1991) *Autism and Asperger Syndrome*. Cambridge: Cambridge University Press.

Frith, U. (2008) *Autism: A Very Short Introduction*. Oxford: Oxford University Press.

Jordan, R. and Jones, G. (2001) *Meeting the Needs of Children with Autistic Spectrum Disorders*. London: David Fulton.

Pashley, S. (2013) *OMG! I've Got Asperger's*. European Union: united p.c. publisher.

Sainsbury, C. (2012, second edition) *Martian in the Playground: Understanding the Schoolchild with Asperger's Syndrome*. London: Sage.

Stanton, M. (2000) *Learning to Live with High Functioning Autism: A Parent's Guide for Professionals*. London: Jessica Kingsley Publishers.

Chapter 8, Auditory Processing Disorder

Foli, K. J. (2002) *Like Sound Through Water: A Mother's Journey Through Auditory Processing Disorder*. London: Atria Books.

Heyman, L. K. (2010) *The Sound of Hope: Recognizing, Coping with, and Treating Your Child's Auditory Processing Disorder*. New York, NY: Ballantine Books.

Chapter 9, Specific Language Impairment

Monschein, M. (2008) *The 50 Best Games for Speech and Language Development (50 Best Group Games)*. Buckingham: Hinton House Publishers.

Speake, J. and Barnes, R. (2003) *How to Identify and Support Children with Speech and Language Difficulties*. Wisbech: LDA.

Chapter 13, Teaching Tips

Fisher, R. (2001) *Teaching Children to Learn*. Cheltenham: Stanley Thornes (Publishers) Ltd.

Fisher, R. (2005, second edition) *Teaching Children to Think*. Cheltenham: Nelson Thornes.

Chapter 14, Tips for Reading

Madsen, N. (1987) *Teach Your Child to Read Properly*. Brighton: Elliot Right Way Books.

Topping, K. (1995) *Paired Reading, Spelling and Writing: The Handbook for Teachers and Parents*. London and New York, NY: Cassell.

Chapter 18, Tips for Maths

Boaler, J. (2009) *The Elephant in the Classroom*. London: Souvenir Press.

Eastaway, R. and Askew, M. (2013) *Maths for Mums and Dads*. London: Square Peg, Random House.

Eastaway, R. and Askey, M. (2013) *More Maths for Mums and Dads*. London: Square Peg, Random House.

Chapter 21, Tips to Enhance Language and Communication Skills

Fisher, R. (2013) *Teaching Thinking: Philosophical Enquiry in the Classroom*. London: Bloomsbury Publishing.

Chapter 22, Tips for Motivation

Dweck, C. S. (2012) *Mindset: How You Can Fulfil Your Potential*. London: Robinson.

Chapter 23, Tips for Confident Learners

Dweck, C. S. (2012) *Mindset: How You Can Fulfil Your Potential*. London: Robinson.

Chapter 24, Habits, Strategies and Study Skills

Buzan, T. (2005) *Mind Maps for Kids: Max Your Memory and Concentration*. London: Thorsens.

Cogan, J. and Flecker, M. (2004) *Dyslexia in Secondary School: A Practical Handbook for Teachers, Parents and Students*. London: Whurr.

USEFUL RESOURCES, ORGANISATIONS AND WEBSITES

Chapter 2, Working Memory

A number of computer-based programs have been developed with a view to improving the working memory capacity of school-aged children. Cogmed and Jungle Memory are two which are accessible and user friendly. See:

www.cogmed.com

www.junglememory.com

These are not the only programs around but they have been in operation for long enough to have had their efficacy researched. The results of studies to see if they do improve working memory have been published, but overall the research literature on brain training remains rather contradictory. There are many claims for dramatic improvements but then there are critics who suggest that initial gains are not sustained, do not transfer from the skills learnt as part of the program to other skills which also involve working memory, and finally that the studies themselves are flawed in one way or another. So, it is not easy to ascertain whether engagement with one of these programs is going to help any one particular child.

It is fully understandable if you, as a concerned parent, are interested in giving your child a chance to take part in a working memory improvement program. It may bring about excellent improvements. Your child is an individual, and if one of these programs works well for him or her it can only be a bonus.

Chapter 3, Dyslexia

The organisations listed below whose descriptions are followed by a star, *, are also relevant to dyspraxic pupils and their parents.

The British Dyslexia Association (www.bdadyslexia.org.uk) provides advice and support for all those affected by dyslexia. It runs courses and training and works to influence practice and legislation. Find out if there is a local support group near you.

The Council for the Registration of Schools Teaching Dyslexic Pupils, or CReSTed (www.crested.org.uk), helps parents and also those who advise them choose an educational establishment for children with specific learning difficulties. It lists and rates a good number of schools, so try this site if you are looking for a specialist school which caters for dyslexic children.*

Dyslexia Action (www.dyslexiaaction.org.uk) is a national charity that takes action to change the lives of people with dyslexia and literacy difficulties.

The Dyslexia-SpLD-Trust (www.thedyslexia-spldtrust.org.uk) is a collaboration of voluntary and community organisations with funding from the Department for Education to provide reliable information to parents, teachers, schools and the wider sector. It acts as a communication channel between government, leading dyslexia organisations, parents, schools, colleges, teachers and the sector.

The dyslexic.com website (www.dyslexia.com) is provided by, and is a trade name of, iansyst Ltd. Iansyst provides the training and educational software and hardware. Its core focus is on technology to help people with dyslexia make the most of their abilities. This has widened to include other assistive technology.*

Dystalk (www.dysTalk.com) is for parents of children who are looking for information on how to optimise their child's learning. Top professionals in the learning difficulties world have been filmed as they speak to parents. These lectures can now be watched online for free. The site also contains a resources section including useful books, links, professionals and schools.*

The Helen Arkell Centre (www.arkellcentre.org.uk) supports all those impacted by dyslexia, whether pupils, adults or parents of those with dyslexia. The centre can arrange assessments and specialist teaching; it runs training courses for specialist teachers and puts on talks and events.*

The International Dyslexia Association (www.eida.org) is an international organisation that concerns itself with the complex issues of dyslexia. It actively promotes effective teaching approaches and related clinical educational intervention strategies for people with dyslexia.

The Dyslexia Teaching Centre, Kensington (www.dyslexiateachingcentre. co.uk) is a teaching and assessment centre which provides highly qualified, specialist support for children and adults of all ages, enabling individuals to acquire the skills needed for success in education, the workplace and everyday life. The centre also provides bursaries for those who need help but are unable to fund assessment or tuition themselves.*

Patoss (www.patoss-dyslexia.org) is the Professional Association for Teachers and Assessors of Students with Specific Learning Difficulties. It provides advice and support for parents as well as for teachers and other professionals.*

Chapter 4, Dyspraxia

The Dyspraxia Foundation (www.dyspraxiafoundation.org.uk) is a national foundation whose aim is to:

- support individuals and families affected by dyspraxia
- promote better diagnostic and treatment facilities for those who have dyspraxia
- help professionals in health and education to assist those with dyspraxia
- promote awareness and understanding of dyspraxia.

MindGenius (www.mindgenius.com)

Inspriation (www.inspiration.com)

Food and Behaviour Research (www.fabresearch.org) provides a wealth of useful information on research into nutrition and human behaviour.

Chapter 5, Dyscalculia and Other Maths Difficulties

Learning Works (www.learning-works.org.uk)

The Mathematical Brain (www.mathematicalbrain.com) is the website of Brian Butterworth, the UK's leading expert on dyscalculia. It has updates on the latest research and links to resources.

Dyscalculia.org (www.dyscalculia.org) contains many useful links to teachers (for those in the US). The author of this site is a US special educator, Renee Newman.

The Dyscalculia Centre (www.dyscalculia.me.uk) is sponsored by the publisher First and Best in Education Ltd, and has links to resources for parents and teachers.

Chapter 6, Attention Deficit Disorder with or without Hyperactivity – ADHD

If you type 'ADHD support groups' into a search engine numerous sites come up. This is an interesting reflection of the burgeoning interest in the topic over the past decade. It must also reflect the need that many parents feel for support in understanding and helping their ADHD offspring. It may also reflect the growing awareness of adults who have experienced ADHD traits for many years and who are now able to find out more.

I have selected two UK national sites, ADDISS and CHADD, both of which have been established for many years. I am sure that many other sites will provide parents and teachers with insights and help.

ADDISS, the National Attention Deficit Disorder Information and Support Service (www.addiss.co.uk), is a registered charity providing information and resources about ADHD for parents, sufferers, teachers and health professionals.

CHADD, Children and Adults with Attention-Deficit/Hyperactivity Disorder (www.chadd.org)

Another useful site, Fintan O'Regan's Behaviour Management Training (www.fintanoregan.com), provides training, coaching and consultancy in the area of ADHD.

Chapter 7, Autism Spectrum Disorder

The National Autistic Society (www.autism.org.uk)

NHS Choices (www.nhs.uk/conditions/Autistic-spectrum-disorder)

YoungMinds (www.youngminds.org.uk)

Asperger's Syndrome Foundation (www.aspergerfoundation.org.uk)

To find a local support group try www.aspergersupport.org.uk

Chapter 8, Auditory Processing Disorder

Audiology Online (www.audiologyonline.com)

Contact a Family (www.cafamily.org.uk) has medical information on auditory processing disorder.

Great Ormond Street Hospital (www.gosh.nhs.uk) also has medical information on auditory processing disorder.

The National Coalition on Auditory Processing Disorders (www.ncapd.org)

National Deaf Children's Society (www.ndcs.org.uk/family_support/ auditory_processing_disorder/index.html)

NHS Choices (www.nhs.uk/conditions/auditory processing-disorder)

Phonak (www.phonak.com) will give information about the EduLink wireless system which can be used in school.

Fast ForWord listening program – a speech and language therapist can tell you more about this program. It is available from a number of suppliers. Further information is available on the web.

Chapter 9, Specific Language Impairment

Christopher Place (www.speech-language.co.uk) is a speech, language and hearing centre for babies and children under five who have hearing impairment, delay in speech, language and communication, or more complex needs.

I CAN (www.ican.org.uk) is a children's communication charity.

Talking Point (www.talkingpoint.org.uk) is an information website which is part of the I CAN organisation.

The Royal College of Speech and Language Therapists (www.rcslt.org)

Chapter 10, Visual Processing Difficulty

The British Association of Behavioural Optometrists (www.babo.co.uk)

The website for Keith Holland Associates (www.keithholland.co.uk) has much useful information.

Chapter 11, An Educational Psychologist's Assessment
How to find an independent EP who
can carry out an assessment
You may find that your child's school has a list of EPs who they like to recommend or you may have a friend who has had a good experience and can recall the name of the EP they found useful. If not, then a quick web search for independent educational psychology assessments brings up numerous sites, for example www.psychologydirect.co.uk/educational-psychologist.

If you approach an individual or group practice which has not been personally recommended to you I do suggest that you ask all the questions that you want before booking an appointment. It is an expensive venture and you need to feel satisfied that it will be of value to you and your child.

Exam concessions/access arrangements

These refer to the examination adjustments agreed for candidates based on evidence of need and normal way of working. Details can be found on the Joint Council for Qualifications website (www.jcq.org.uk).

Chapter 14, Tips for Reading

The dyslexic.com website (www.dyslexia.com) is provided by, and is a trade name of, iansyst Ltd. Iansyst provides the training and educational software and hardware. Its core focus is on technology to help people with dyslexia make the most of their abilities. This has widened to include other assistive technology.

Toe by Toe (www.toe-by-toe.co.uk) is a systematic page-by-page and step-by-step series of activities in one book, delivered one to one, with instructions for the 'coach' provided for each activity. It takes learners right back to the beginning of phonics and works up from there. It is intended that learner and coach should work through the entire scheme, however long that takes, and then graduate to simple reading books.

Barrington Stoke (www.barringtonstoke.co.uk) publishes dyslexia-friendly books which are designed to break down the barriers to reading and learning to read. So often the poor reader is bored by the simple books which he or she can access and where the story is aimed at a much younger child. Barrington Stoke commissions great books from well-known authors with the brief that the stories have interest and excitement but the language and writing enables the poor reader to cope.

Modern technology has produced some great innovations. For many poor readers the pen which reads words aloud is a good resource. Available from:

- www.livescribe.com/solutions/learningdisabilities
- www.readingpen.co.uk
- www.wizcomtech.com

Chapter 15, Tips for Spelling

Franklin has a range of interactive spell checkers and children's dictionaries (available on Amazon).

Wordshark (www.wordshark.co.uk) provides motivating spelling activities.

To find the 100 most commonly used words in English go to www.englishclub.com/vocabulary/common-words-100.htm.

Chapter 16, Tips for Writing

Mind maps, when taught and used well, can be helpful to many pupils. Useful sites to visit include:

- www.tonybuzan.com
- www.examtime.com/mind-maps

Voice recognition has improved dramatically and is a further aid for the pupil who struggles to get pen to paper. Products include Dragon Dictation, Voice Texting Pro and iSpeech.

Chapter 17, Handwriting Tips

National Handwriting Association (www.nha-handwriting.org.uk)

TTS Group (www.tts-group.co.uk)

Chapter 18, Tips for Maths

Maths is Fun (www.mathsisfun.com)

Nrich (www.nrich.maths.org)

iCoachmath (www.icoachMath.com)

Wolfram Alpha (www.wolframalpha.com) provides examples and explanations of all that is covered in the national curriculum.

Mangahigh (www.mangahigh.com)

Numberphile (www.numberphile.com)

Chapter 21, Tips to Enhance Language and Communication Skills

Debate Mate (www.debatemate.com)

Stagecoach (www.stagecoach.co.uk)

Chapter 24, Habits, Strategies and Study Skills

There are several software programs for mind mapping, for example www.thinkbuzan.com and www.dyslexic.com.

General

Diagnostic and Statistical Manual of Mental Disorders (DSM-5) (www.dsm5.org)

Independent Parental Special Education Advice (IPSEA) (www.ipsea.org.uk)

Information, Advice & Support Services Network (www.iassnetwork.org.uk)

Understood (www.understood.org) covers almost everything which parents might want to know about in relation to learning difficulties and school.

INDEX